STUDIES IN
THAI HISTORY

COLLECTED ARTICLES

by

David K. Wyatt

SILKWORM BOOKS

First published in paperback in 1994 by
Silkworm Books
54/1 Sridonchai Road, Chiang Mai 50100, Thailand

National Library of Thailand Cataloguing in Publication Data

    Wyatt, David K.
       Studies in Thai History
       I.   Thailand-History
       II.   Title
       959.3
       ISBN : 974-7047-19-5

Design by T. Jittidejarak
The texts were set in Adobe issue of Galliard Roman, and composed on an
Apple Macintosh using the PageMaker program.
Printed in Thailand

PREFACE

It is tempting to see the publication of such volumes as this as a "vanity trip" for their authors. After all, they consist of no more than than articles reprinted from earlier in the author's career, most of them ten or twenty years old and now badly outdated. Such relics of an earlier scholarship are perhaps better forgotten: certainly if they were still in currency there would be no need to reprint them.

And so I thought. I had long resisted any idea of publishing such a volume until a recent trip to Thailand brought home to me the fact that frequently I was called upon to make arguments I had long since ceased even to think about, because I thought I had said all I needed to say on the subject. I then realized that many of the articles making these points had never been available in Thailand, and that much of the rest of the world probably had not seen them.

Most of the articles in this collection were written as "occasional" pieces; that is, they were written for particular occasions—as conference papers, as contributions to the birthday celebrations of respected teachers, as articles written out of a sense of duty, or as minor pieces hurriedly dashed off for a conference. Some were written to counter arguments of others which I considered to be ill-considered; and others were intended to make what I hoped might be a definitive statement on one issue or another.

The process of working through these pieces to prepare them for publication has been an interesting one, akin perhaps to reliving one's intellectual biography. I have not attempted to change them, though a few of them are badly in need of serious revision in the light of subsequent scholarship. I have attempted to regularize the romanization of Thai, and on this occasion have made a few changes to reflect my current thinking about romanization—substituting *c* for the hard *ch* sound, *ò* for the sound like that of the initial syllable of *awful*, and *ü* for the vowel sound sometimes rendered *ue* or *eu*. In a few cases I have updated bibliographical references, especially in cases when books later appeared out of items that I had cited as dissertations or articles.

These articles are arranged here in rough chronological order of the subject, not in the order in which they were written. They fall naturally into five groups, each of which has its own concerns and its own subtext of argument with existing scholarship.

The first six articles all deal in some way with the sources of the early history of Siam In general, they deal with inscriptions, Pali and Thai chronicles, and laws, both of Lan Na and of Siam. They cumulatively try to make the point that there is much more material for earlier history than is generally believed, and that these sources must be taken seriously and treated with a great deal of respect.

The second group of articles consists of three pieces set in the late Ayudhya and early Bangkok periods, all dealing with what I then called "family politics." The intention here was to move away from the strict focus on the royal family that too often marks the study of Thai history, and to explore the relationships among the leading noble families that made them such an enduring force in the politics and economics of Thai society in the pre-modern period. The main sources used here were biographical and genealogical, although the first of the three articles shows how a long-forgotten Persian-language source can be used to corroborate the Thai sources.

Of the following three articles, each is very different from the others. The "Subtle Revolution" article—the longest in this volume—was intended as an exploration into Thai intellectual history through an examination of the writings of the First Reign of the Bangkok Period. The argument that lies behind this article is that the Thai handling of their encounter with the West in the nineteenth century can best be understood in terms of the developing intellectual style of the kingdom's élite, as this this took shape out of the chaos and crisis of the wars with Burma in the late eighteenth century. The next article, "Siam and Laos," is a much more straightforward, narrative article, the first that I wrote and published (1963). And the third article in this group is at the other end of the chronological span, written in 1988 and published only in 1989. It foreshadows work that I am doing now, and ultimately has to do with the question of how older texts might be read "between the lines."

The four articles in the fourth group all derive from my work in the 1960s on the origins of modern education in Thailand. The first piece, on the Buddhist monkhood and social mobility, was written as an act of homage to those in the National Archives who assisted my research there in 1962-63. It was written in Thai, and the English version is a close translation of the Thai version. It seems never to have been superseded, and is occasionally cited in ways that indicate that some have found it useful. "Education and the Modernization of Thai Society" was written as an act of homage to Lauriston Sharp, who served on my doctoral committee at Cornell; and one thing it tried to do was to show Sharp some measure of my intellectual debt to him. Both this article and the two that follow ("Samuel McFarland" and "Ban Phraya Nana") try to make the point that the early modern schools had a good deal to do with defining and shaping the Thai élite of the turn of the century and beyond; and ultimately they had something to do with preparing the way for the political changes of the twentieth century.

The final two articles both try to summarize my thinking about the importance of the reign of King Chulalongkorn. It should be remembered that both articles were written at the height of the Vietnam War controversy in the United States (and Thailand). One of the overriding intellectual fashions of that day was a general underestimation of the positive features of the old monarchy. In these two pieces, one published in Thailand and the other in the United States, I wanted to make the point that Chulalongkorn's power was won in the face of great resistance to change, and not the contrary. At the same time, I wanted to avoid being drawn into controversy about the roles of subsequent absolute monarchs.

The articles published here constitute only a small portion of my work over the years. In particular, I have held back a large group of articles and other writings on the subject of Thai chronicles, save only for the first item in this collection. I have held these back partly because some of the items are very lengthy, but mainly because the subject is something on which I continue to work, and concerning which my thinking has radically changed in recent years.

Such utility as the articles included here may have surely should encourage the reader to take Thai history more seriously than it all too often has been taken. Thai history is not something that has been completed, not does it consist solely of a tedious collection of names and dates. These articles encompass an enormous range of sources, from inscriptions and chronicles to archival records and newspapers. In all cases, the sources are hardly transparent: they can be read in a multitude of different ways, and there is always more to be learned from an "old" source—as, for example, from the inscription of King Ram Khamhæng. The sources may be old, but the questions that can be addressed to them are constantly new and changing, and I hope that I may have suggested in this collection that we still have much to learn of the Thai past.

In closing, I am delighted to have the opportunity to extend my thanks to those who have helped me. I am grateful for the continuing collegial friendship of my friends in the Southeast Asia Program and the Department of History at Cornell University. I have not had to badger the Cornell University Librraries to locate books for me because Giokpo Oey and John Badgley and their staff have done such a superb job at maintaining the high level of the John M. Echols Collection on Southeast Asia. Countless students have stimulated my thinking. Especially over the past six years I have benefited from the friendship and hospitality of M.R. Rujaya Abhakorn and Aroonrut Wichienkeeo, to single out but a few of many, in Chiang Mai; and I am especially thankful to my publisher, Trasvin Jittidecharaks, for her enthusiasm and encouragement.

DAVID K. WYATT

Ithaca
July 1993

TABLE OF CONTENTS

CHRONICLE TRADITIONS
IN THAI HISTORIOGRAPHY*

Among D.G.E. Hall's many important contributions to the development of the study and teaching of Southeast Asian history is his work in connection with the series of conferences on historical writing on the peoples of Asia, the Southeast Asia section of which met in 1956. The volume which he edited from the proceedings of that conference, *Historians of South-East Asia*,[1] made a significant impression on the many students then just beginning their studies in the field. Some of us may surely have been somewhat intimidated by the volume's description and analysis of the voluminous sources in the many vernacular languages of the region, only a few of which any of us could hope to master in a lifetime. At the same time, most of us then could gain some encouragement that our arduous language training and study of standard European sources were leading us along a course which could only be rewarding in the long run. We looked forward to immersing ourselves in the mysteries of Javanese chronograms; or Burmese *yazawin* and *a-yei-bon* and *ei-gyin;* or Malay *hikayat* and Javanese *babad*. And we came even more to appreciate the enormous accomplishments of European scholarship on the history of Southeast Asia, upon which Professor Hall's own *History* was so splendidly built (and continued to grow so gracefully).

---

* In *Southeast Asian History and Historiography: Essays Presented to D.G.E. Hall,* ed. C. D. Cowan and O. W. Wolters (Ithaca: Cornell University Press, 1976), pp. 107-122. Reprinted with the permission of the Cornell University Press.

[1] London, 1961.

It is surely among the highest of compliments to Professor Hall's work to note now that the *Historians* volume has in numerous respects been superseded by more recent work, just as the successive editions of his *History* have had to incorporate much substantial revision. Our field of historical studies has moved very rapidly, and very far, in the past decade or two. We have available now a great many new monographs in previously unexplored fields and editions and translations of previously neglected texts. Nonetheless, not all branches of our field have moved ahead at the same pace. More has been done with modern history than with that of earlier periods; and much more work has been done on the history of Malaysia, Indonesia, and the Philippines than all the other countries of the region. Probably the most dramatic improvement has come with respect to the history of Thailand, which seems to have been in such a languid state in 1956 that it proved impossible to include chapters on Thailand in the *Historians* volume. Since that time, one can enumerate nearly thirty completed doctoral dissertations dealing with Thai history submitted to American, British, Australian, and Continental universities, as well as a considerable number now in progress. With an increasing pool of research being published on the basis of this and the authors' subsequent work, one can expect substantial revisions to our present understanding of modern Thai history in the near future.

Work on earlier Thai history, however, has yet to receive the attention it deserves. A great deal of excellent work has been accomplished concerning the early kingdom of Sukhothai, on the basis of its epigraphy, by A. B. Griswold and Prasert na Nagara;[2] and their work on several occasions has ventured into the history of the kingdom of Ayudhya (AD 1351-1767).[3] Very little has yet

---

[2] In a series of articles entitled "Epigraphic and Historical Studies," beginning in vol. 56 of the *Journal of the Siam Society*, and separately published under the same title in 1992.

[3] Including "A Fifteenth-Century Siamese Historical Poem," in *Southeast Asian History and Historiography*, ed. C. D. Cowan and O. W. Wolters (Ithaca: Cornell Univ. Press, 1975), pp. 123-163; and "Devices and Expedients, Vat

been done, however, on Thai history prior to the fourteenth
century, especially on the early kingdoms of northern Siam, or on
the internal history of Ayudhya itself. That this has been so stems
largely from the nature of the sources themselves. These include
a wide range of materials, including inscriptions, miscellaneous
records, literary sources, local legends and oral traditions, and
foreign accounts. The core of this material, however, is an
extraordinarily rich chronicle tradition.

Two separate sets of problems are involved here. Those for the
Ayudhya period are in some ways more manageable. The royal or
dynastic chronicles—well known to Western scholars since the
seventeenth century—might be considered to consist of a single
linear tradition, with two major variants on a single theme.
Though somewhat sparse and specialized in the sorts of
information they convey to the historian, they can be checked
against other sources, and particularly foreign accounts, and
certainly can yield a connected narrative of major events in the
history of the kingdom. This basically is what was done by
W. A. R. Wood in the 1920s with his History of Siam.[4] Much
more care has yet to be taken, however, in collating various
versions of the Ayudhya chronicles with each other and with other
documentary sources, as well as in exploiting more systematically
the nuances of meaning and subtle turns of events which can be
discovered from careful consideration of the nature of such
chronicles as historical sources and of the unspoken values and
intentions of their compilers.

In dealing with the pre-Ayudhya history of Siam, quite
another set of problems arises. Rather than a single chronicle
tradition, there are dozens, deriving from various localities,
written from disparate points of view, and raising severe problems
of dating and chronology. They have tended to be dismissed as
worthless or unreliable, or to have been ignored for extraneous

---

Pa Mok 1727 A.D.," in *In Memoriam Phya Anuman Rajadhon,* ed. Tej Bunnag
and Michael Smithies (Bangkok, 1970), pp. 147-220.

[4] W. A. R. Wood, *A History of Siam from the Earliest Times to the Year A.D.
1781* (London, 1925; reprinted Bangkok, 1959).

reasons. Without them, however, no solutions are possible to many of the basic problems of Thai historiography.

It has for some time—apparently from the middle of the nineteenth century—been customary for Thai authors to distinguish between two basically different types of chronicles: between *tamnan* and *phongsawadan*. Both are essentially annals, arranging events chronologically and concerned not at all with analysis or interpretation, save implicitly. Although *tamnan* seemingly began to be written earlier, certainly by the fifteenth century, both were being composed as late as the nineteenth century. They may be distinguished by the purposes for which each was written, the identity of their authors, and their relative scope in time and space.

Tamnan History

What might be termed the "earliest" chronicle traditions indigenous to Siam are the *tamnan* (stories, legends) associated with the localities and principalities of northern Siam and generally (but not exclusively) with the predecessors of the major Buddhist kingdoms of Sukhothai, Lan Na Thai (Chiang Mai), and Ayudhya. As a genre of historical literature, these "chronicles" usually are characterized first and foremost by their Buddhist associations. In this connection, many such *tamnan* are cast explicitly within Buddhist chronological and geographical frameworks. Many begin in the time of the Buddha, or earlier Buddhas, and some go so far as to prophesy to the end of the current Buddhist Era. They frequently cover earlier events in the history of Buddhism in India and Ceylon and trace the extension of the religion to the locality, region, or institution with which they are concerned. Many may be considered to have been written by Buddhist monks.

The subjects of such *tamnan* are usually Buddhist principalities, religious institutions or foundations, images, or relics and reliquaries. They could be considered as having been composed, in a sense, to legitimize their subjects by demonstrating the means by which they are linked to the Buddha, or showing how their subject has become and remains a repository of merit. They can thus be seen as having also a certain didactic value. While most such texts are quite localized in their subject, they are at the same time universal in quality: for those who wrote and read them, these were truly universal histories.

When written down, most *tamnan* almost certainly were incised in Siamese, Northern Thai (Tai Yuan), Lao, or Khmer script on carefully prepared palm leaves.[5] Few of these survive from much before the seventeenth century,[6] yet we know that many were written earlier. It thus is necessary to assume that most actual manuscripts are later copies, as some explicitly state.

There is sufficient variation in existing texts to suggest a variety of means by which *tamnan* may have been compiled. Many contain local origin legends and myths, the best-known archetype of which is the Khun Borom story from Laos, which has all the Tai peoples issuing from a pumpkin or gourd.[7] Similar stories are to be found incorporated in such texts as the Nan chronicle.[8] It seems likely that much of the earlier narrative in many *tamnan* must derive from oral traditions.

Another component of many *tamnan* is the succession of rulers, often related in the form of a list embellished with brief tales of their exploits as well as their services to the religion. These have much in common with the indigenous historiography of such Tai peoples as the Ahom of Assam, the Shan of Burma and Yunnan, the Lao of northern Siam and Laos, the Lü of southwest China,

---

[5] See Montgomery Schuyler, Jr., "Notes on the Making of Palm Leaf Manuscripts in Siam," *Journal of the American Oriental Society*, 29 (1908), 281-283; and Christian Velder, "Die Palmblatt-Manuskript-Kultur Thailands," *Nachrichten der Gesellschaft für Natur- und Volkerkunde Ostasiens* 89/90 (1961), 110–114.

[6] Cf. Charles F. Keyes, "New Evidence on Northern Thai Frontier History," *In Memoriam Phya Anuman Rajadhon*, p. 225.

[7] René de Berval (ed.), *Kingdom of Laos* (Saigon, 1959), pp. 379-381; and C. Archaimbault, "Religious Structures in Laos," JSS, 52, 1 (April 1964), 57-74.

[8] "Rüang ratchawongpakòn, phongsawadan müang Nan," *Prachum phongsawadan*, pt. 10 (Bangkok, 1918; reprinted Bangkok: Kaona, 1964, IV, 333-542); partial English version published as *The Nan Chronicle*, trans. Prasœt Churatana, ed. D. K. Wyatt (Ithaca, 1966), a new edition of which is now (1993) in press.

and the various upland Tai peoples of Laos, northern Vietnam, and southern China.[9] These customarily feature a chronological system employing concurrent ten- and twelve-year cycles, in which the same combination of two named years occurs only once in each sixty-year cycle.[10] On the whole, this chronology demands treatment with the utmost respect: when tested against similarly-dated inscriptions it is not often found erroneous.

Their general characteristics notwithstanding, the qualities and nature of the various *tamnan* texts that are presently available vary widely. Out of a considerable quantity known to exist,[11] only a relatively small proportion has been published; and only a handful have received the editorial care they demand. The most prominent among these may be divided into three groups: first, the *tamnan* of the distant past in extreme northern Siam; second, the "universal histories" in Pali and Thai, the product of the Buddhist efflorescence in Lan Na Thai in the fifteenth and sixteenth centuries; and third, the "monumental *tamnan*" of Buddhist images, relics, and institutions.

Tamnan of the Distant Past

This group of texts, of uncertain date, provenance, and authorship, deals with early states of extreme northern Siam and adjacent areas in the period prior to the thirteenth-century foundation of such states as Lan Na Thai, Sukhothai, and Nan. All of them are the subjects of considerable puzzlement and controversy among

---

[9] This subject is much too vast to be discussed here. The reader is referred to the following: (Ahom) N. N. Acharyya, *The History of Medieval Assam* (Gauhati, 1966), pp. 17-30; (Shan) J. G. Scott and J. P. Hardiman, *Gazetteer of Upper Burma and the Shan States*, I, 1 (Rangoon, 1900), esp. chap. 6; and (Lao) L. Finot, "Recherches sur la littérature laotienne," *BEFEO* 7, 5 (1917), esp. pp. 149-154.

[10] See Prince Phetsarath, "The Laotian Calendar," in de Berval, pp. 97-125.

[11] See G. Cœdès, "Documents sur lûhistoire politique et religieuse du Laos occidental," *BEFEO*, 25, 1-2 (1925), 172-174; and Pierre-Bernard Lafont, "Inventaire des manuscrits des pagodes du Laos," *BEFEO*, 52 (1965), 429-546.

those who have studied them, owing to their relatively weak links with subsequent Thai history. All were written originally in Tai Yuan. The *Tamnan Muang Suwannakhomkham*,[12] which deals with the legendary origins and history, over numerous millennia, of a state apparently in the extreme north-central region of the Indochina Peninsula, in the Mekong Valley, is remarkable for several reasons. First, other texts (particularly the Singhanavati chronicle) refer to Suwannakhomkham as a historical antecedent of the kingdoms of Chiang Sæn, Chiang Mai, and Phayao, in northern Siam. Second, its references to the *kròm* people usually are taken to refer to the Khmer of Angkorian Cambodia.[13] The apparent impossibility of either dating or localizing the subject of this text is a source of considerable frustration to those who would seek to ascertain the history of the Thai in the middle Angkorian period, prior to their rapid rise to power in Siam. This text invites serious study, especially within the context of vaguely similar Lao traditions associated with the region of That Phanom and Nakhòn Phanom in northeastern Thailand,[14] and the so-called "Annals of the North" (*Phongsawadan nüa*),[15] both of which share with it several points of similarity and congruity.

---

[12] In *Prachum phongsawadan,* pt. 72 (Bangkok, 1939; reprinted Bangkok Khurusapha, 1969, XLV, 132-240). A French translation was published by Camille Notton, *Annales du Siam, I: Chroniques de Suvanna Khamdeng, Suvanna Khom Kham, Singhanavati* (Paris, 1926), pp. 82- 135.

[13] See also G. H. Luce, *Old Burma—Early Pagan* (Locust Valley, N.Y., 1969), 1, 21-23.

[14] See Phra Phanomchediyanurak, *Urangkhanithan (tamnan phrathat phanom phitsadan)* (Bangkok, 1949); Sila Viravong (ed.), *Urangkhathat thetsana* (printed on palm leaves, Bangkok, 1943); and Ch. Archaimbault, *Contribution a l'étude d'un cycle de légendes lau* (Paris, 1980; Publications EFEO, CXIX).

[15] C. Notton, *Annales du Siam, IV: Legendes sur le Siam et le Cambodge* (Bangkok, 1939). Many Thai editions exist, of which the most accessible is included in *Phraratchaphongsawadan Krung Si Ayutthaya ... læ phongsawadan nüa,* 2 vols. (Bangkok, 1961), 11, 316-406. Note Prince Damrong Rajanubhab's comments on it, "The Story of the Records of Siamese History," *JSS,* 11, 2 (1914/15); reprinted in *Selected Articles from the Siam Society Journal,* I (Bangkok, 1954), 81.

Two extremely important texts associated with the same area, and with a protohistorical period prior to the thirteenth-century founding of Chiang Mai, are the *Tamnan Singhanawatikuman* and the *Tamnan Müang Ngœn Yang Chiang Sæn*. The former first became generally known with the publication of a French translation by Notton in 1926;[16] the second became available only with the publication of Thai editions of both in 1936.[17] Their relatively late availability had the consequence of keeping them from the serious scholarly attentions of Prince Damrong Rajanubhab and George Cœdès when they worked on some of the texts of earlier Siamese history in the first three decades of this century.

The *Tamnan Müang Ngœn Yang Chiang Sæn* might be an extremely late work, as the last date mentioned in it is equivalent to AD 1905. This appears, however, in what must be considered an appendix to the main text, the bulk of which is concerned primarily with the history of extreme northern Siam from its legendary beginnings down to Mangrai's founding of Chiang Mai in 1296. The remaining third of the text centers mainly on Phayao, on King Ngam Müang and his successors down to modern times. Although, like the Singhanawati chronicle, it contains numerous Buddhist references, it seems best to classify it with that text as part of a group of chronicles sharing a common geographical focus, a single genealogical line, and a characteristic chronological framework featuring three separate eras: *pathama-*, *dutiya-*, and *tatiya-sakaraja* ("first," "second," and "third" eras). All these features similarly are shared with the early section of the Nan chronicle, also a later compilation, which must be based on similar texts.[18]

The *Tamnan Singhanawati* also deals with the Chiang Sæn region, but does so in a more explicitly Buddhist framework. Its early portions deal with pre-Buddhist and early Buddhist times,

---

[16] Notton, *Annales du Siam*, I, 141-202.

[17] *Prachum phongsawadan*, pt. 61 (Bangkok, 1936; reprinted Bangkok: Khurusapha, 1969), XXXIII, 197-287; XXXIV, 1-204.

[18] Cited in n. 8, above.

and in places it can be seen to be based on Pali Buddhist texts. The author's concerns here are to link the upper Mekong region with universal (Buddhist) history and to account for local states and sacred shrines by relating their foundation to Buddhist prophecies and mythology. In the process, a sacred and semi-political geography is described which extends from the Chiang Sæn-Chiangrai region northward into southern Yunnan. The latter portion of the text has certain points of contact with the *Tamnan Suwannakhomkham* mentioned above, as it begins with the seizure of the Chiang Sæn state by a "Kròm" prince living at Umongsela.[19] Subsequent passages dealing with a Khòm (Khmer) occupation of Yonakanagara, the northern Tai state in present-day Thailand, and with a later Burmese or Mon invasion, cry out for careful study.

The *Tamnan Singhanawati* is by far the most interesting— and potentially important—of this genre, primarily because it purports to be a full chronological record. Its very dates, however, seem to have given rise to the disdain commonly accorded it. Three dating systems arc employed in the text, and each date also is rendered with its place in the sixty-year cycle. Beginning with Nottonûs French edition, many have taken the dates employed in the latter portion to be dates expressed in the Mahasakaraja Era (MS + 78 = AD), owing to such equivalences being explicitly made there.[20] The chronicle thus appears to cover a period from 674 BC to AD 637 (by Notton's calculations) and it has been accordingly dismissed as fabulous. These calculations seem to be based on mistaken conversions made by some late copyist of the text.[21] References to an invasion from Burma and episodes dated in other chronicles in the eleventh century AD, which in the Singhanawati chronicle are expressed with dates in the fourth and fifth centuries of an unspecified era, encourage a belief that these dates should

---

[19] Notton, *Annales du Siam*, I, 185; Chanthit Krasæsin, "Tamnan Chiang Sæn," *Thalæng ngan prawattisat ekkasan borankhadi*, 4, 2 (May 1970), 137, writes "khòm." Compare this passage with the Suwannakhomkham: Notton, p. 120; Thai edition (1969), p. 206.

[20] See, for example, Notton, ibid., p. 201.

[21] Notton's version derives from a copy made in 1880 (ibid., p. 202).

be taken as Lesser Era (Culasakaraja + 638 = AD) dates. One recent editor of the text has done so, attempting also to unravel the chronology of the entire chronicle.[22]

Of the host of local *tamnan* covering later history, some written in comparatively recent times, one demands special mention here: the chronicle of Chiang Mai. It clearly falls within this tradition, set within universal Buddhist history in its early portions yet concerned primarily with the history of a particular locality in historical times. The chronicle of Chiang Mai long was known only in its French edition, translated by Notton and published first in 1932.[23] Only recently has a Thai version, transcribed from Tai Yuan, become available.[24] A colophon to the Thai edition suggests it was composed in 1827, yet Notton's French version goes only to 1805, the remainder being filled out with sections of the modern *Phongsawadan Yonok*. The two clearly treat the same text: they are identically divided into "books" (*phuk*); but Notton has only seven, while the recent version comprises eight. They form a connected narrative of the history of Chiang Mai, after a brief introductory passage in Book I which moves from the Buddha's predecessors to the reign of Asoka. The early portions draw briefly on the standard Pali sources and on the Suwannakhomkham, Singhanawati, and Camadevi chronicles, and then devote the fullest attention to the period from the end of the thirteenth century to the end of the eighteenth, with particular emphasis upon King Mangrai (1259-1317, Book II), King Tilokarat (1442-1487, Books IV-V), and relations with the Burmese. As the chronicle of a major

---

[22] Manit Wanliphodom, *Tamnan Singhanawatikuman, chabap sòp khon* (Bangkok, 1973). Another edition, without attempts to unravel the chronology, has been completed by Chanthit Krasæsin, "Tamnan Chiang Sæn (Tamnan Singhanawati) ...," *Thalængngan prawattisat ekkasan borankhadi,* 3, 3 (Sept. 1969), 131-151; 4, 1 (Jan. 1970), 141-156; and 4, 2 (May 1970), 133-148.

[23] *Annales du Siam, III: Chronique de Xieng Mai* (Paris, 1932). Notton's translation should not be accepted uncritically.

[24] *Tamnan phün müang Chiang Mai,* ed. Sanguan Chotisukkharat (Bangkok, 1971). This edition is very sloppily done.

state which was incorporated into the kingdom of Siam only in the nineteenth century, the history of which is hardly given its due in the royal chronicles of Ayudhya, the *tamnan* of Chiang Mai must be considered a major source for the history of Thailand.

Such texts as these doubtless have been around for a very long time, in some form or another. Their three types of content—miraculous legend, lists of rulers, and Buddhist embellishments and additions—suggest a sequence in which individual texts might have taken shape over the centuries. They contain both a degree of precision with respect to rulers and the length of their reigns and a degree of historical plausibility which have been neglected. Concluding as they commonly do with events prior to known events of the thirteenth century, they suggest the extent to which Thai historiographers (and presumably others) regarded that period as constituting a break in the continuity of Thai history. Even more importantly, with the demise of the "Nan-chao myth"[25] they suggest an alternative field of inquiry for those concerned with what one Thai historian has called the "Beachhead states";[26] namely, early Thai states in the upper Mekong region in the several centuries prior to the thirteenth, having some connections with Angkorian Cambodia and Pagân Burma, as well as with other Tai states of northern Southeast Asia.

"Universal Histories"

The Buddhist historiography of northern Siam is extraordinarily rich and relatively well known, especially from the work of Cœdès in the 1920s. His monumental "Documents sur l'histoire politique et religieuse du Laos occidental" of 1925 brought to full scholarly attention two major Pali historical works produced at Chiang Mai in the early sixteenth century.

---

[25] See Hiram Woodward, "Who are the Ancestors of the Thais: Report on the Seminar," *Sangkhomsat parithat*, 2, 3 (Feb. 1965), 88-91; F. W. Mote, "Problems of Thai Prehistory," ibid., 2, 2 (Oct. 1964):100-109, and "Prehistory of the Thai People," ibid., special no. 3 (June 1966), 24-31.

[26] Kachorn Sukhabanij, "The Thai Beachhead States in the 11th-12th Centuries," *Sinlapakòn*, 1, 3 (Sept. 1957), 74-81, and 1, 4 (Nov. 1957), 40-54.

There are, however, several others. These include "universal histories" written in Pali, both then and later; one in Thai; and several "monumental" *tamnan* to be discussed below.

The best-known of the Pali "universal histories" are the two works partially published and translated by Cœdès. The first, the *Camadevivamsa*, was written by Mahathera Bodhiransi around the beginning of the fifteenth century.[27] A work of considerable length, its fifteen chapters begin with the time of the Buddha, and presage later Tai Yuan history with a prophecy as to the future establishment of the kingdom of Haripuñjaya, present-day Lamphun. Much of the text (fascicles 4-11) is devoted to the reign of Queen Camadevi, who was brought by ascetics from Lavo (Lopburi). Her successors, perhaps of the period AD 825–1050,[28] are much more quickly dealt with, and the chronicle ends with the rediscovery of relics of the Buddha, deposited in Haripuñjaya much earlier by his disciples, by King Adityaraja, who is thought to have reigned there in the mid-twelfth century.[29] The purpose of this chronicle thus might be considered to be to explain the presence at a major shrine in Lamphun of Buddhist relics, and its function to be the linking of that region, in which the text's author lived almost four centuries later, with the person of the Buddha, earlier Buddhist states in the region, and "universal history"— that is, the origins and progress of Buddhism.

The *Jinakalamali* was written in Chiang Mai by Mahathera Ratanapañña in AD 1516.[30] It is certainly the best example of its type, providing a synoptic history of Buddhism from the

---

[27] *Rüang Chmmathewiwong, phongsawadan muang Hariphunchai* (Bangkok, 1921; reprinted, with Thai translation only, 1930 and 1967); partial romanized Pali text and French translation, Cœdès, "Documents," pp. 141-171; and also Notton, *Annales du Siam, II: Chronique de La:p'un, Histoire de la dynastie Chamt'evi* (Paris, 1930).

[28] Kachorn, I, 4:50.

[29] Ibid., p. 51; and G. Cœdès, *The Indianized States of Southeast Asia* (Honolulu, 1968), pp. 194-195

[30] Partial Pali text and French translation in Cœdès, "Documents," pp. 36-140; full romanized text ed. A. P. Buddhadatta Mahathera (London, 1962); English translation by N. A. Jayawickrama, *The Sheaf of Garlands of the Epochs of the Conqueror* (London, 1968).

Buddha's resolution to become a Buddha through the history of Buddhism in India and Ceylon and the establishment of Buddhism in Siam, particularly the spread of Sinhalese Buddhism from the thirteenth century up to the author's own lifetime in Chiang Mai. Although its coverage of secular affairs is peripheral to its primary concern with the history of Buddhism, its utility as an accurate source for Siamese history has frequently been demonstrated, and it must be numbered among the classics of Thai historiography.

One other work, exceptional in some ways, also deserves special mention here. This is the *Sangitiyavamsa*, composed in Pali by the Bangkok monk Somdet Phra Wannarat (also known as Phonnarat) in 1789.[31] Written in honor of King Rama I immediately after his famous revision of the Pali canon, this is a history of the successive Buddhist councils at which the Tipitaka was revised. Its first two chapters discuss the first seven councils convened in India and Ceylon, and then the spread of Buddhism in South Asia is treated. There is extensive discussion of the history (treated dynastically) of northern Siam, Ayudhya, and early Bangkok (chapters 6-8), and it contains an especially moving description of the fall of Ayudhya in 1767. Its classification as "universal history" is problematic, yet it does, in classical fashion, treat of the chronological development of a world structured by a common religious heritage in such a manner as to suggest no other world exists. Similarly, its temporal framework, like that of the other texts, is at least implicitly delimited in both finite and infinite Buddhist time: that is, the current epoch extending five thousand years forward from the Buddhaûs enlightenment is set within the abstract infinitude of cosmic time in which there are earlier buddhas and buddhas-to-be.[32]

The Singhanawati chronicle, already discussed, might seem a likely candidate for inclusion in the category of Thai "universal

---

[31] *Sangkhitiyawong, phongsawadan rüang sangkhayana phrathammawinai* (Bangkok, 1923; reprint Bangkok, 1978); Pali text and Thai translation in parallel columns.

[32] My discussion of this point owes much to the recent work of Charnvit Kasetsiri, Anan Ganjanapan, and Koson Srisang.

histories." Its place here, however, is debatable owing to the strong possibility that it is a composite work, perhaps a local historical tradition blown up to fit a broader Buddhist framework. A much clearer example of this genre, one more certainly an original work, is the *Mulasasana*.[33] This work, still seriously neglected, is thought to have been compiled in Lan Na Thai just prior to the *Camadevivamsa* and *Jinakalamali*,[34] and perhaps to have served as a source for them. The main portion of the text was written by a monk, Buddhañana, in the mid-sixteenth century, later material being added by another monk, Buddhabhukama.[35] In structure their work is similar to the two main Chiang Mai texts, extending in time from the Buddha's resolve to become a Buddha to the early sixteenth-century kings of Chiang Mai. It has in addition, however, a long discursive closing section dealing with Buddha relics and the future course of the religion.

"Monumental" Tamnan

There is another class of *tamnan* which shares with the "universal histories'" a common Buddhist framework but whose scope is very much more restricted. These are the *tamnan* of Buddhist images, monuments, and institutions, particularly common in northern Siam but also known elsewhere. One group of these chronicles is of particular interest as deriving from the same environment, and even the same individuals, as some of the "universal histories."

The *Sihinganidana* was written in Pali by Mahathera Bodhirangsi, who is also the author of the *Camadevivamsa*, and it may be considered to date from around the beginning of the fifteenth century, AD 1402-1442.[36] It is the story of the Sihinga

---

[33] *Tamnan mulasasana* (Bangkok, 1939; new ed. Bangkok, 1975).

[34] Cf. Cœdès, *Indianized States,* pp. 136; 322, n. 30. The latest date mentioned in the text is equivalent to A.D. 1510 (p. 260).

[35] I am indebted to A. B. Griswold for advice on this point.

[36] Dhanit Yupho, in the foreword to a new edition of the text, translated from Pali by Sæng Monwithun, *Nithan phraphutthasihing* (Bangkok, 1963). This edition gives the full Pali text, pp. 1-32.

Buddha image, which by legend was cast in Ceylon; it was subsequently brought to Sukhothai via Nakhòn Si Thammarat in the reign of King Ramkhamhæng and then taken to Ayudhya in 1378. In the warfare of the succeeding decades it was moved to Kamphængphet (1382), Chiangrai (1388), and, finally, Chiang Mai (1407). Bodhirangsi probably wrote in celebration of its arrival in Chiang Mai. Because of the image's involvement in the wars of this period, the chronicle is a useful supplementary historical source.[37]

The most famous Buddha image in Siam is the so-called Emerald Buddha, now housed in the Temple of the Emerald Buddha within the walls of the Grand Palace. Its history, written by a young Chiang Mai monk named Brahma-rajapañña, is of considerable interest. The date of his work is unknown: we know only that he based it upon an already-existing version in Thai, and that only his Pali version existed by the reign of Rama 'I 1782-1809), founder of the present dynasty. Titled in Pali *Ratanabimbavamsa*, it has been frequently translated.[38] Because of the image's considerable "wanderings" in Siam, Cambodia, and Laos prior to its installation in Bangkok in 1782, the chronicle has much to say to the historian.

Tamnan of Buddhist religious monuments are numerous, and indeed continue to be written today. The best-known (and perhaps the earliest) of these have been collected in a single volume by Thailand's Fine Arts Department.[39] This collection includes only chronicles of reliquaries (*phrathat*), most of which

---

[37] An English translation by Camille Notton was published in Bangkok in 1933 under the title *P'ra Buddha Sihinga*.

[38] The Pali text is available only in a volume edited by the Fine Arts Department, *Tamnan Phra Kæo Morakot chabap sombun* (Bangkok, 1961), pp. 312-384. This volume also includes a Pali version and explanation by King Mongkut, and several modern versions including the translation into Thai made for King Rama I in 1788. The best modern translation in Thai is by Sæng Monwithun, *Ratanabimbavamsa, tamnan Phra Kæo Morakot* (Bangkok, 1967). There exists an English translation by the indefatigable Camille Notton, *The Chronicle of the Emerald Buddha* (Bangkok, 1932).

[39] *Prachum tamnan phrathat, phak thi 1 læ phak thi 2* (Bangkok, 1970).

have been transcribed from palm-leaf manuscripts written in northern Thai script. The ten *tamnan* are (with probable dates of composition, when known, in parentheses) from Chiang Sæn (1515?), Lamphun (1606), Lampang (1830), the Chumphit Nakhòn Reliquary (1543), Doi Puphuthap in Phræ province, the Chò Hæ Reliquary in Phra (1864), That Phanom in the northeast (1838), Nakhòn Si Thammarat (c. 1553),[40] Dòi Suthep in Chiang Mai (1825), and the Chæ Hæng Reliquary in Nan (1704). In most cases, these are chronicles of the palladia of individual *mü ang*, and the fortunes of both are closely interrelated. Thus they have much to offer the historian whose interests lie in more secular directions. These texts almost always contain numerous dates, expressed in their fullest form. Because they often overlap with local histories and chronicles, they may profitably be employed in cross-checking other sources.[41] This genre of works remains relatively unexplored and deserves careful scholarly attention.[42]

Phongsawadan History

The major differences between *tamnan* and *phongsawadan* historical traditions are obvious only through a comparison of the most extreme examples of the two types: the comparison is blurred when one considers later examples of *tamnan* such as the Chiang Mai chronicle, which contains elements of both types. Taking as extreme examples the Mulasasana and Jinakalamali *tamnan* and any of the versions of the *phongsawadan* of Ayudhya, their differences are clear. Instead of treating "universal," Buddhist history, the royal chronicles (*phraratchaphongsawadan*) of Ayudhya deal with dynastic, or, more properly, kingly history: the deeds of

---

[40] See D. K. Wyatt, *The Crystal Sands: The Chronicles of Nagara Sridharrmaraja* (Ithaca, 1975).

[41] For example, the chronological puzzles of the Nan chronicle can be solved by reference to the Chæ Hæng Reliquary chronicle.

[42] Only one chronicle of this type so far has appeared in translation: E. W. Hutchinson, "The Seven Spires: A Sanctuary of the Sacred Fig Tree at Chiang Mai," *JSS*, 39, 1 (1951), 51-68. A wider sampling of this literature is available in condensed form in Sanguan Chotisukkharat, *Tamnan müang nüa*, 2 vols. (Chiang Mai, 1955-1960).

the rulers of Ayudhya. Their inherent continuity is secular, not religious, save insofar as the compilers were concerned with the enduring "merit" of Ayudhya itself. Rather than being written by Buddhist monks, they were written by scribes or officials at the royal court. Although too few early examples survive to allow easy generalization, it would appear that they were composed primarily for the edification of the ruler and his successors, though it has also been suggested that a ruler might have considered the royal chronicles as part of his royal regalia.

It is not known for certain when the first chronicle of Ayudhya was written, although it is quite certain that the basic sources for early texts must have been kept from an early time in the form of astrologersû notebooks of extraordinary events.[43] The earliest full version of Ayudhya history presently known was compiled in 1640 by the Dutch merchant Jeremias van Vliet. Beginning with three variant legends concerning the origins of the founder of Ayudhya, it then gives a reign-by-reign chronicle of notable events down to the date of composition. As no dates are given in this version, but only reign lengths, and because of the discursive style in which it was written, pending further study it may be considered to be based primarily upon oral, rather than written, records of Siamese history.[44]

The earliest, the best known, and the only full translation of Siamese royal *phongsawadan* is the so-called Luang Prasert version of c. 1680, first published in Thai in 1907 and in English translation in 1909.[45] This chronicle is known to have been compiled in the reign of King Narai the Great (1657-1688) by

---

[43] Examples of these are available in printed form: "Cotmaihet hon" and "Cotmaihet hon khòng chamün Kongsin," *Prachum phongsawadan*, pt. 8 (Bangkok, 1917; reprinted Bangkok: Kaona, 1961, IV, 86-162); and *Cotmaihet hon chabap Phra Pramuanthanarak* (Bangkok, 1921).

[44] Following a lead from Seiichi Iwao, this text was first discovered and photographed by Kachorn Sukhabanij. It is published as *The Short History of the Kings of Siam*, trans. Leonard Andaya, ed. D. K. Wyatt (Bangkok, 1975).

[45] *Phraratchaphongsawadan krung kao chabap luang Prasœt'aksònnit* (Bangkok, 1907), included in *Prachum phongsawadan*, pt. 1 (Bangkok, 1914; reprinted Bangkok: Kaona, 1963, 1, 113-138); and translated by O. Frank

a court astrologer, Phra Horathibodi. Although it ceases with events in the year 1604, Prince Damrong Rajanubhab was of the opinion that a second volume of the text once existed to carry events into Narai's reign.[46]

The Luang Prasœt version of the Ayudhya *phongsawadan* is quite skeletal, giving only the barest details of events, and it is particularly thin on the earliest periods. Its chief virtue has always been held to be its chronological accuracy, attested to by comparison with foreign sources. It bears such strong similarities in structure to the later "abridged chronicle," noted below, that it is tempting to consider it as such, perhaps a version intended to answer foreigners' questions concerning Siamese history.

Prince Damrong's useful article of 1915, translated from comments in his introductory section of the "Royal Autograph Edition" of the *phongsawadan*, generally describes the various versions of the Ayudhya chronicles.[47] It is necessary to cover the same subject again, however, owing to considerable advances in the study of the subject in the past half-century. As Dr. Busakorn Lailert recently has explained, there are nine extant versions of the Ayudhya chronicles besides the Luang Prasert version, all of which postdate the fall of the kingdom to the Burmese in 1767.[48]

Of the earliest version, that of Culasakaraja (CS) 1136 (AD 1774), only one small fragment has survived.[49] This covers only the years CS 926-931 (AD 1564–1569) and is too fragmentary to shed much light on the *phongsawadan* as a whole. Of a slightly later version of CS 1145 (AD 1783), we similarly have only small fragments, dealing with portions of the reigns of Maha Chakraphat

---

furter, "Events in Ayuddhya from Chulasakaraj 686–966," *JSS* 6,3 (1909), 1-21, reprinted in *Selected Articles from the Siam Society Journal*, I (Bangkok, 1954), pp. 38-62.

[46] Damrong, "Story of the Records," p.84.

[47] Ibid.

[48] "Phraratchaphongsawadan Krung Si Ayutthaya," *Sinlapakòn*, 12, 2 (July 1968):89-93.

[49] "Phraratchaphongsawadan khwam kao," *Prachum phongsawadan*, pt. 4 (Bangkok, 1915; reprinted Bangkok: Kaona, 1964, II, 113-132).

and Maha Thammaracha (AD 1549–1590). This version has never been published.

Only with the later versions of the reign of King Rama I (1782-1809) does a fuller picture of *phongsawadan* history begin to emerge. The earliest full version, the Phan Canthanumat version of CS 1157 (AD 1795),[50] clearly indicates that its compiler worked from an earlier version written in the reign of King Borommakot (1733-1758) and revised in the reign of King Taksin (1767-1782).[51] In CS 1169 (AD 1807), Rama I had a leading Buddhist monk, Somdet Phra Phonnarat, the author of the *Sangitiyavamsa*, undertake a thorough revision of the chronicles, basing his work primarily upon the CS 1157 version but heeding the king's sensibilities on certain delicate episodes.[52] This version, of which the best manuscript is in the British Museum, must be considered the last great example of the *phongsawadan*.[53] Two features of its composition are especially remarkable. First, it is unusual in having a short introductory section dealing with the legendary events leading up to the foundation of Ayudhya in 1351. This material is reminiscent generally of the *tamnan* traditions concerning northern Siam, with which it has some points of connection, and of the compiler's previous work within that tradition as expressed both in his *Sangkhitiyavamsa* and in two fragments of a more lengthy work on the pre-Ayudhya period, the *Culayuddhakaravamsa*.[54] It is worth remarking that this introduction was deleted from subsequent reworkings of his *phongsawadan*. Secondly, it is somehow appropriate to note

---

[50] *Phraratchaphongsawadan krung Si Ayutthaya chabap Phan Canthanumat (Cœm) kap phra Cakkraphatdiphong (Cat)* (Bangkok, 1964); two versions in one volume.

[51] Busakorn, p. 90.

[52] Ibid. pp. 91-93.

[53] The manuscript was discovered by Kachorn Sukhabanij; and is published as *Phraratchaphongsawadan krung Sayam chak tonchabap thi pen sombat khong British Museum krung London,* ed. Tri Amatyakul (Bangkok, 1964).

[54] *Culayuddhakaravamsa phuk 2 rüang phongsawadan Thai* (Bangkok, 1920); and "Culayuddhakaravamsa khwam riang (ton ton)," *Prachum phongsawadan* pt. 66 (Bangkok, 1937; reprinted Bangkok: Khurusapha, 1969, XI., 260–278).

the specific initiative taken by King Rama I in ordering the compilation of this chronicle, an act perfectly in character for a monarch also responsible for the total revision of the Pali canon, the recodification of Thai law, and the composition of the most complete version of the Ramayana known in Siam.

Until the publication of the "British Museum" manuscript of the chronicle, that version was known only through subsequent versions based upon it, of which the most prominent was the edition published in two volumes by the American missionary Dan Beach Bradley in the reign of King Mongkut. This edition was commonly attributed to Prince Paramanuchit Chinorot, who had been a pupil of Somdet Phra Phonnarat. Inasmuch as, with the exception of the deleted pre-Ayudhya portion, it is virtually identical to the "British Museum" manuscript in which authorship is explicitly attributed to Somdet Phra Phonnarat, that long-standing misapprehension has been removed.[55] It remains highly likely that it was Prince Paramanuchit who prepared Bradley's version for printing, just as it is almost certain that this same version is that which served as the basis of the version edited personally in 1855 by King Mongkut, the "Royal Autograph Edition."[56] From one, or a combination, of these texts, Prince Paramanuchit himself compiled two abridged versions, probably in Mongkut's reign, which are unique in having in some places a chronology all their own.[57]

---

[55] The authorship question was first solved by Tri Amatyakul, "Phutæng nangsü phraratchaphongsawadan chabap phim 2 lem," *Sinlapakòn*, 5, 6 (March 1962), 43–50, and 6, 1 (May 1962), 25-34. The Bradley "two-volume" edition has been published as *Phraratchaphongsawadan Krung Si Ayutthaya chabap Somdet Phra Phonnarat, Wat Phra Chetuphon* (Bangkok, 1962).

[56] The latest edition is the first to be encompassed within the covers of a single volume: *Phraratchaphongsawadan chabap phraratchahatlekha* (Chonburi, 1968) Mongkut's version here has had additional editorial attention from Prince Damrong Rajanubhab, to whose energy we owe the fact that almost all the texts mentioned in this article are available in print.

[57] These were first published in the Bradley edition of the mid-nineteenth century. The most accessible texts are those included in *Phrar atcha phongsawadan krung Si Ayutthaya chabap luang Prasœtaksònnit, chabap*

Two recent works have begun the important task of demonstrating that there is much more to be learned from the Ayudhya *phongsawadan* than Wood even hinted.[58] Certainly they are heavily concerned with king and court and more interested in warfare than in peace; in short, they are what King Chulalongkorn termed tales of "dynasties and battles" (*wong wong cak cak*). They reveal little of provincial affairs, of economic life, or even of religion. They have, nonetheless, a great deal—perhaps much more than has been suspected—to tell the modern reader about a historically-important segment of Thai society, about its political values, its modes of behavior, and its style of rule. Until this material has been thoroughly analyzed, we will still lack all but the most elementary skeleton of Ayudhya history within which to place such other material as is beginning to come to light.

Neither *tamnan* nor *phongsawadan* has disappeared from Thai historiography. They continue to be issued and read, and there are still many—provincial monks, retired officials, journalists—whose writings contain elements of one or both traditions. When a historian is pressed to apply a more "modern" analytical approach to their materials, they might suggest that he supply his own interpretations. Those who in the decades to come carry forward the work Professor Hall has so long promoted might begin by making these basic sources of Siam's history better known and more accessible.

... *kromphra Paramanuchit Chinorot læ phongsawadan nüa* ..., 2 vols. (Bangkok, 1961), II, 281-315. A translation of the longer of these, by the present author, is published as "The Abridged Royal Chronicle of Ayudhya of Prince Paramanuchit Chinorot," *JSS* 61, 1 (Jan. 1973), 25-50.

[58] Busakorn Lailert, "The Ban Phlu Luang Dynasty, 1688–1767: A Study of the Thai Monarchy during the Closing Years of the Ayuthya Period" (Ph D. diss., University of London, 1972); and Charnvit Kasetsiri, *The Rise of Ayudhya: A History of Siam in the Fourteenth and Fifteenth Centuries* (Kuala Lumpur, 1976).

MAINLAND POWERS
ON THE MALAY PENINSULA,
AD 1000-1511*

It has long seemed natural for historians of the Sultanate of Malacca to look to Siam and to mainland Southeast Asia for evidence which might throw light on the references in Malay, Chinese, and Portuguese sources to Thai activities and influence in the Malay Peninsula between the end of the fourteenth century and the beginning of the sixteenth. It was Colonel G.E. Gerini who first seriously began this search through mainland sources at the turn of the century and came up with a limited number of references to Thai activities.[1] On the basis of a vague claim of Thai suzerainty over Nagara Sri Dharmaraja (Ligor) and land extending "to the sea which marks the frontier" in the postscript to the 1292 Sukhothai inscription of King Rama Khamhæng; a Mon reference to Thai military expeditions down the peninsula in 1278-80; scattered thirteenth century references to Nagara Sri Dharmaraja in the sixteenth-century Pali chronicles of Chiang Mai; and an Ayudhya claim to vassals in the southern portion of the peninsula in the "Palatine Law," the date of which he read as AD 1358, Gerini built a case which sought to assert the "unquestionable" possession of the entire Malay Peninsula by the Thai kingdoms of Sukhothai

---

* Paper presented to the International Conference on Asian History, Kuala Lumpur, Malaysia, August 1968. (Paper no. 63.) This paper was written jointly with Dr. J.S. Bastin. I include here only the first portion, which I wrote. Not previously published.

[1] G.E. Gerini, "The Nagarakretagama List of Countries on the Indo-Chinese Mainland (circa 1380 A.D.)," *Journal of the Royal Asiatic Society [JRAS]* 1905, 485-511.

and Ayudhya from the middle of the thirteenth century until the Portuguese conquest of Malacca in 1511.[2]

Gerini wrote at a time when the issues he raised—of Thai suzerainty over portions of the Peninsula peopled by Muslim Malays—struck tender emotional and political nerves in the years just prior to the Anglo-Siamese Treaty of 1909. C.O. Blagden's response, published the following year, in 1906, was in many respects an overreaction.[3] Despite intermittent excursions into the problem since that date by others,[4] it still stands essentially as Gerini and Blagden left it in 1906. No more has been established than isolated indications of Thai activities at a limited number of widely-scattered dates between the middle of the thirteenth century and the beginning of the sixteenth. The core of the problem remains untouched: the problem of establishing how, why, and when the Thai came to be involved in relations with the Malay states of the peninsula.

To define this problem in terms of "Thai" activities, however, is both misleading and less productive than it need be. First, to put ethnic labels on the participants in a power struggle during this particular period of time is to imply a rigid contrast between the Theravada Buddhist Thai and Muslim Malay which was, if not absent, then politically unimportant before the fifteenth century; second, to restrict the scope of this examination to specifically "Thai" activities is to beg questions of ethnic identification and composition in the formative years of Siam's history; and it tends to the neglect of important strands of continuity which linked the early Thai kingdoms with the activities of their predecessor states. Reduced to simplest terms, the ethnic identities of soldiers, diplomats, monks, and officials who were active on the Malay Peninsula between the years 1000 and 1500 are not as important as the simple fact that they came as agents of a power or powers

---

[2] *Ibid.*, p. 491.

[3] C.O. Blagden, "Siam and the Malay Peninsula," *JRAS*, 1906, 107-19.

[4] Notably Kenneth R. Hall and John K. Whitmore, "Southeast Asian Trade and the Isthmian Struggle, 1000-1200 AD," in *Explorations in Early Southeast Asian History: The Origins of Southeast Asian Statecraft*, ed. Kenneth R. Hall and John K. Whitmore (Ann Arbor, 1976), 303-340.

of mainland Southeast Asia; and it is to the problem of the origins of such involvement that this paper is directed.

In seeking answers to these problems, two alternative avenues of approach commonly have been followed, each for a separate period of time. The first, and the most substantial in the literature on the subject, has been to focus attention upon the peninsular state of Tambralinga, as the nexus of conflict between Srivijaya and the Khmer Empire between the eleventh and thirteenth centuries.[5] For the period beginning around the middle of the thirteenth century, a totally different approach commonly has been followed; to seek evidence of the activities of the mainland states, i.e. Sukhothai and Ayudhya, in the records of their respective capitals.[6] A substantial body of new evidence, only a small proportion of which can be considered here,[7] makes possible a fresh examination of the earlier period and an extension of the local history approach into the later period. While the fruits of this new research can by no means conclusively establish solutions to the numerous questions posed by the complexity of this vast period, this evidence does at least give some body and life to what has hitherto been ephemeral, if not chimerical.

The Eleventh and Twelfth Centuries.

The local focus of mainland ambitions on the Malay Peninsula in the eleventh and twelfth centuries undoubtedly was the peninsular state of Tambralinga, located in the vicinity of modern Nagara Sri Dharmaraja (Nakhòn Si Thammarat or Ligor). Intermittently mentioned among the dependencies of the Khmer

---

[5] Notably by G. Cœdès, "A Propos de la chute du royaume de Srivijaya," *Bijdragen*, 83 (1927), 459-72; and more recently by L.P. Briggs, "The Khmer Empire and the Malay Peninsula," *Far Eastern Quarterly*, 9:3 (May, 1950), 256-305, and O.W. Wolters, "Tambralinga," *Bulletin of the School of Oriental and African Studies*, 21 (1958), 587-607.

[6] E.g., G.E. Marrison, "The Siamese Wars with Malacca during the reign of Muzaffar Shah," *Journal of the Malayan Branch of the Royal Asiatic Society*, 22, pt. 1 (1949), 61-66.

[7] It is more fully presented in this author's *The Crystal Sands: The Chronicles of Nagara Sri Dharrmaraja* (Ithaca, 1975).

empire in Chinese accounts, Tambralinga appears to have taken advantage of the weakness of her neighbors to pursue an independent course at the beginning of the eleventh century. It has long been supposed that Tambralinga was the origin of an attempt against the Angkorian throne in 1002; and on the basis of the understanding that the Tambralinga candidate, Suryavarman I, was successful in seizing the throne, which he held for nearly half a century, it was assumed that at least the northern half of the peninsula thereby would have remained within the Khmer empire.[8] In his 1964 analysis of the Prasat Ben inscription, however, Professor Cœdès has shown that, on the contrary, the Tambralinga pretender was Jayaviravarman, who was unsuccessful and was expelled from Angkor by Suryavarman towards 1008.[9] Thus although Tambralinga might have been included within the Khmer empire during Jayaviravarman's short and contested reign, there is no reason to believe that it remained within the empire after his demise; and, indeed, it would be reasonable to suppose that Suryavarman's campaigns in the valley of the Caophraya River and his request for Cola aid "against an enemy who threatened his kingdom" in 1012 are reflections of his attempts to carry the struggle against Jayaviravarman and Tambralinga back into the territory of the latter.[10] Under these circumstances, it would have been natural for Tambralinga to turn for aid to Srivijaya and to Kadaram, Srivijaya's peninsular outpost, or perhaps to the Mon country of Lower Burma. It may be significant that both Srivijaya and Tambralinga were active in strengthening their diplomatic contacts with China during this period, especially in the years 1016-17.[11] The Cola invasions which soon followed

---

[8] Cf. Briggs, *op. cit.*, p. 286; and Wolters, *op. cit.*, p. 598.

[9] G. Cœdès, *Inscriptions du Cambodge,* VII (Paris, 1964), pp. 167-72.

[10] R.C. Majumdar, "The Overseas Expeditions of King Rajendra Cola," *Artibus Asiæ,* 24 (1962), pp. 3~8-420 Majumdar interprets this request for Cola aid as a response to a threat from Kadaram/ Srivijaya.

[11] Tambralinga sent missions to China in 1014 and 1016, and Srivijaya in 1017: Wolters, "Tambralinga," p. 595; and W.P. Groeneveldt, "Notes on the Malay Archipelago and Malacca, Compiled from Chinese Sources," *VBG,* 39, pt. 1 (1877), p. 650.

included among their objects Tambralinga and other isthmian states—Langkasuka, Kadaram, and Takkola—as well as the Sumatran seat of the Srivijayan empire and Papphala in the region of Pegu in Lower Burma.[12]

It is possible that the Cola expeditions resulted in the re-introduction of Khmer influence in the isthmian region during the second quarter of the century, although the westernmost inscriptions of Suryavarman I[13] are those of Lopburi of 1022-25, and there is no direct evidence that his troops moved thence further southwards. If the Khmer were active in the isthmian region again by the middle of the century, it would appear that they were there not independently, but rather within the context of a multi-partite contest for control over a trade route which was an alternative to the Straits of Malacca still dominated by Srivijaya.

The first new mainland power to become involved in the affairs of the peninsula was probably the kingdom of Pagân. King Aniruddha (1044-77), Luce believed,[14] followed up his conquest of Thaton in 1057 by moving his armies as far to the south as Mergui, and "possibly even ... south of the isthmus of Kra."[15] If so, it would seem at least possible that his Mon predecessors in Lower Burma may have established peninsular interests as well, during the previous quarter century; and it would be well to bear in mind in this connection the inclusion of Burma ports among the targets of the first Cola expeditions; namely Papphala on the

---

[12] G. Cœdès, *Les états hindouises d'Indochine et d'Indonesie* (2e ed.; Paris, 1964), pp. 261-63.

[13] Apart from the inscriptions of Prachinburi, only two inscriptions of Suryavarman I have been found in Central Siam, two from Lopburi of A.D. 1022-25. Cf. the chronological list of Khmer inscriptions in Cœdès, *Inscriptions du Cambodge*, VIII (Paris, 1966).

[14] G.H. Luce, "Some Old References to the South of Burma and Ceylon," *Felicitation Volumes of Southeast-Asian Studies Presented to His Highness Prince Dhaninivat* (Bangkok, 1965), vol. II, pp. 270.

[15] *Ibid.* In a later article, Luce changes this statement-to suggest that it is "probable that they, Aniruddha and Saw Lu (or Kyanzittha), crossed the isthmus of Kra." "The Career of Htilaing Min (Kyanzittha)," *JRAS*, 1966, p. 59.

Pegu coast, and presumably Takkola.[16] In the following decade, the affairs of the peninsula were further complicated by the activities of Ceylon, the Colas, and Srivijaya. King Vijayabahu I (1055-1110) of Ceylon, embroiled in conflict with the Colas, requested aid from Aniruddha "shortly before 1067," and the latter responded with a large shipment of what Luce terms peninsular products, which he interprets as an indication that Aniruddha may then have been campaigning "in the far south."[17] Almost immediately thereafter, in 1067, the Colas launched another expedition against Kadaram, this time in aid of its ruler (or a claimant to its throne) who had been forced to flee his country and sought Cola aid.[18] Cœdès is inclined to interpret this incident as a revolt against Srivijaya by Kadaram,[19] while Paranavitana puts yet another interpretation on these events by identifying Kadaram as Srivijaya.[20] Cola intervention, however, was short-lived—the Cola protégé almost immediately turning out his benefactors[21] —and, when the Colas returned to warfare on Ceylon which was going against them and which two years later was to bring to an end their seventy-seven year occupation of the island,[22] the pressure on the isthmian region appears at least temporarily to have been relaxed. Since the middle of the century, Angkor had been preoccupied with internal conflict and with war on her eastern frontiers; Aniruddha was busy with the internal consolidation of his empire; and Srivijaya was quiescent in decline. It was at this moment, in 1070, that Tambralinga sent what was to be her last embassy to China, her

---

[16] Cœdès, Les états, p. 262. One is also led to query whether peninsular interests were involved in a Khmer invasion of Lower Burma around 1050; see G.H. Luce, "A Cambodian (?) Invasion of Lower Burma," JRAS, 12, pt. 1 (1922), pp. 39-45; and Luce, "Career of Htilaing Min," pp. 57-58.

[17] Luce, "Some Old References," p. 271, based upon Culavamsa, LVIII, vv. 8-10.

[18] Cœdès, Les états, p. 272.

[19] Cœdès, Les états, p. 272.

[20] S. Paranavitana, Ceylon and Malaysia (Colombo, 1966), pp. 51-52.

[21] Paranavitana, Ceylon and Malaysia, p. 52.

[22] See C.W. Nicholas and S. Paranavitana, A Concise History of Ceylon (Colombo, 1961), pp. 191-92.

first since 1016.[23] It is possible that this embassy signaled the beginning of a new period of independence for the isthmian state, but with the general falling-off in Chinese overseas contacts in this period, evidence is lacking from that source; and we are left with a number of scattered references which do not necessarily add up to a coherent or continuous narrative of the events of the period.

For the period extending from the Tambralinga embassy of 1070 until the beginning of the thirteenth century, there are three somewhat contradictory sets of evidence which, taken separately, might prove the cases for Khmer or Burmese suzerainty over the isthmian region or for a lengthy period of independence, respectively.

The case for a continuation or resumption of Khmer suzerainty is based almost entirely on two Chinese references to Tambralinga as "Teng-" or "Tan-liu-mei."[24] Chao Ju-kua, in his *Chu-fan chih* of 1225, followed the *Ling wai tai ta* of 1178 in including Teng-liu-mei among the dependencies of the Khmer empire (and at least the later account included Pagân[25]), although Chia-lo-hsi, usually associated with Chaiya, north of Ligor, was stated to be a dependency of Srivijaya[26] and the Khmer empire was said to border on Chia-lo-hsi in the south.[27] The removal of the

---

[23] Wolters, "Tambralinga," p. 598. Wolters' suggestion that this embassy might be interpreted as an attempt to throw off the Angkorian connection established by Suryavarman I must be re-examined in the light of the Prasat Ben inscription.

[24] I accept Wolters' ("Tambralinga," pp. 592-95) argument for discarding "Tan-mei-liu" as a scribal error in the *Sung shih*. See, however, Paul Wheatley, *The Golden Khersonese* (Kuala Lumpur, 1961), pp. 65-67.

[25] F. Hirth and W.W. Rockhill, *Chau Ju-kua: His Work on the Chinese and Arab Trade in the Twelfth and Thirteenth Centuries, Entitled* Chu-Fan-Chi (St. Petersburg, 1911; Taipei, 1965), pp. 54, 56 note 10. But cf. L.P. Briggs, *The Khmer Empire* (Philadelphia, 1951), pp. 216-17; and G.H. Luce, "The Early Syam in Burma's History: A Supplement," *JSS*, XLVII, pt. 1 (June, 1959), pp. 60-61.

[26] Hirth and Rockhill, *Chau Ju-kua*, p. 62.

[27] Hirth and Rockhill, *Chau Ju-kua*, pp. 54, 66 n. 10. On these difficulties, see J.G. de Casparis, "The Date of the Grahi Buddha," *JSS*, LV, pt. 1 (Jan. 1967), p. 39 n. 27.

Grahi Buddha inscription (Cœdès' No. XXV) from this period by Dr. de Casparis precludes its consideration here as evidence either for the continuation of Khmer influence or for the establishing of a new link with Sumatra.[28] Khmer epigraphy is silent on this subject; and although the Preah Khan inscription of the last decade of the twelfth century does, perhaps significantly, appear to include among its toponyms several localities at the head of the Gulf of Siam which would have controlled the northern land access to the isthmus, including Ratburi and Phetburi,[29] it provides no definite indication of events in the isthmian region itself. One is left only with Aymonier's completely undocumented reference of 1904 to Jayavarman VII's campaigns on the peninsula in 1195 which are supposed to have resulted in the incorporation into the empire of Chen-li(-fu) and Tambralinga, among other places.[30] It would seem that the likelihood of Khmer influence on the peninsula is strongest for the reign of Jayavarman VII, towards 1200; but concrete evidence on this point is lacking.

The case for a period of Burmese suzerainty has been urged by Professor Luce; most succinctly in 1959 with his suggestion that "the isthmus of Kra ... appears to have been under the control of Pagân from about 1060 to 1200 AD"[31] This suggestion is based primarily upon fragmentary epigraphic evidence, including the finds of votive tablets which date from the reigns of Aniruddha, his successor Saw Lu, and Kyanzittha, as far south as Mergui.[32]

---

[28] G. Cœdès, *Recueil des inscriptions du Siam*, II (2 ed.; Bangkok, 1961), pp. 29-31; and Casparis, "Grahi Buddha," pp. 31-40.

[29] G. Cœdès, "La stele de Preah Khan d'Angkor," *BEFEO*, XLI (1941), vv. 116-117.

[30] E. Aymonier, *Le Cambodge*, III (Paris, 1904), p. 528. Aymonier here appears to have been utilizing mainly Cham inscriptions and, perhaps, the Vietnamese chronicles. In covering the same period, Maspero, *Le royaume de Champa* (Paris, 1928), pp. 165-66, states that Jayavarman VII sent missions to Dai Viet in 1194 and 1198, and it may be that in the latter he announced his successes. I have been unable to check his references: *Viet su luoc*, quyen III, p. 17b; *Dai Viet su ki toan tho*, quyen IV, p. 22b; and *Kham dinh Viet su thong giam cu'o'ng muc*, quyen V, 27b.

[31] Luce, "Early *Syam*: Supplement," pp. 60-61.

[32] Luce, "Some Old References," esp. pp. 271-73; and see Luce, "Dvaravati and Old Burma," *JSS*, LIII, pt. 1 (Jan., 1965), esp. pp. 16-19.

The Burmese presence in the isthmian region was undoubtedly more forceful by the middle of the twelfth century, when it led to conflict between Ceylon and Pagân. After King Narathu had restricted trade with Ceylon, captured a princess the ruler of Ceylon was sending to "Kamboja," and blocked Ceylon's trade across the Isthmus of Kra,[33] a Sinhalese force invaded Lower Burma in 1165, capturing Bassein, Pagân, and Papphalama, and killing the Burmese king. Luce conjectures that Ceylon thereby gained control of the isthmus; but following the death of King Parakramabahu I of Ceylon in 1186, his successor, Vijayabahu II, concluded a treaty of peace with Burma.[34] By the end of the next Sinhalese reign in 1196, King Narapatisithu or Cañsu II of Pagân (1174-1211) was laying claim to a large tract on the peninsula which included, among other less legible toponyms, Tavoy, a town near Mergui, Tenasserim, Takua-pa, Phuket,[35] and a place-name ending in -*nakuiw* (= -*nagara*).[36] After this time, however, the evidence for Burmese activities and influence in the region immediately declines.[37]

The third alternative or component of the tale, the evidence for an independent Tambralinga, is even less tidy than the case for the Khmer and Burmese alternatives. It rests in the first place upon

---

[33] *Culavamsa*, LXXVI, vv. 10-75. The last of these assertions made by Luce ("Some Old References," p. 275), is conjectural, apparently based upon references to the interception of a Sinhalese princess en route to Kamboja (v. 35), probably via the isthmian route, and the imprisoning in a "fortress in the Malaya country" of Sinhalese envoys sent to Kamboja (v. 22). The Kamboja references here are tantalizing: they seem to suggest that Ceylon was courting an alliance with Angkor, and that the object of these moves was at least partially economic, concerned with trade across the isthmus. See also Paranavitana, *Ceylon and Malaysia*, p. 69. Note the totally variant account of this period given in the *Hmannan yazawin daw gyi*, sec. 142 (*Glass Palace Chronicle*, tr. Luce and Pe Maung Tin, pp. 133-34).

[34] *Culavamsa*, LXXX, vv. 6-8; and Luce, "Some Old References," p. 277.

[35] *Salankre*. Could this possibly be Salan (= Ujong Salang = Thalang = Phuket Island) + Kra?

[36] Luce, "Some Old References," p. 276. This fragmentary toponym suggests "Siridhammanagara," the form used for Ligor in the sixteenth century Pali chronicles of Siam.

[37] See Luce, "Some Old References," pp. 277-78.

a number of references in the historiography and literature of Ceylon to a state which Paranavitana took to be Tambralinga. The best of these references is in an inscription of the reign of King Vikramabahu I (1111-32) of Ceylon which states that "a great dignitary of the Ceylon Sangha, by name Ananda, was instrumental in purifying the order in Tambarattha,"[38] the identity of Tambarattha and Tambralinga being argued from an elaborate cross-checking of Pali and Sinhalese sources.[39] Two other twelfth-century reference to Tambarattha in the Pali literature of Ceylon (where Sinhalese versions of the same works usually write Tamalingamu) also speak of that locality as if it were an important center of Buddhist scholarship in close contact with Ceylon.[40] The import of these references is simply that, unless Professor Paranavitana's identification is erroneous, Tambralinga during the twelfth century was not only a center of religious activity, but also, as evidenced by that activity, a political entity enjoying some considerable measure of autonomy.[41] If it did not have such a status or similar pretensions, overseas religious and diplomatic contacts would have had to be channeled through Tambralinga's suzerain.

These three alternative explanations of the period extending from 1070 to about 1200 are not mutually exclusive; and all three might be accepted as representative of discontinuous fragments of the time scale. One might, for example, posit that Tambraling a was independent from the time of the embassy to China (1070) until shortly after the only dated Pali reference (1111-32); that a three-cornered struggle for hegemony in the isthmian region between Ceylon, Pagân, and Angkor ensued through the middle of the century, resulting in a Burmese victory in the time of Narapatisithu; and that Khmer hegemony was very briefly established there in the later years of Jayavarman VII's reign (1181-1215+). This sequence of events could account for all the references, Chinese, Burmese, Pali, Sinhalese, and Khmer.

---

[39] *Ibid.*, pp. 78-81.
[40] *Ibid.*, p. 80.
[41] The descriptive "-*rattha*" ("reign, kingdom, empire; country, realm"—P.T.S. Pali-English Dictionary—of "Tambarattha" clearly has such connotations.

The Ligor Chronicles

Partial confirmation of this interpretation of the events of the twelfth century comes from two versions of the Thai chronicles of Nagara Sri Dharmaraja.[42] The events related in the first portion of these chronicles[43] are, on the face of it, fanciful and beyond comment; but their structure is striking. The first episode they deal with, ostensibly based upon the chronicle of the Tooth Relic,[44] is an invasion of a town on the Malay Peninsula by forces coming from the south, before which a prince and princess of the ruling house fled to Ceylon, carrying with them a Tooth Relic of the Buddha which they temporarily secreted on the future site of Nagara Sri Dharmaraja.[45] The ruler of Ceylon assisted their return to their home, although not to their patrimony, and apparently imposed his suzerainty on the new rulers of the state, while at the same time he seems to have had copies of the original relic installed there and at the future site of Nagara Sri Dharmaraja. After an indeterminate interval, the chronicles begin a second episode with the expedition southwards of a King Narapati of Pegu (Hongsawadi), who discovered the deserted site which was to become Ligor and obtained from Ceylon permission to found a city on that site and a Buddhist patriarch for the new city. After an epidemic defeated his first attempt to found a city there, he began construction again in the year Mahasakaraja (MS) 1098 (= AD 1176).[46]

---

[42] The "Tamnan müang nakhòn Si Thammarat" (here termed "Version A"), probably of the latter half of the seventeenth century and first published in 1938; and the "Tamnan phra that müang nakhòn Si Thammarat" (here termed "Version B"), probably of the reign of King Narai (1657-88), first published in 1928; both of which have been reprinted in a collection edited by the Thai Fine Arts Department, *Ruam rüang müang nakhòn Si Thammarat* (Bangkok, 1962), pp. 46-63 and 78-95, respectively. The MS. of the first is in the National Library, Bangkok, numbered "Phongsawadan, 36/C." I was unable to locate the MS. of the second in November 1966.

[43] Version A, paras. 1-7; Version B, paras. 1-8.

[44] See B.C. Law, ed. and tr., *The Dathavamsa (A History of the Tooth Relic of the Buddha)* (Lahore, 1925).

[45] Version A. para. l; Version B, paras. 1-3.

[46] Version A, paras. 2-3; Version B, paras. 4-5. The date is given only in B, while Version A indicates the era but omits the digits.

There follows[47] a puzzling episode in which envoys from India (*madhayamapradesa*) requested the king to provide their country with Buddhist relics and such relics magically were provided to fulfill their demand. Following this,[48] there is a list of the twelve tributaries of Nagara Si Thammarat, after which the narrative again is broken by an epidemic which led to the desertion of the city.

Using the single date included in this section as a point of departure, the following sequence emerges: a period of independence disrupted by warfare (?1070-?1130), a period of Sinhalese hegemony during which Sinhalese Buddhism is established (?1130-1176), and Burmese suzerainty substituted for that of Ceylon by King Narapati(sithu) of Pagân in 1176—a date which falls within his regnal years (1174-1211) and makes sensible the Dhammarajaka inscription of 1196-98—, followed by the abandonment of the city after 1196, perhaps to hostile forces. The Ligor Chronicles here are by no means conclusive, but they should suffice to cast doubt upon any attempt to see the history of Tambralinga in the twelfth century solely in terms of that state's relationship with Angkor. The additional evidence provided by Burmese, Pali, and these Thai sources makes clear the necessity to examine the history of Tambralinga in the eleventh and twelfth centuries in terms of multi-partite conflict over the neck of the Malay Peninsula. It should be clear from the examination of the sources to this point that contacts and conflicts involving the isthmian region—and specifically Tambralinga—were relatively constant over the period; and the potential for exclusive control of the region by a single power was present at any time when a balance of interests might fail of execution.

The second major conclusion which emerges from a study of the Ligor Chronicles is the indication of the form which an isthmian state based on Nagara Sri Dharmaraja had assumed by about AD 1200, as furnished by the list of tributaries. These were as follows:

---

[47] Version A, paras. 4-6; Version B, paras. 6-8.
[48] Version A, para. 7; Version B, para. 8.

Saya(puri) (Telubin)	Trang
(Pa-)tani	Chumphòn
Kelantan	Panthai Samò (Pantai Samò)[49]
Pahang	Sa-ulau (unidentified)
Sai(-puri) (Kedah)	Takua-pa
Phatthalung	Kra

Most of the places included in this list require no comment: if one excludes the two unidentified toponyms,[50] the list covers all the traditionally "Thai" portion of the peninsula south of Chumphon, together with those of the Malay states which were most closely associated with Siam in the Malacca period and in the history of each of which there is a legendary Buddhist period, as in the *Kedah Annals,* focused northwards (as opposed to the Malacca tradition, which points in the opposite direction). This is eminently a modest tributary list, which the chronicle comes to enlarge upon in later sections, as one might expect. In this list, the southern limits are defined by Pahang, Kelantan, Patani, and Kedah, the northern limit by Chumphon; and all these states were, by their participation in the building of the Great Reliquary of Nagara Sri Dharmaraja, bound by religious as well as political ties to the ruler of that city.

From Narapati to Ayudhya, 1200-1350

Whatever may have been the status of Tambralinga at the end of the twelfth century, the pressure on that state was very soon reduced by events which overtook its neighbors. Jayavarman VII

---

[49] "Pantai" surely is modern Khmer "Banteay," meaning "fortress"; while "Samò" strikes one as the way in which the Thai might render "Chmar," "small" (similar to the way in which Khmer "Stung" has become Thai "Cading" in the toponym Cading Phra, north of Songkhla), giving us a toponym similar to that of old Battambang, "Banteay Chmar." Cf. S. Lewitz, "La toponymie khmère," *BEFEO,* LIII (1967), p. 398. A poetic (*klòn*) version of the Ligor Chronicles composed by a lady pupil of Sunthòn Phu (*Tamnan phra borommathat nakhòn Si Thammarat,* Thonburi, 1957, p. 128) gives the same tributary list, but substitutes "Pandaya Matra" (a faulty rendering of Banteay Mas?) for "Pantai Samò".

[50] There are two notable gaps in this tributary list, Chaiya and Songkhla, which the two unidentified toponyms may or may not fill.

may have gained a momentary success on the peninsula around 1195, but he certainly was unable to maintain his position there for long, for in 1200 the Khmer dependency of Chen-li-fu, probably in the northwestern corner of the Gulf of Siam and in a position to block land access to the peninsula from that quarter, appears to have asserted its independence by sending the first of three embassies to China.[51] Whether or not Jayavarman VII managed to restore Khmer authority there after the last of these embassies in 1205, the empire was very soon to sink into that final decline which was to render so swift and easy the Thai upsurge in the valleys of the Menam Caophraya. Similarly, both Pagân and Srivijaya were entering quiescent phases in their history, and Srivijaya her final oblivion.

In the most general sense, the thirteenth century was a period of extreme localism in Southeast Asia, a period of low pressure during which none of the old established empires of the region was able to exert itself effectively at any distance from its capital. Leaving aside the question of the ethnic identities of the states involved, the efforts of this situation were nowhere more conducive to the foundation and development of new states than along the central north-south axis of Southeast Asia from the southern border of Yunnan to the tip of the Malay Peninsula. The products of this situation are well-known: the foundation of Sukhothai and Lan Na Thai and the extension of the power of the former in the latter half of the century at least half-way down the Malay Peninsula to Nagara Sri Dharmaraja and perhaps beyond.[52] As for the isthmian region in particular, the most notable event of the century undoubtedly was the well-known double invasion of Ceylon by Candrabhanu of Tambralinga, in 1247 and again around 1260.[53] With reference to the subject at hand, the key

---

[51] O.W. Wolters, "Chen-li-fu: A State on the Gulf of Siam at the beginning of the 13th century," *JSS*, XLVIII, pt. 2 (Nov., 1960), pp. 1-35.

[52] A graphic—if not perfectly accurate—illustration of the way in which Thai power split Southeast Asia in the thirteenth century is given by the end-paper map of "Southeast Asia in the Late Thirteenth Century" in the *Atlas of South-East Asia* (London, 1964).

[53] See Cœdès, *Les états*, pp. 336-37; and Nicholas and Paranavitana, *Concise History of Ceylon*, pp. 281-89.

question of the century is the relationship between these two events, if any.

The Ligor Chronicles are singularly unhelpful in unraveling the mysteries which still surround the personage of Candrabhanu, although they do provide some information about him, without referring to the Ceylon expeditions. For the period from the beginning of the thirteenth century to the middle of the fourteenth, however, these chronicles are apparently episodic and unconnected; and it seems advisable at this point simply to extract from them generalized themes and information rather than specific details which may prove misleading. Bearing in mind these cautions, the Ligor Chronicles state that there was a dynasty ruling in Nagara Sri Dharmaraja in the latter half of the thirteenth century[54] of which each ruler was named "Phraya Sri Dharmasokaraja" and two of whose crown princes were named "Candrabhanu," a practice of nomenclature which supports Professor Paranavitana's suggestion that "Candrabhanu" was much more a title than a personal name.[55] The first of these succeeded his elder brother as ruler, and then his younger brother, "Phraya Phongsasura became Phraya Candrabhanu." Then, "Later, Thao Sri Thammasoka [i.e. the former Candrabhanu who had become ruler] died, and his younger brother, Phraya Candabhanu, became ruler."[56] Only one date is here given, the year 1200, for the death of the first of the line, without any era being specified. As the Mahasakaraja Era is used earlier in Version A, one may assume that it is this Era which the Chronicle's compilers intended to apply here. If so, the intended year is AD 1278.

AD 1278 is rather late for the accession of Candrabhanu, particularly if one wishes to identify this ruler with the man who attacked Ceylon in 1247 and around 1260. However, it is not unlikely that his elder brother who had preceded him as ruler had also at some point held the same title of "Candrabhanu." To this elder brother, Thao Sri Dharmasokaraja, a considerable portion

---

[54] Following the chronicles' own dates.
[55] Paranavitana, *Ceylon and Malaysia*, p. 77.
[56] Version A, para, 10; Version B, para. 13.

first Version B of the chronicles is devoted.[57] He is said to have been a ruler of Indapatapuri—a common name for the Cambodian capital[58]—and to have fled an epidemic in his capital to come and rebuild Nagara Sri Dharmaraja.[59] For reasons unexplained, when news of the rebuilding of the Great Reliquary of Ligor[60] and the issuance of invitations to the twelve tributaries to participate in its inaugural fete reached "Thao Bijaiyadeba Jianbhava, the father of Thao U Thòng, the ruler of Krung Sri Ayudhya. Thao U Thòng raised an army"[61] and engaged Ligor in warfare, the final outcome of which was a diminution in Ligor's status,[62] an agreement whereby the two parties engaged each to send tribute to the other, and the delimitation of their common frontier at Pan Tabhara (Bang Taphan). If one takes Thao U Thòng

---

[57] Version B, paras. 10-13. Version A is defective here, an indeterminate portion being missing; and as the text at both ends of the lacuna is virtually identical to parallel portions of Version B, I take the two to have been identical here.

[58] See G. Cœdès, "The Origins of the Sukhothai Dynasty," *JSS*, XIV, pt. 1 (1921)-, pp. 8-9; C. Notton, *Annales du Siam*, I (Paris, 1926), pp. 99, n.2, and IV (Bangkok, 1939), pp. 95-96; and A. Leclère, *Histoire du Cambodge* (Paris, 1914).

[59] Note again here the occurrence of an epidemic. I am inclined to think that epidemics might have been used in these chronicles as literary devices to explain discontinuities, signaling the end of one episode and, so to speak, clearing the ground for the next.

[60] Paranavitana notes that religious intercourse between Ceylon and Tambralinga continued through the interval between Candrabhanu's attacks. *Ceylon and Malaysia*, p. 79. On the Great Reliquary and Ligor's conversion to the Theravada "around 1200," see A.B. Griswold, "Siam and the Sinhalese Stupa," *Buddhist Annual* (Colombo, 1964), pp. 75-80.

[61] Version B, para. 12.

[62] This is an inference from a passage in Version B, para. 12, which occurs in relating the encounter of Thao Sri Dharmasokaraja and Thao U Don:

"When Thao U Don and Thao Sri Dharmasokaraja were to come to terms, and Thao U Don had ascended the dais, Phraya Sri Dharmasokaraja would not go up, so Thao U Don led him by the hand. King Sri Dharmasokaraja's crown then fell from his head. Then Thao Sri Dharmasokaraja promised that "As long as I and my younger brother live, we will be as of the same golden plate. If you desire anything, you need only tell me. In future, I will be tributary to Krung Sri Ayudhya. As for Thao U Don, he agreed to friendship."

to be Ramadhipati, the first king of Ayudhya (1351-1369), then this account of Candrabhanu's father, Thao Sri Dharmasokaraja, is grossly anachronistic. If, on the other hand, one accepts the argument of Dhanit Yupho and others, based upon the *Phongsawadan nüa* and some versions of the Ayudhya annals, as to the origins of Ramadhipati and his wife in the Sririjaiya Jiansen dynasty which ruled a principality in the western reaches of the Caophraya delta from the end of the twelfth century,[63] then this account is a plausible one. Two elements of the Ligor Chronicle's account demand attention. First, the chronicle is ambiguous. It states that "news of this [the inauguration of the Great Reliquary, etc.] reached Thao Bijayadeba Jianbhava, the *father of* Thao U Thòng...," so that in the succeeding phase it is unclear whether it was Thao U Thòng or his father (or father-in-law?) who sent the armies south to attack Nagara Sri Dharmaraja. It could as well be the father as the son, bearing the same title. Secondly, the reference to Thao U Thòng's father by name or title is extremely interesting: "Thao Bijayadeba Jianbhava" is a perfect equivalent for "Thao Sirijaiya Jiansen."[64] One might suppose that the compiler of the Ligor Chronicle picked up this information from the *Phongsawadan Nüa* or other of the standard Thai chronicles; but, had he been familiar with this literature, it is unlikely that he would have missed other information which these sources contain. One is forced, then, to regard the Ligor Chronicles as independent, if aberrant, sources. If one accepts the data and chronology of the Ligor Chronicles for the first three quarters of the thirteenth century, as many problems are created as benefits are gained. The chronicles offer an explanation for "Candrabhanu" as a name or title which was used by more than one generation of rulers, but they do not mention the raids on Ceylon. They ascribe

---

[63] See Dhanit Yupho, *Rüang müang Traitrüng u don læ ayodhya* (Bangkok, 1960), esp. pp. 26-29; and Prince Damrong Rajanubhab, "Siamese History Prior to the founding of Ayuddhaya," *JSS*, XIII, pt. 2 (1919), reprinted in *Selected Articles from the Journal of the Siam Society*, III (Bangkok, 1959), esp. pp. 66-74.

[64] I am grateful to A.B. Griswold for calling this equivalence to my attention.

to Candrabhanu's line what would appear to be a Cambodian origin, without explaining it. They give a continuity to the political configuration of the state by mentioning again the twelve tributaries and the delimitation of a northern frontier, and they indicate in a very tempting manner the fashioning of a link between Nagara Sri Dharmaraja and a principality in Central Thailand.

On the other hand, if one rejects the problematic evidence of the Ligor Chronicles for the events of the thirteenth century, one can fall back upon the traditional evidence which long ago was brought forward by Cœdès.[65] This is the evidence of two Pali chronicles of north Siam, both composed early in the sixteenth century, which tell of the coming of the Sihinga Buddha image to Siam from Ceylon. According to this tale, in AD 1256 King "Rocaraja" or "Sayaranga"[66] of Sukhothai went with his armies to "Siridhammanagara" (Ligor) where "Siridhammaraja" was reigning, and was there told of the magical properties of the Sihinga Buddha image which was in Ceylon. The two men sent a message to Ceylon requesting the image, and after considerable trials the image arrived in Nagara Sri Dharmaraja from whence, after it had been venerated for seven days and nights in the city, it was sent to Sukhothai.[67] Cœdès chose to regard this episode as indicative of the background to the *first* raid on Ceylon, while ignoring the involvement of Sukhodaya.[68] The Ligor Chronicles take a somewhat ambivalent attitude. They record the arrival of the

---

[65] Especially in his "Chute du Srivijaya." Cœdès used the *Jinakalamali*, the relevant portion of which he translated in his "Documents sur l'histoire politique et religieuse du Laos occidental," *BEFEO*, XXV (1925), esp. pp. 98-99. The *Jkm*, appears to have been based upon the more detailed *Sihinganidana*, which has been translated into English by Camille Notton, *P'ra Buddha Sihinga* (Bangkok, 1933), esp. pp. 19-28.

[66] *Jkm*. gives the date as B.E. 1880 (1256), while the *Sihin*. has B.E. 1500 (A.D. 956). The former has "Rocaraja" where the latter has "Saiyaranga," which is a Pali translation of the usual nickname for Rama Khamhæng and other Sukhothai rulers, "Phra Ruang."

[67] The full account is in the *Sihinganidana, loc. cit.*, while the *Jkm*. abbreviates the tale considerably.

[68] Cœdès, *Les états*, pp. 336-37; and see Briggs, "The Khmer Empire and the Malay Peninsula," p. 301.

Sihinga Buddha, unbidden, in the time of Narapati;[69] and then state that between 1196 and 1198 (which might be read as AD 1274-76), during the ruler of a ruler named Sri Saiyanaranga[70] who "came from the west," the image was sent to Chiang Mai.[71] This event would have occurred two years before the advent of the "Candrabhanu" line. Neither approach appears at present to be productive of an explanation of the Thai expansion in the latter years of the thirteenth century.

Version B of the Ligor Chronicles notes that, during the reign of the second Candrabhanu (post-1278), Nagara Sri Dharmaraja was defeated by a force from Java and became a tributary of that state, Javanese hegemony finally being thrown off by a local hero using means reminiscent of Sri Rana Wikrama's strong man, Badang.[72] Similarly, Cœdès calls attention to the military expedition sent by King Krtanagara of Singhasari (Java) against Sumatra and the Malay Peninsula in 1275.[73] Javanese influence in the peninsula at this date, however, cannot have been either forceful or sustained, particularly by the 1290s, when Java was under pressure from the Mongols.

That the Thai took advantage of the rise of the Mongols in China is beyond question. The problem of the last two decades of the thirteenth century is to explain how Nagara Sri Dharmaraja came to be included among the tributaries of Sukhothai mentioned in the postscript to Rama Khamhæng's inscription of 1292. Two answers generally have been offered to this question. First, Blagden drew attention to the evidence of the Mon chronicle, *Rajadhiraja*, which records that the ruler of Sukhothai was absent from his capital on a military expedition to the south "not long before 1280."[74] This Mon account is quite specific: it

---

[69] Version A, para. 3; Version B, para. 5.

[70] Identical to the ruler of Sukhothai mentioned in the Sihinganidana.

[71] Version A, para. &; Version B, para. 9.

[72] C.C. Brown, tr., "Sejarah Melayu," *JMBRAS*, 25, pts. 2-3 (Oct. 1952), pp. 35-40.

[73] *Les états*, p. 361.

[74] C.O. Blagden, "The Empire of the Maharaja, King of the Mountains and Lord of the Isles," *Journal of the Straits Branch of the Royal Asiatic Society*, no. 81 (March, 1920), p. 25.

states that a letter arrived informing the King of Sukhodaya that a Javanese force had attacked his dependencies and urgently requesting aid to repel them. The king organized land and naval forces, and left his palace in charge of the Mon Magado.[75] This account lends weight to the Ligor Chronicle's reference to warfare with Java, as well as to the *Nagarakrtagama*; but the implication of the reference is that Nagara Sri Dharmaraja was *already* a dependency of Sukhothai in the 1270s.

The second answer to the question of the origins of Sukhodaya's connection with Nagara Sri Dharmaraja has come from Chinese sources. The ruler of the kingdom of "Hsien" sent embassies to the Mongol court in 1292 and again in 1294; but on the latter occasion the mission was stated as having come from the "kan-mu-ting" (*kamraten*) of Phetburi.[76] In the following year (1295), the Chinese records reported that "the people of Hsien and Ma-li-yu-erh had long been quarreling and fighting with each other. Now both submitted." And the Imperial order went out to "Hsien:" "Do not injure Ma-li-yuerh. Do not trample on your promise."[77] The obvious interpretation of these references is to see in them reflections of a period of warfare between Sukhodaya and a Sumatran state, in the course of which Ram Khamhæng came down to Phetburi to direct the campaigns.[78]

This is a perfectly plausible explanation of the events of the period; but one section in the Ligor Chronicles makes one hesitate to accept the equivalence between the "*kan-mu-ting* of Pich'a-pu-li city" and the "*kan-mu-ting*, king of Hsien Kingdom," besides the peculiarity of the Chinese source in its failure to mention "Hsien" in connection with the "Pi-ch'ia-pu-li" mission. After the "Candrabhanu" dynasty and the war with Java, the Ligor chronicles state that an epidemic wiped out the city, bringing an end to the

[75] From a Thai translation executed for King Rama I in 1795: *Rajadhiraja* (Bangkok, 1962), pp. 9-10. The reference to naval forces clearly indicates that Java was meant, and not Müang Savâ or Javâ (Luang Prabang).

[76] P. Pelliot, "Deux itineraires de Chine en Inde à la fin du VIIIe siècle," *BEFEO*, IV (1904), pp. 242-43; and G.H. Luce, "Early Syam," p. 10.

[77] Luce, "Early *Syam*," *loc. cit.*

[78] Cf. Cœdès, *Les états*, p. 373.

line. The next section, which appears only in one version of the chronicles, deals with a prince, Phra Banamadahle Sri Mahesvasti-dradhirajaksatriya, grandson of the ruler of Sukhodaya,[79] who was ruling in Phetburi and evidently supplying his grandparents with salt from the Pan Taban region. A Chinese envoy arrived, and was sent back to China with tribute of sappanwood, in return for which the Emperor of China sent his daughter[80] to wed the "king" of Phetburi. The latter then sent his son, Phra Banamavan, to found a new city in the region of Ligor, *müang* Nagara Ton Phra, in the Year of the Horse, 1588, of an unspecified era.[81]

Were it not for the ostensible date of this episode, AD 1045 or 1666, these paragraphs might fit perfectly with the evidence of the Mon chronicles, the Sukhothai inscription, and the *Yuan shih*. The problem of the date, however, is not capable of easy solution. Version A contains no later dates, so that there is no internal check on this one: indeed, the only other date mentioned in Version A is (MS) 1196 for the coming of "Phraya Saiyanaranga" from the west, which could be equivalent to AD 1274.[82] On the other hand, the interval between that episode and the Phetburi one does not appear to be a Jong one. Version B does not include the Phetburi episode at all.

---

[79] Phra Banamadahle is referred to only as the "grandson of the king." That this king was the king of Sukhothai is an inference from the statement that Phra Banamadahle sent the ruler of Müang Sukkramabata (?) to govern Müang Phræk (Paknambho), a town included among Sukhodaya"s tributaries in the inscription of 1292. He would have to have been the ruler of an inland kingdom, else he would not have depended on an outpost like Phetburi for salt. Lopburi would have obtained salt from the Samut Sakhon or Chonburi region.

[80] She, Nang Candradevi Sri Padarajaputri Dònsamudra, was said to be the daughter of the emperor of China by a concubine (Nang Candramauli Sri Padarajaputri Sri Dònsamudra) who was the daughter of Nang Candramauli Sri Padanarthasuravamsa, who in turn had been born in Champa and sent as a concubine to China.

[81] Version A, para. 10; Version B, para. 15, both state that the Candrabhanu line came to an end through an epidemic. Version A continues with the Phetburi episode (para. 11), the exchange of embassies with China (para. 12) and the sending of Phra Banamavan to Nagara Ton Phra (para. 12).

[82] Para. 3.

A solution to the problem, however, may be reached on broader grounds, by a general examination of the historiography of South Thailand. Version A, in treating the reign of Phra Banamavan and his son, enters into considerable detail concerning the economic structure of the principality which becomes Nagara Sri Dharmaraja; in particular, the parceling out of rice-lands among members of the ruling family and for the support of religious establishments.[83] Because of the obvious importance of this division of land, and particularly the donation of support for Buddhist monasteries, the acts of donation and demarcation have remained vivid in the historical memory of the people of the area. Virtually every account of the history of the region includes mention of a man called "Nai Sam Còm," who surveyed the land arrangement and formalized it, his survey serving as the basis for a great many subsequent appeals. A "chanting verse (*klòn suat*)" version of the Ligor Chronicles composed in Nagara Sri Dharmaraja at the end of the eighteenth century refers to "Phra Sam Còm" or "'Nai Hansa Sam Còm" in the period immediately preceding the war with Thao U Thòng.[84] His name occurs repeatedly throughout a series of seventeenth-century documents dealing with disputes over monastery lands in Phatthalung, where his is the ancient "Domesday Book" by which all such disputes must be settled.[85] Version B of the Ligor Chronicles is even more specific, in explaining that there were two such surveys, the first undertaken "in the year 1815" by "Nai Sam Rajahansa" following complaints that previous agreements had been violated; and then again in "Mahasakaraja 1550" by Nai Sam Còm; shortly after which the ruler who had approved the second of these surveys died, "in the year 1861."[86] The second of these three dates will

---

[83] Paras. 13, 19-33.

[84] Thailand, Fine Arts Dept., eds., *Tamnan phra borommathat müang Nakhon Si Thammarat, klòn suat* (Amphœ Khanom, Nakhon Sri Thammarat, 1961), pp. 92fi93.

[85] Thailand, Commission for the Publication of Historical, Cultural, and Archeological Records, eds., *Prachum phra tamra ?borommarachuthit phüa kalpana samai Ayudhya, phak 1* (Bangkok, 1967), e.g. pp. 10, 11, 14, 16, 22, etc. in the Thai-Khmer document, p. 63 in the second document, and p. 71 in the third.

not fit between the other two unless it is taken as a misreading for 1850. None of the three dates is sufficiently specific (providing neither the name of the animal year nor the year of the decade) to give an internal check for consistency. As they stand, they would read as AD 1271, 1306, and 1317.[87] Further confirmation of this chronological sequence comes from a copy of a seventeenth century manuscript in the National Library branch in Nakhòn Sri Dharmaraja which states that "In the year 1813, Year of the Lesser Dragon, tenth of the decade, Nai Sam Còm arrived from Krung Thep Mahanakhòn to make a survey ..."[88] This date comes closest of any of the dates to being verifiable, or at least to pass the test of internal consistency,[89] and is equivalent to AD 1269.

Again on the chronological argument, there is one further piece of information which adds something to the study of this period. In the highly problematic "Chronicle of the Brahmans of Nagara Sri Dharmaraja" there are a number of dates, including the date of the foundation of Ayudhya repeated several times, only one of which seems to have any significance for this period. It is a statement concerning the recognition and "chartering" of the court Brahmans of Ligor by Ligor's overlord, whose capital is not specified, on Wednesday the third day of the waxing moon of the fifth month in the year Mahasakaraja 1219, Culasakaraja 659,

---

[86] Version ~, paras. 19, 21 and 23.

[87] Converted to AD by treating them as dates in the Buddhist Era, figured after the Sinhalese fashion. It would be possible, by dropping the thousand-digit, to treat them as Lesser Era dates, which would yield dates of AD 1453, 1488, and 1499. I discard this possibility for two reasons: first, I know of several cases where thousand-digits need to be added to dates, but none where they need to be dropped; and, second, to treat them as CS dates would destroy their congruity with the date which follows.

[88] Untitled, undated MSS. in black ink on *samut khòi,* 34 x 11 cm. Obverse contains a text dated A.D. 1844. The passage cited is from folio 28.

[89] No Lesser Dragon year was ever tenth of the decade. Buddhist Era 1813 was, however, "first of the decade," and there easily could have been a short period at the beginning of the year which was "still tenth of the decade." None of the other possibilities—reading the date as CS 813 or as MS 1513—yields a Year of the Lesser Dragon.

Year of the Cock, ninth of the decade; a date which checks out in every detail, and is equivalent to a day in April, 1297.[90]

Not everyone will accept these thirteenth century dates, for they run counter to several generations' careful examination of the events of the period. They do, however, deserve very serious scrutiny, for they reflect a consistent attitude taken by the historiography of south Thailand with respect to the end of the thirteenth century which, reduced to simplest terms, implies (and asserts) that the major dividing line in the history of the isthmian state of Nagara Sri Dharmaraja comes at the end of the thirteenth century when a new ruling class came in, land was divided up to their benefit, Buddhist monasteries received their endowments, the local Brahmans were recognized and chartered, and the state was put into a relationships of semi-dependency (or perhaps something stronger) with a state in the lower basin of the Caophraya River.[91] In short, this was the period of the Thai takeover.

Ethnic designations are not used in the earlier portions of any of the Ligor Chronicles; but they begin to be employed in Version A during the reign of Phra Banamavan, and in Version B during the structurally-similar period outlined above, although they are overt only in Version A. In Version B, in the period delimited by the land surveys of "1815" and "1861," a great many individuals are named as holders of lands or contributors to the work of reconstructing the Great Reliquary, each name with its proper prefix. There are the Thai "cao," "khun," "mæ nang," "nai," "ban," and "amtæng"[92] as well as a number of men referred to as "raja" or "sultan," rulers of Kedah, Kelantan, Phatthalung, and Chaiya.[93]

---

[90] *Tamnan phram müang nagara Si Thammarat* (Bangkok, 1930), pp. 38-39

[91] An "Ayodhya," predecessor of Ayudhya, or Phetburi, Suphanburi, and Lopburi, all are possible contenders for this role. Given the rate at which interest in and research on this subject is proceeding in Thailand, an answer to the problem. should be forthcoming before long.

[92] Note that none of the elaborated bureaucratic hierarchy of even fourteenth century Ayudhya is present—no "luang," "phra," or "phraya."

[93] Version B, paras. 19-22, passim. Note that "rajas" were here listed as rulers *of* Chaiya and Phatthalung.

Version A is considerably more specific. Phra Banamavan was sent from Phetburi with a force which included fifty Malays (*khæk*), and was told to put the Malays to rule over towns which became his vassals, sending him tribute in gold.[94] He arranged for nine boats for the Malays, and sent them to rule over the Malay domains: 'Che Uma to Yihon (in the region of Narathiwat), 'Che Ravansa to Canadeba (south of modern Songkhla), and others to Patani, Pahang, Telubin, Phatthalung, Kedah, La-ngu (near Satul), Chaiya, Noce(?), and Phlu(?), each of these sending him annually three cartloads of cowries "in friendship."[95] He appointed two men whose function it was to travel to the tributaries each year to collect their tribute, elsewhere mentioned as being ten *tamlüng* (600 grams) of gold.[96] His arrangements for the governance of the Malay states were confirmed by his son and successor,[97] during whose reign all the tributaries assisted in the reconstruction of the Great Reliquary, as named in the following list.[98]

Yihon	Pahang	Kelantan
Phlu	Ace[99]	Canadeba
Telubin	Patani	La-ngu
Kedah	Trang	Chaiya
Sah Ulau	Chumphòn	Ban Saphan

This is a detailed, specific account; but again, it is a moderate one. Malacca is nowhere claimed among the dependencies of Nagara Sri Dharmaraja. The southern Malay vassals are named and claimed, but beyond sharing in the work of constructing the Great Reliquary of Ligor they hardly figure in the narrative of their chronicles. The manner in which Version A relates the story of Phra Banamavan arranging for boats to take the Malay "rajas" to their states and for their tribute to be collected indicates that his

---

[94] Para. 12. Note the *tuan* of Sukhothai inscription XXXVIII, A, 15.
[95] Para 17.
[96] Para 18.
[97] Para 19.
[98] Para 22.
[99] This reads like "Aceh," but might it be a variant of "Noce," mentioned above?

role was something of the intermediary between these states and a power in the Caophraya delta. Beyond this, the Ligor Chronicles are silent on the critical events of the fourteenth and fifteenth centuries. The real contribution they make to an understanding of that later period comes from the light they shed on the development of a regional polity in the isthmian region and of the manner (and the time) in which that polity became linked to Ayudhya and its predecessor states in the Caophraya valley.

Clearly, Ligor was an important center of power and conflict on the Malay Peninsula during the thirteenth century. Less certain is the sequence of events which brought Nagara Sri Dharmaraja within the influence of her northern neighbors by the end of the century, although, from the above examination of a wide variety of sources, certain fixtures within that sequence are evident. First, there appear to be no valid grounds for disputing the historicity of the two expeditions to Ceylon by Candrabhanu, in 1247 and around 1260. Second, the Ligor Chronicles add weight to the evidence of Mon and Javanese sources suggesting that there was a Javanese attack upon parts of the Malay Peninsula in the 1270s. Thirdly, the Javanese episode assists us in placing within this chronological framework the "Candrabhanu" dynasty of the Ligor Chronicles (Version B). Fourthly, the Phetburi dynasty of Version A and a parallel portion of Version B fit both logically and chronologically into the 1280s and 1290s, requiring that the date in Version A (1588, Year of the Horse, which is self-contradictory) be dispensed with. For these dates, those of Version B may be substituted: a ruler being sent to Nagara Sri Dharmaraja by an unnamed king in an unnamed capital in 1272, immediately after which the first land survey was made; Nai Sam Còm being sent to make a new survey on the appointment of a new ruler in 1306; and a further ruler being named in 1317. The year 1306 appears to be a date which links the two versions of the chronicles: it was a Year of the Horse, 1228 of the Mahasakaraja, which just conceivably could have been mis-copied as 1588 in Version A. If this chronology holds, it would suggest that the Phetburi connection went back earlier in time than the known Chinese embassy of 1294; and this suggestion, in turn, might assist in explaining how "Hsien" might have been "trampling on their promise" (obviously made some time earlier) by 1295. Certainly if one is to interpret the Chinese records as meaning that a state called "Hsien" in the western valley of the Menam Caophraya was actively pursuing an expansionist policy on the Malay Peninsula by the 1290s, and if that state or another of similar complexion was, according to the Mon source, undertaking similar activities as early as the 1270s, it is necessary to posit that that state enjoyed a position of power and influence at Nagara Sri Dharmaraja by the 1270s. The Ligor Chronicles make it possible, though not easy, for us to do so.

CONTEXTUAL ARGUMENTS
FOR THE AUTHENTICITY OF
THE RAMKHAMHÆNG INSCRIPTION*

For more than a century, those concerned with the history of Thailand have used the first Sukhothai inscription as their most important primary source for the earliest history of the Tai in the Chaophraya River basin, dating it, following the inscription, to the very end of the thirteenth century. It has become one of those hoary chestnuts, to be pulled out of the fire at the drop of a hat (to coin several phrases) to fit any occasion, though like the Bible in the West it is more often referred to than read. It might quietly slip from memory or from public attention had not several iconoclasts within the past several years questioned its authenticity by suggesting that it is a "Piltdown Skull," a forgery from the nineteenth century. Were these claims true, historians of Thailand would have to go back to square one (wherever that is), and re-think and re-work thirteenth-century Sukhothai history.

I do not think such claims are sustainable. Other scholars have presented a variety of arguments that, it seems to me, support the authenticity of the inscription.[1] The most telling of these, in my view, are those from the discipline of linguistics. For what they are worth, please allow me to present another perspective, from an historian viewing the inscription as a text; that is, as a coherent structure of words and logic. I want to present the view that Sukhothai Inscription Number 1 has a rhetoric and a logic

---

* In *The Ram Khamhæng Controversy: Collected Papers,* ed. James R. Chamberlain (Bangkok: Siam Society, 1991), pp. 439-450. Originally presented as a paper at the annual meetings of the Association for Asian Studies in Washington, D.C., in March, 1989. Reprinted with the permission of The Siam Society.

[1] In *The Ram Khamhæng Controversy.*

states medieval, not modern; and that it speaks with a voice that
is medieval, not nineteenth century.

Let us begin with the structure of the inscription as a whole
and examine what Alton Becker once called the "text-building
strategy" of its author or authors. Appended below is the full text
of the inscription as translated by A.B. Griswold and Prasert na
Nagara, slightly revised, to which I have added paragraph
numbers that I will refer to in the course of the remarks that
follow.[2] (The paragraphing of the inscription is that added by
Griswold and Prasert.) And to simplify matters, let us assume,
following the judgments of most who have studied the stone, that
all or part of Face 4 of the inscription consists of one or more
postscripts, added to the main portion of the inscription some
time after the first three faces were engraved on the stone. I will
confine my remarks to the first three faces (paragraphs 1-11 only).

The point to which the logic of the inscription leads is
paragraph #11. This paragraph describes the ritual occasion for
which the inscription was engraved—rather like a cornerstone-
laying ceremony in the West. On this occasion in a year equivalent
to AD 1292, the inscription says, the king had a slab of stone carved
as a throne on which he daily sat to deliberate the business of the
kingdom, except on the four holy days of each month when a
Buddhist monk preached from the same throne. To mark this
occasion, the stone says the king had four inscriptions engraved,
only one of which—Sukhothai Inscription #1—has survived.

The point of the inscription thus is reached only in the last half
of the third face of the inscription: it took the author 80 finely-
chiseled lines of text to get there. The first question we must ask
is, In what context did the inscriptionûs author choose to set the
ritual occasion of the inauguration of his throne?

Consider the logic through which the text of the inscription
builds up to the climax of the inauguration of the throne.

The first three paragraphs of the inscription present the case
for the legitimacy of the king based on conditions prior to his

---

[2] Originally in the *Journal of the Siam Society*, 1970.

accession to the throne. Paragraph #1 presents the evidence for legitimacy through birth or descent: Ram Khamhæng was the son of [King] Sri Indraditya. Paragraph #2 presents the evidence for legitimacy by valor in warfare, giving the story of how Ram Khamhæng came to be named "Rama the Brave." Paragraph #3 provides a case for legitimacy by personal virtue, not in this case Buddhist virtue but rather the virtue of what in the Chinese context would be called filial piety: Ram Khamhæng served his father, his mother, and his elder brother. And that virtue, of course, was rewarded: "When my elder brother died, I got the whole kingdom for myself." But it is more than his service to his elder brother that was so rewarded: Ram Khamhæng also became king because of his descent and his kingly valor.

There follow two paragraphs—really, long sections—that deal with defining the kind of polity that Ram Khamhæng created, or at least presided over. Paragraph #4, the longest single section of the inscription (26 lines), deals with the king's policies, portraying him as a wise, just, and benevolent ruler. The section concludes by saying, in effect, that the people praise the king, and that the king nourishes and protects them by providing clear drinking water and fortifying the city. The mutuality of the relationship between ruler and ruled is noteworthy here, and we will need to return to this point.

Paragraph #5 describes the religious life of Sukhothai, focusing particularly upon the annual *kathin* ceremony, when robes and other monastic requisites are given to the Buddhist monks at the end of the rains retreat. This section touches both upon piety—"all have faith in the religion of the Buddha, and all observe the precepts during the rainy season"—and upon the civic expression of that faith; that is, it includes both merit-making and merry-making.

Next, there are five short paragraphs (nos. 6-10) describing the five quarters of the city—the interior and the west, east, north, and south—and concluding with that most curious reference to Phra Khapung, "The divine sprite of that mountain is more powerful than any other sprite in this kingdom."

Now, there is a curious sort of parallelism between the "tour of the city" section and the "policy" section, in that both end up with expressions of mutuality. Note that, just as the "policy" section (Paragraph #4) ends with the people praising the king by planting and the king (in return?) providing them clear water to drink and strong city walls, the "tour of the city" section concludes with the kingûs responsibility to ensure the survival and prosperity of the city by the propitiation of Phra Khapung, that is, by animistic ritual.

What does this logic add up to as we approach the final paragraph of our text? Consider what has to be accounted for in the final paragraph. A throne is being established; a throne that is not just an institution but also a physical object. This throne is to become (quite literally) the seat of government, as well as a physical and symbolic focus for the Buddhist life of the kingdom. The preceding ten paragraphs have attempted to demonstrate that the king undertaking this act is a legitimate ruler, that his kingdom is a credible polity, and that the Buddhism—that is, the moral quality—of this kingdom is sincere and well-developed.

Taken to this relatively abstract level, the logic of the inscription is not particularly striking, though it is for the most part coherent and it is well adapted to the purposes of the inscription's author. Viewed on this level, however, there is nothing particularly thirteenth-century about it.

If we take this approach one step further, however, and look at the individual sections or "paragraphs" of the inscription, quite the opposite conclusion comes to mind, for nearly every paragraph of the inscription has a distinctively early quality to it.

The "legitimacy by descent" paragraph at the opening of the inscription names the king's father but goes no further back in time; and it also mentions his mother and the death of his eldest brother as a child. And of course the choice of language is quite startling: the text uses the first person singular *ku* for (presumably) the king speaking for himself.

The "legitimacy by valor" paragraph describes in most vigorous, active prose an elephant-duel scene that, in my view, reads like an account by a participant. Note, for instance, how for a warrior on elephantback the immediate object of attack is the other manûs elephant, not the man himself.

The "legitimacy by filial piety" paragraph would have been extremely difficult to invent in the nineteenth century, for the actions of the young prince in serving his father were hardly modern activities—hunting and gathering, capturing elephants, and raiding towns and villages.

The logic of the long "legitimacy by policy" paragraph is very complex. First, note that many of the state policies are expressed in terms of what they are not; presumably an implicit contrast with the policies of Angkorian Cambodia is being drawn. To cite one example, "The lord of the realm does not levy toll on his subjects for travelling the roads." (The word used for "toll" is *cangkòp*, a Khmer word.) Second, after the passage about hanging a bell nearby which commoners can ring to gain an instant hearing for their grievances, note how the logic runs: "So the people ... praise him. They plant areca groves and betel groves ... coconut groves and jackgruit groves ... mango groves and tamarind groves." The inscription does not say that people planted rice, though we know that they did. Instead, they planted tree crops that take years to mature, thereby signifying their long-term commitment to this Sukhothai.

There is a logic in the "religious life" paragraph that still puzzles me. The first part of the paragraph is straightforward enough. But note the last few sentences: the people "repeatedly pay homage together, accompanied by the music of instruments and singing. Whoever wants to make merry, does so; whoever wants to laugh, does so; whoever wants to sing, does so." In addition to the interesting parallelism with the trading section of the "policy" paragraph, there seems here to be a contrast implicitly drawn between Buddhism in Sukhothai and religious life elsewhere. The line of this logic leads us not to some conclusion having to do with collective piety so much as it leads to an impression of the collective: "... the city is filled to the bursting point" for festivals.

The "tour of the city" paragraphs are also not without interest for this purpose. Note that two scenes are described as being beautiful: a *vihara* west of the city, and the bucolic farms, orchards, and villages east of the city. The reference to Phra

Khapung is of course quite unusual: there are only two other references to this spirit in the epigraphy, and both those references are to one spirit among many, while the reference of Inscription #1 is to a singular, immediately locatable deity.[3] I find it difficult to believe that a nineteenth-century (or earlier) forger might have given Phra Khapung the place it/he has in this inscription.

Finally, the concluding and climatic paragraph has a very curious logic to it, which is interesting mainly for the puzzles with which it leaves us. Why is the first sentence of this paragraph the first occasion in this text when Ram Khamhæng is identified as the ruler of a *dual* kingdom of Sukhothai and Sri Sajjanalai? Why is reference made to his having planted sugar-palm trees fourteen years earlier? Why the references to the pomp with which the king, mounted on the richly caparisoned elephant Rucasri, goes off to the Araññika twice a month? Why the reference to three other inscriptions (and why were two of the three "planted" in caves)?[4] One might have expected tighter logic from a forger.

To a considerable extent, the logic of the inscription defines the voice of its author; but its voice also is defined by the language employed on the stone. The language can be (and will be) better described by linguists, and I will only mention here the curious first-person beginning of the text, the short, choppy sentences, the archaic vocabulary, and the simplicity of the text.

It would be easier to assess the authenticity of Sukhothai Inscription #1 if we had other contemporary sources against which to measure it. In effect, however, we have used this inscription to define our view of late thirteenth century Sukhothai, so we cannot now reverse the process and measure the stone against the picture that we have created using the stone! At a minimum, I find nothing in the logic, the voice, or the "text" of the text that would support the view that it is inauthentic.

---

[3] See the essay following this one.

[4] In discussing this point in class in late 1992, one student (David Walend) ventured the opinion that all the inscriptions were placed in locations likely to be frequented by the literate.

INSCRIPTION #1 OF SUKHOTHAI

1. [I/1-3] My father was named Sri Indraditya, my mother was named Lady Süang, my elder brother was named Ban Müang. There were five of us born from the same womb: three boys and two girls. My eldest brother died when he was still a child.

2. [I/3-10] When I was nineteen years old, Lord Sam Chon, the ruler of Müang Chot, came to attack Müang Tak. My father went to fight Lord Sam Chon on the left; Lord Sam Chon drove forward on the right. Lord Sam Chon attacked in force; my father's men fled in confusion. I did not flee. I mounted my elephant, opened [a way through] the soldiers, and pushed him ahead in front of my father. I fought an elephant duel with Lord Sam Chon. I fought Lord Sam Chon's elephant, Mas Müang by name, and beat him. Lord Sam Chon fled. Then my father named me Phra Ram Khamhæng because I fought Sam Chon's elephant.

3. [I/10-18] In my father's lifetime I served my father and I served my mother. When I caught any game or fish I brought them to my father. When I picked any acid or sweet fruits that were delicious and good to eat, I brought them to my father. When I went hunting elephants, either by lasso or by [driving them into] a corral, I brought them to my father. When I raided a town or village and captured elephants, young men or women of rank, silver or gold, I turned them over to my father. When my father died, my elder brother was still alive, and I served him steadfastly as I had served my father. When my elder brother died, I got the whole kingdom for myself.

4. [I/18-35; II/1-8] In the time of King Ram Khamhæng this land of Sukhothai is thriving. There is fish in the water and rice in the fields. The lord of the realm does not levy toll on his subjects for traveling the roads; they lead their cattle to trade or ride their horses to sell; whoever wants to trade in elephants, does so; whoever wants to trade in horses, does so; whoever wants to trade in silver or gold, does so. When any commoner or man of rank dies, his estate—his elephants, wives, children, granaries, rice, retainers, and groves of areca and betel—is left in its entirety to his children. When commoners or men of rank differ and disagree,

[the King] examines the case to get at the truth and then settles it justly for them. He does not connive with thieves or favor concealers [of stolen goods]. When he sees someone's rice he does not covet it; when he sees someone's wealth he does not get angry. If anyone riding an elephant comes to see him to put his own country under his protection, he helps him, treats him generously, and takes care of him; if [someone comes to him] with no elephants, no horses, no young men or women of rank, no silver or gold, he gives him some, and helps him until he can establish a state [of his own]. When he captures enemy warriors, he does not kill them or beat them. He has hung a bell in the opening of the gate over there: if any commoner in the land has a grievance which sickens his belly and gripes his heart, and which he wants to make known to his ruler and lord, it is easy: he goes and strikes the bell which the King has hung there; King Ram Khamhæng, the ruler of the kingdom, hears the call; he goes and questions the man, examines the case, and decides it justly for him. So the people of this müang of Sukhothai praise him. They plant areca groves and betel groves all over this müang; coconut groves and jackfruit groves are planted in abundance in this müang, mango groves and tamarind groves are planted in abundance in this müang. Anyone who plants them gets them for himself and keeps them. Inside this city there is a marvelous pond of water which is as clear and as good to drink as the water of the [Me]Khong in the dry season. The triple rampart surrounding this city of Sukhothai measures three thousand four hundred fathoms.

5. [II/8-23] The people of this city of Sukhothai like to observe the precepts and bestow alms. King Ram Khamhæng, the ruler of this city of Sukhothai, as well as the princes and princesses, the young men and women of rank, and all the noblefolk, without exception, both male and female, all have faith in the religion of the Buddha, and all observe the precepts during the rainy season. At the close of the rainy season they celebrate the *kathin* ceremonies, which last a month, with heaps of cowries, with heaps of areca nuts, with heaps of flowers, with cushions and pillows: the gifts they present [to the monks] as accessories to the

kathin [amount to] two million each year. Everyone goes to the Araññika over there for the recitation of the *kathin*. When they are ready to return to the city they walk together, forming a line all the way from the Araññika to the parade-ground. They repeatedly pay homage together, accompanied by the music of instruments and singing. Whoever wants to make merry, does so; whoever wants to laugh, does so; whoever wants to sing, does so. As this Sukhothai has four very big gates, and as the people always crowd together to come in and watch the King lighting candles and setting off fireworks, the city is filled to the bursting point.

6. [II/23-27] Inside this city of Sukhothai, there are viharas, there are golden statues of the Buddha, there are statues eighteen cubits in height; there are big statues of the Buddha and medium-sized ones; there are big viharas and medium-sized ones; there are monks, Nissayamuttas, Theras, and Mahatheras.

7. [II/27-33] West of this city of Sukhothai is the Araññika, built by King Ram Khamhæng as a gift to the Mahathera Sangharaja, the sage who has studied the scriptures from beginning to end, who is wiser than any other monk in the kingdom, and who has come here from Müang Sri Dharmmaraja. Inside the Araññika there is a large rectangular vihara, tall and exceedingly beautiful, and an eighteen-cubit statue of the Buddha standing up.

8. [II/33-35] East of this city of Sukhothai there are viharas and monks, there is the large lake, there are groves of areca and betel, upland and lowland farms, homesteads, large and small villages, groves of mango and tamarind. [They] are as beautiful to look at as if they were made for that purpose.

9. [III/1-3] North of this city of Sukhothai there is the bazaar, there is the Acan statue, there are the *prasadas*, there are groves of coconut and jackfruit, upland and lowland farms, homesteads, large and small villages.

10. [III/3-10] South of this city of Sukhothai there are kuti with viharas and resident monks, there is the dam, there are groves of coconut and jackfruit, groves of mango and tamarind, there are mountain streams, and there is Phra Khaphung. The divine sprite of that mountain is more powerful than any other

sprite in this kingdom. Whatever lord may rule this kingdom of
Sukhothai, if he makes obeisance to him properly, with the right
offerings, this kingdom will endure, this kingdom will thrive;
but if obeisance is not made properly or the offerings are not
right, the sprite of the hill will no longer protect it and the
kingdom will be lost.

11. [III/10-27] In 1214 saka, a Year of the Dragon [AD
1292], King Ram Khamhæng, lord of this kingdom of Sri
Sajjanalai and Sukhothai, who had planted these sugar-palm trees
fourteen years before, commanded his craftsmen to carve a slab of
stone and place it in the midst of these sugar-palm trees. On the
day of the new moon, the eighth day of the waxing moon, the day
of the full moon, and the eighth day of the waning moon, [one
of] the monks, theras, or mahatheras goes up and sits on the
stone slab to preach the Dharma to the throng of laypeople who
observe the precepts. When it is not a day for preaching the
Dharma, King Ram Khamhæng, lord of the kingdom of Sri
Sajjanalai and Sukhothai, goes up, sits on the stone slab, and lets
the officials, lords, and princes discuss affairs of state with him.
On the day of the new moon and the day of the full moon, when
the white elephant named Rucasri has been decked out with
howdah and tasseled head cloth, and always with gold on both
tusks, King Ram Khamhæng mounts him, rides away to the
Araññika to pay homage to the Sangharaja, and then returns.
There is an inscription in the city of Chaliang, erected beside the Sri
Ratanadhatu; there is an inscription in the cave called Phra
Ram's Cave, which is located on the bank of the River Samphai;
and there is an inscription in the Ratanadhara Cave. In this
Sugar-palm Grove there are two pavilions, one named Sala Phra
Masa, one named Buddhasala. This slab of stone is named
Manangasilabat. It is installed here for everyone to see.

12. [IV/1-4] All the Ma, the Kao, the Lao, the Tai of the land
under the vault of heaven and the Tai who live along the U and
Khong come and do obeisance to King Sri Indraditya's son King
Ram Khamhæng, who is lord of the kingdom of Sri Sajjanalai
and Sukhothai.

13. [IV/4-8] In 1207 saka, a Year of the Boar [AD 1285], he caused the holy relics to be dug up so that everyone could see them. They were worshipped for a month and six days, then they were buried in the middle of Sri Sajjanalai, and a cetiya was built on top of them which was finished in six years. A wall of rock enclosing the Phra Dhatu was built which was finished in three years.

14. [IV/8-11] Formerly these Tai letters did not exist. In 1205 saka, a Year of the Goat [AD 1283], King Ram Khamhæng set his mind and his heart on devising these Tai letters. So these Tai letters exist because that lord devised them.

15. [IV/11-27] King Ram Khamhæng was sovereign over all the Tai. He was the teacher who taught all the Tai to understand merit and the Dharma rightly. Among men who live in the lands of the Tai, there is no one to equal him in knowledge and wisdom, in bravery and courage, in strength and energy. He was able to subdue a throne of enemies who possessed broad kingdoms and many elephants. The places whose submission he received on the east include Sra Luang, Song Khwæ, Lum Pa Cai, Sakha, the banks of the Khong, and Viang Can-Viang Kham, which is the furthest place. On the south, [they include] Khanthi, Phra Bang, Phræk, Suphannaphum, Ratchaburi, Phetchaburi, Sri Dharmaraja, and the seacoast, which is the farthest place. On the west, [they include] Müang Chot, Müang......n, and Hamsavati, the seas being their limit. On the north, they include Müang Phlæ, Müang Man, Müang N[an], Müang Phlua, and, beyond the banks of the Khong, Müang Sava [Luang Phrabang], which is the farthest place. All the people who live in these lands have been reared by him in accordance with the Dharma, every one of them.

THREE SUKHOTHAI
OATHS OF ALLEGIANCE*

Among the inscriptions of the early Thai kingdom of
Sukhothai included in a collection recently published by the Thai
Government[1] are three fragmentary inscriptions of the fourteenth
century; two from Sukhothai itself (nos. XL and XLV) and one
from the northern town of Nan (no. LXIV), which bear what
might be termed "oaths of allegiance." In terms more magico-
religious than penal and corporal, they specify the punishments
due to those who break their vows of loyalty to the rulers of
Sukhothai; and one (no. LXIV) reproduces the text of an oath
taken by King Sai Lü Thai (Dharmarâja II, c1369-c1399) upon
entering into an alliance with the ruler of Nan. In addition to
considerable political information, these inscriptions provide
valuable indications of the course of development and
elaboration of the cosmological and moral foundations of the
kingdom in the last third of the fourteenth century; a magico-
religious structure which remains important to the present day.

Cœdès has noted the significance of a reference in the
inscription of King Ram Khamhæng (AD 1292) to Phra Khaphung,
the lord of the mountain-top, the protective and tutelary deity
who symbolized the unity of the territories controlled by that

---

* Paper presented to the XXVII International Congress of Orientalists,
Ann Arbor, Michigan, August 13-19, 1967. Not previously published. This
essay is probably the most outdated of those published here, as it was written
several years before A.B. Griswold and Prasert na Nagara began their series of
studies of the inscriptions of Sukhothai in the *Journal of the Siam Society*, and
the inscriptions themselves subsequently have been re-edited and re-published.

[1] Thailand, Office of the Prime Minister, Commission for the Publication
of Historical, Archeological, and Cultural Documents (eds.), *Prachum sila carük
phak thi 3* (Bangkok, 1965).

king in the closing decades of the thirteenth century.[2] At that point, early in the history of Sukhothai, the king expressed a somewhat crude cosmological foundation for unity which attempted to override political and religious localism in a mode consciously different from that previously upheld in the same region by the Khmers.[3] This was a task particularly difficult in an age of evangelistic and particularistic[4] Theravada Buddhism when that religion's accommodation to the previously "indianized" political orders of mainland Southeast Asia was as yet but imperfectly accomplished, and in an era of great ethnic, linguistic, and religious diversity; and one hardly would be tempted to attribute Ram Khamhæng's successful political and military expansion solely to the cosmological formulae he devised. Certainly the tenuous quality of Sukhothai's unity under Ram Khamhæng was revealed when his empire began to crumble under his immediate successors.[5]

It is from the period of decline in Sukhothai's fortunes in the reign of King Dharmarâja II, who succeeded to the throne ca. 1369, that the three inscriptions date. Number XL, found in 1956 at Wat Mahathat in Sukhothai, consists of three fragments of an undated stele in the Siamese language and script, and seems to date from the beginning of the reign.[6] Number XLV, also found in 1956 at Wat Mahathat, similarly consists of three fragments of

---

[2] G. Cœdès, *The Making of South-East Asia,* tr. H. M. Wright (London, 1966), pp. 142-43.

[3] See G. Cœdès, "L'art siamois de l'époque de Sukhodaya," *Arts asiatiques,* I:4 (1954), pp. 281-302.

[4] I use this word here in a restricted and immediate political sense, to refer to a period during which I feel that the political effects of Buddhism were at least temporarily negative and localized lacking specific geographical and political foci. This situation began very rapidly to change at the beginning of the fourteenth century.

[5] See Prasert na Nagara, "Kanchamra prawattisat Sukhothai," *Sangkhomsat parithat,* special no. 3 (June 1966), 43-52.

[6] Mainly because it refers to a King Dharmarâja (line 8), apparently recently deceased, who can only have been Lü Thai. Number XL was later edited and published by Griswold and Prasert, "A Pact Between Uncle and Nephew," *Journal of the Siam Society* 1969; and in their *Epigraphical and Historical Studies* (Bangkok: Siam Society, 1992), 159-184.

three faces in the Siamese language and a script more formalized than that of number XL. It bears a date, AD 1392.[7] Inscription LXIV was found in the late 1950s at Wat Chang Kham in Nan.[8] It consists of one fragment of a large stele, on which only twenty-six lines are legible, with the addition of a brief insertion inscribed on the reverse of the stone. It is in Siamese, in a script which *Maha* Cham Thongkhamwan, the epigrapher of the Thai Fine Arts Department, characterizes as mid-fifteenth-century; but, although undated, internal evidence would suggest assigning it to the reign of King Dharmarâja II and associating it with the Mount Sumanakut Inscription (no. VIII) which Cœdès suggests dates from about 1370.[9]

All three inscriptions specifically contain oaths of allegiance. To describe its own contents, inscription XL uses the terms "solemn vow"[10] and "covenant of truth;"[11] while numbers XLV and LXIV use the more familiar terms *sabatha*[12] and *sapala*,[13] both of which might generally be translated by the word "oath." Each of the three oaths is distinctive. I wish here specially to call attention to the sanctions threatened in each case against those who would break their vows of loyalty to the ruler and state; for

---

[7] Number XLV was later studied by Griswold and Prasert as "The Pact Between Sukhodaya and Nan," *Journal of the Siam Society* 1968; in their *Epigraphical and Historical Studies,* pp. 67-107.

[8] Number LXIV is referred to by Griswold and Prasert, "A Declaration of Independence and its Consequences," *Journal of the Siam Society* 1968; in their *Epigraphical and Historical Studies* (Bangkok: Siam Society, 1992), 1-42, esp. pp. 11-12.

[9] G. Cœdès, *Recueil des Inscriptions du Siam,* I (Bangkok, 1924), p. 124, and below, note 27 It is similarly dated by Prasoet, *op. cit.,* p. 48. To do justice to *Maha* Chamûs opinion (stated only generally in the title of the inscription, "Inscription in Sukhothai Script of the B.E. 2000 style") the script is unlike some others of the same period and locality—e.g., no. VI—but, admittedly on the basis of poor photographs, it would appear very similar to the- script of the Wat Chang Lòm inscription of 1384, published in *Sinlapakòn* X:1 (May 1966), 63-73.

[10] *satya paratijña*—lines 9, 13.

[11] *parigana sandhisatya*—line 12.

[12] No. XLV, face A, lines 1, 23; LXIV, face A, line 8.

[13] No. XLV, face C, line 15; LXIV, face A, line 8.

those sanctions provide direct indications of the ways in which, over a period of time, the rulers of Sukhothai attempted to define the nature of their state in ultimate terms by invoking the cosmological forces and moral ideas which maintained its being.[14]

Ironically, it is what is probably the latest of the three inscriptions, number XLV, dated 1392, which seems the most archaic in content. This inscription contains the only known reference to Phra Khaphung apart from the Ram Khamhæng inscription of a century earlier. Here he is mentioned in a list of spirits among whose duties it was to punish those who offended against their oath of loyalty to the rulers of Sukhothai. Perhaps the most fascinating aspect of this list is that it contains what reads as a patrilineal genealogy of the ruling house of Sukhothai. Unfortunately, the names of these "grandfather spirits," altogether nineteen in number, do not appear to be in chronological order, and most of the names are otherwise unknown in Thai historical literature.[15]

The commitments required of those taking the oath of Inscription XLV were simple: loyalty to the "grandfather and grandson"[16]—the ruling house of Sukhothai—was expected generally of all,[17] and specifically of those called upon to serve the state in war and peace.[18] In return for such loyalty, the inscription promised impartial justice, with appeals apparently supervised by high dignitaries of the monkhood.[19] The sanctions threatened against those who broke their vows were twofold. First, there was

---

[14] In considering this interpretation, I have benefited greatly from the comments and advice of A. Thomas Kirsch.

[15] This list was first referred to in English in an article by Kachorn Sukhabanij, "The Thai Beach-Head States in the 11th-12th Centuries," *Sinlapakòn* I:3 and 4 (Sept. and Nov., 1957), note 9. It since has been considered by, among others, Prasert na Nagara, *op. cit.*, p. 49.

[16] Face A, line 17. The use of kinship terminology to refer to the ruling line of Sukhothai is characteristic of many of the inscriptions of the period. Interesting is the manner in which the "father image" of Ram Khamhæng is supplanted by the "grandfathers" in the fourteenth century inscriptions.

[17] Face A, lines 17-18.

[18] Face C, lines 2-17.

[19] Face A, lines 32-37.

the animistic sanction: the necks of the disloyal would be broken by the "flock of spirits."[20] Secondly, there were Buddhist sanctions: evildoers would be condemned eternally to hell,[21] losing all hope of ever attaining noble rebirth,[22] and with being cast beyond the saving powers of the Triple Gems.[23] Physical and penal sanctions may also have been included, judging from indications on the third face, but this is by no means clear.

Sukhothai Inscription XL is very similar, although much more abbreviated. The oath called for specific assurances of loyalty from the ruler's servants in their past, present, and future actions and intentions. The sanctions threatened against the disloyal were overtly only Buddhist, although there was an implicit penal threat. They were threatened with the extinction of hope for worldly attainments in their next reincarnation[24] and with being cast into outer darkness, where all is "dark, indifferent, and confusing."[25] As in the 1392 inscription, there is a reference to the adjudicating role of the monkhood in determining cases of infractions against the oath.[26]

The Nan inscription, number LXIV, provides a contrast which stems largely from the specific conditions under which it appears to have been framed, and which require some explanation. It bears every indication of growing out of the period of warfare between Sukhothai and Ayudhya in the latter half of the fourteenth century and the former's attempts to seek alliances with its northern neighbors.[27] The inscription itself clearly indicates that the Sukhothai monarch involved was King Sai Lü Thai (Dharmarâja II);[28] and the Nan Chronicle would suggest

[20] Face A, line 18.
[21] Face A, line 20.
[22] Face A., lines 18-19.
[23] Face A, lines 21-23.
[24] Line 19.
[25] Line 23.
[26] Lines 15-16.
[27] See Prasoet, op. cit., p. 48; and, later, Griswold and Prasert, "King Lödaiya of Sukhodaya and His Contemporaries," and "The Epigraphy of Mahadharmaraja I of Sukhodaya," in *Epigraphical and Historical Studies*, pp. 291-570.
[28] Ibid.

Chao Pha Kòng (1361-1386), whose predecessor is said to have died at the hands of an Ayudhyan assassin,[29] was the Nan ruler concerned. It is clear from Inscription VIII that these two rulers did reach some understanding and a delimitation of their frontiers around the year 1370.

The extant portion of the Nan inscription begins with the sanctions: the threat of being cast beyond the reach of the saving grace of Religion—the Triple Gems and Saivism[30]—and its bearers, the monkhood.[31] The Sukhothai ruler then swore positive promises to the ruler of Nan: to rule justly and righteously, to protect Nan, and to consider the domains of Nan and his own as one.[32] He concluded by calling upon Nan for its loyalty and assuring Nan of his own, and by pointing to the common moral benefits which both would share.[33]

It has long been possible, on the basis of the first volume of Sukhothai inscriptions, published by Cœdès in 1924, to trace in Sukhothai's history a steady progression of the state's cosmological

---

[29] *The Nan Chronicle*, tr., Prasoet Churatana (Ithaca, 1966), pp. 11-12. This inscription fits very well with Inscription VIII, where (face C) the borders of Sukhothai ca. 1370 are described and this ruler of Nan specifically named: "To the north, the Nan River forms the border with the territory of Chao Phraya Pha Kon, chief of müang Nan" (tr. by Cœdès, *Recueil*, I, pp. 128-29). Alternatively, this inscription could reflect a later integration of Nan into the Sukhothai state; but the frontiers of Sukhothai as defined in the Pali face of the Wat Asokaram inscription of 1406 (*Sinlapakòn*, IX:3, Sept. 1965, p. 76), would militate against such an interpretation: the. northern boundary of Sukhothai then was still in the Uttaradit region.

[30] The reference here (lines 4-6) is phrased in the following terms: "The religion of Siva (saibagama = saivagama), / the Lord Buddha, the Dharma, the Sangha; all these will he pass beyond: may he not know them. The myriad / of faces of the Lord Buddha, may he not know them. Religion, including the religion of Siva, may he not know the sastras / ...." Saibagama is identified as the Atharva-veda both by *Maha* Cham in his notes and by McFarland's Thai dictionary. This name, however, is not one commonly associated with the Atharvaveda in Indian tradition: see M. Bloomfield, *The Atharvaveda* (Straßburg, 1899), pp. 7-11. Maha Cham's reading thus would appear to be based on the term's *later* usage in Thailand.

[31] Lines 4-7.

[32] Lines 10-15, plus the insertion on face B.

[33] Lines 18-26.

foundations from the mixture of animism and relatively-simple Buddhism in the reign of Ram Khamhæng (Inscription I) to the combination of highly-intellectualized Buddhism with classical Hinduism in the reign of Lü Thai (e.g., Inscriptions III and IV); and to link this sequence of development with similar religious formulae of the early Ayudhya empire.[34] Rather than fit within that sequence of development, however, these late Sukhothai inscriptions extend it in time and to a certain extent reveal what would seem to be an ideological regression. Inscription XL and the Nan Inscription (LXIV) fit reasonably well with the tenor of King Lü Thai's reign, but the cosmological appeals made in the later 1392 one (XLV) are closer to Ram Khamhæng's inscription of 1292 than to the inscriptions of the 1370s or 1380s.

In attempting to explain this sequence of development progressing from Ram Khamhæng's somewhat crude attempt to upgrade animistic tutelary deities to serve as universalistic symbols of Sukhothai's unity, to Lü Thai's wonderfully universalistic mixture of Buddhism and Hinduism, and thence regressively to the 1392 inscription's almost pathetic appeal to local spirits, one might speculate—and speculation it must remain—that competition and the exigencies of immediate political situations were just as, if not more, important in determining the form which magico-religious appeals would take in late Sukhothai than doctrinal or intellectual considerations.[35] By 1351, the Thai challenge to Khmer authority on the plains of central Siam was a century old, and the successes won early by the Thai rulers of Sukhothai were being exploited by their fellows to the south. The foundation of Ayudhya in that year transformed a loose multilateral confederation[36] into a bitter bipartite competition for leadership

[34] See D.K. Wyatt, *The Politics of Reform in Thailand: Education in the Reign of King Chulalongkorn*, pp. 1-7.

[35] On such relationships between politics and cosmology, see, for example, Charles Archaimbault, "Religious Structures in Laos," *Journal of the Siam Society*, LII, i (April, 1964), 57-74.

[36] Such is the analysis of the situation initially put forward some decades ago by Phya Anuman Rajadhon, *Phra* Borihan Thepthani, and Dhanit Yupho; later by Kachorn Sukhabanij; and within the past two years argued in the

of the struggle against a Khmer empire which was to collapse two decades later.[37] It was necessary for both Sukhothai and Ayudhya to attempt to define the nature of that competition, to clarify the nature of the states they were and were building.

In formulating their politico-cultural appeals, both Sukhothai and Ayudhya began from a similar starting point; upholding a universalistic synthesis composed of Hinduistic and Buddhist elements which complemented each other to buttress the authority of the kingship while maintaining the moral individualism which so suited Thai social structure in this age of warfare. Within two decades, however, Ayudhya's physical force, augmented by a more favorable situation, superior techniques of organization, and greater resources on which to draw, shifted the basis of this competition. Sukhothai, her boundaries shrinking as vassals and provinces fell away, increasingly must have been forced into a position where intellectual and sophisticated religious appeals and sanctions could help her little, and where personal loyalties counted for everything. It would have done Sukhothai little good to threaten recalcitrant vassals with metaphysical punishments when they were faced with Ayudhya's armies. Ayudhya could offer northern princes and nobles the same religious comforts and threats as Sukhothai could. The 1392 inscription might be taken as evidence that, in such a position, Sukhothai abandoned a hopeless competition with Ayudhya which had been waged on common ground, defined in universalistic terms, and fell back upon the only secure ground left which was uniquely her own: personal loyalties, and the ever-present and powerful spirits of the primeval animistic world, localized on her own home territory. Thus, in thought as much as by deed, were the "Universal Monarchs" of Sukhothai reduced again to local princes.

---

journals *Sangkhomsat parithat, Chòfa,* and *Borankhadi* by a younger generation of Thai historians [in the mid-1960s]. The argument over the antecedents of Ayudhya is far from concluded, but certainly the effects of the foundation of Ayudhya are quite clear.

[37] As recently established by O. W. Wolters, "The Khmer King at Basan (1371-3) and the Restoration of the Cambodian Chronology During the Fourteenth and Fifteenth Centuries," *Asia Major* n.s. XII, pt. 1 (1966), 44-89.

The significance of the three oath inscriptions is that they furnish an indication of the changing complexion of the moral order of the universe upon which the rulers of Sukhothai, by reason both of belief and of circumstances, felt they could call in a situation of central importance: the ritual strengthening and renewal of unity.

Their value, however, should not be exaggerated. Like Sukhothai (and, indeed, like the kingdom of Luang Prabang),[38] Ayudhya—and Bangkok after her—developed an oath of allegiance tradition which called upon the spirits of ancestors and localities; and, if Thai literary historians are correct, she did so in the reign of Rama Thibòdi, the first king of Ayudhya.[39] This call to the spirit world was included in the imprecation which empowered the waters drunk in the oath of allegiance ceremony by all the officers of the kingdom.[40] There was, however, one vital difference which

---

[38] See Pierre Nginn, "Invocation aux Devata dans le ceremonie du serment," *France-Asie* VII, nos. 66-67 (Dec. 1951), 573-76, which gives the text of the invocation used in the oath of allegiance ceremony at Luang Prabang, similar in many respects to that in the inscription of 1392.

[39] The Thai oath of allegiance ceremony was the subject of an exhaustive study undertaken by King Chulalongkorn in 1877 and first published in 1920 under the title *Phraratchakaranyanuson* (reprinted, Bangkok, 1964). It appears in abridged form in the king's *Phraratchaphithi sipsong düan* (1960 edn., pp. 222-71). Speculations concerning the date of the imprecation seem to be based on a reference in the closing stanza to a King Rama Thibodi (of which there were at least two), and on the fact that the imprecation is composed in a style and vocabulary very archaic. See Plüang na Nakhòn, *Prawat wannakhadi Thai* (2nd ed.; Bangkok, 1955), pp. 52-53; and P. Schweisguth, *Étude sur la littérature siamoise* (Paris, 1951), pp. 47-48. Schweisguth mistakenly identified this imprecation as a ritual command for the waters to recede at the end of the rainy season, and was unaware of its association with the oath of allegiance ceremony. See also H. G. Quaritch Wales, *Siamese State Ceremonies* (London, 1931), pp. 193-98, for a general discussion of the ceremony.

[40] The text of this imprecation is given in Prince Sommot Amòraphan *Prakat kan phraratchaphithi*, vol. I (Bangkok, 1916), pp. 21-26; Chulalongkorn, *Phraratchakaranyanusòn*, 1920 edn., pp. 133-38, or 1964 edn., pp. 172-78. Its text defies even translation into modern Thai, and Plüang, *op. cit.*, gives a very useful summary of its contents. On the oath, see especially Cit Phumisak, *'Ongkan chæng nam læ khokhit mai nai prawattisat Thai lum nam Caophraya* (Bangkok: Duang Kamon, 1981).

distinguished the Ayudhya ceremony both from the oath traditions of her hinduized predecessors in Southeast Asia, notably Angkor and Srivijaya,[41] and from the oath traditions of Sukhothai and Luang Prabang. Whereas the Khmer and Srivijaya oaths were almost exclusively hindiustic in their sanctions, and the Sukhothai and Luang Prabang oaths Buddhist and animistic, the Ayudhya and Bangkok oath was a well-proportioned synthesis of the Brahmanical and animistic traditions; a balance between the Brahmanical ritual of universal unity and the particularistic immediacy of animistic religious traditions. In devising this oath and formulating this appeal, Ayudhya showed a cultural creativity, born of pragmatism, which was rare for its day and which, in the final analysis, may well provide one key to an understanding of the reasons for Ayudhya's success and Sukhothai's failure.

---

[41] On the Angkorian oath, contained in eleventh century inscriptions of Suryavarman I, see Cœdès, *Inscriptions du Cambodge*, III (Paris, 1951), pp. 209-10; and an English translation in Wales, *op. cit.*, pp. 195-96. On Srivijaya, see J. G. de Casparis, *Prasasti Indonesia*, II (Bandung, 1956), esp. pp. 27-32, 36-46.

LAWS AND SOCIAL ORDER
IN EARLY THAILAND:
AN INTRODUCTION TO THE *MANGRAISAT**

Over the past several decades a considerable body of scholarly literature has accumulated concerning the evolution of Thai social and political patterns, behavior, and values, and our study of Thai society now is much more solidly-based than it was only a generation ago. One might legitimately begin to wonder, however, whether we might not "have it all wrong." The question is not entirely flippant. Much of what has been written on such subjects has little solid historical depth. Historians' study of Thailand prior to the nineteenth century remains relatively superficial, based on very scanty sources; and to the extent that social scientists and others have depended on the historians, none would argue that they have been completely well-served. Even more seriously, however, one can argue that there has been a good deal of reading contemporary and recent situations back into the past; and even historians' analyses of pre-Chakri social and political history have been all too readily the prisoner of a narrow, linear view of Thai history as the political succession of kingdoms from Sukhothai to Ayudhya to Bangkok.

Consider the sharp contrast that conventionally is drawn between Sukhothai and Ayudhya—a contrast between the informal, personal, and paternalistic social and political style of Sukhothai, and the formalistic, impersonal, and bureaucratic structures characteristic of the Ayudhya period. On the basis of this contrast, it has become customary to view Ayudhya's initiation in the fifteenth century of an elaborate system of socio-political hierarchy (the *sakdi na* system attributed to King Borommatrailokanat) as

* *Journal of Southeast Asian Studies* 15:2 (September 1984), 245-252. Reprinted with permission.

a dramatic and sudden change that thrust Ayudhya's development forward, but at the same time created dynamic tensions within the society, between rigid hierarchy and more 'loosely-structured' behavior, that were to bedevil Siamese history into the twentieth century. Against such an approach, it is possible to argue that the supposed continuity between Sukhothai and Ayudhya is more a product of twentieth-century historiography than of any past reality: the peoples of Sukhothai and Ayudhya were of different stocks and came out of different historic experiences, and the kingdoms were contemporary rivals, rather than successive generations in a line of political (or social or cultural) descent. If, for a moment, we forget the supposed continuity from Sukhothai to Ayudhya, we can then open the possibilities, otherwise neglected or closed, of exploring other continuities and discontinuities that separately link Sukhothai and Ayudhya with *different* pasts—Ayudhya with the long, slow khmerizing process that had been going on in the Caophraya Valley from the tenth or eleventh century, and Sukhothai with more narrowly Tai streams of development that had been flowing in the interior valleys of mainland Southeast Asia from even earlier.

The general problem raised by this example is the problem of social and political evolution among the Tai (and neighboring) peoples from, let us say, the ninth or tenth to the fifteenth century. Few would deny that the Tai peoples underwent considerable social change during this period. The common hypothesis is that the various Tai groups (and some more than others) then developed increasingly more complex social organization, that the vertical (hierarchical) dimensions of their societies developed at the expense of the horizontal, and that they became increasingly differentiated socially. In considerable measure, these changes have been explained primarily as the product of changes in scale as groups of the Tai peoples moved from isolated, small interior valleys to broader plains capable of supporting much larger populations; plains perhaps already including numerous non-Tai indigenous inhabitants. In the all-too-few pages most of us can allot to the treatment of such complicated developments, we move within a "few hundred" years from rude, simple, "democratic," semi-tribal village. communities to complex, sophisticated, hierarchical, bureaucratic societies. It goes without saying that, not only was the transition between these two polar opposites probably very complex, but neither opposite was nearly as neat as it might now at first glance appear to be. In short, we still have a great deal to do before we can understand the processes of "state-building" among the Tai peoples.

With respect to premodern times this process has not been easy to study, at least in part for lack of reliably contemporaneous sources. To date, the most successful attack on the problem has been made using legal sources: M.R.W. Akin Rabibhadana's seminal work on *The Organization of Thai Society in the Early Bangkok Period, 1782-1873.*[1] Quite apart from his major contribution to our understanding of the nineteenth-century social order, Akin also had much to say about social organization in the Ayudhya period, based upon his reading of the surviving laws of the Ayudhya period, as gathered together into the monumental legal compilation of 1805, the *Three Seals Laws* of King Rama I. In the process, he had to confront the formidable difficulties of working with that legal code as an historical source, the chief among which is the simple fact that, though many of the laws included in that corpus bear earlier dates, they most likely were revised at the time of the 1805 compilation, and therefore they cannot with absolute certainty be considered reliable sources for any earlier period without a good deal of qualification. Notwithstanding these difficulties, Akin draws a convincing explanation of changing social and political organization in the late Ayudhya period which remains the standard introduction to the subject.

Akin's analysis of the Ayudhya system, however, not least because of its basis in the legal corpus of 1805, as well as because of his structural approach, is essentially a static, steady-state model of social organization in the fifteenth through eighteenth centuries. He is less successful in tracing major changes in that system than in analyzing the dynamic tensions that underlay it without fundamentally changing it either in the direction of

---

[1] Ithaca: Cornell University Southeast Asia Program, 1969; Data Paper 74.

greater institutional strength or greater personal mobility. Here he is clearly the prisoner of his sources; and until such time as the *Three Seals Laws* are critically edited and their chronology unraveled we will not be able fully to exploit their potential as sources for the study of changes in the social and political patterns of the Ayudhya period. Some hope is offered by the completion of a joint project of the Southeast Asia Studies Centre of the Kyoto University and the National Museum of Ethnology in Osaka to produce a computerized index to every word in the *Three Seals Laws*. This index should make it possible to trace changing social and political terminology through laws of different dates, for example. It should be of use in unwinding anachronisms, although, because it was not based on a close reading of the original manuscripts of the laws, it will not be a definitive source for the study of changes in the language and orthography.

Legal texts are of obvious utility to the historian and social scientist interested in earlier social and political conditions and institutions. Their very subject is the regulation of the society; and though they often may reflect better a society's aspirations than the realities of its existence, few other sources are of greater significance. It might seem surprising, therefore, that so little work has been done on Thailand's legal history. The reason for this paradox would appear to stem from the linear view of Thai history mentioned earlier: Historians and legal scholars have confined their attention to the surviving records of Sukhothai, Ayudhya, and Bangkok; and they have therefore been confined to the problematic study of the *Three Seals Laws*.

One extremely important target of opportunity for the historian and social scientist is the legal tradition of what is now northern Thailand, but was until the nineteenth century the sometimes-independent, sometimes-tributary-to-Burma Kingdom of Lan Na. The only well-known representative of this tradition is the *Mangraisat,* an early legal text of uncertain date attributed, at least in its origins, to King Mangrai of Chiang Mai, who reigned from 1259 to 1317. It was largely neglected until recently, when Prasert na Nagara edited a version of the text in Thai, a small portion of which was subsequently translated and published by Dr. Prasert and A. B. Griswold in 1977.[2]

The manuscript of the *Mangraisat* presented by Griswold and Prasert is based upon a copy from Lopburi, with a date equivalent to AD 1800, long posterior to its supposed date of composition. Griswold and Prasert suppose that the text was copied for the use of a local (Lopburi) population of Lan Na prisoners of war who settled in that region and required their own customary law for the regulation of their life. The manuscript includes more than 200 clauses, but Griswold and Prasert translate only the first twenty-two, which for various reasons they believe to be much older than the rest of the code. This portion of the text concludes with a "peroration" identical to that given at the end of the entire manuscript, and strengthens their assumption that the original text ended there. In editing their version, they also consulted a variant version dating probably from the period AD 1614-26, and made unsystematic reference to two other versions from Chiang Mai, one at Wat Chiang Man and the other at Chiang Mai University. They do not, however, claim to have undertaken a thorough critical study of the text and its antecedents and textual context.

Not surprisingly, even the first twenty-two clauses of the *Mangraisat* make fascinating reading to those interested in the structure and functioning of early Tai societies. Even in treating the most mundane matters, the text reveals much of both belief and practice. Considering now only that first section of the text, its twenty-two clauses may be described as being divided into eleven sections, as follows:

(i) Legitimation by history (Preamble)—Here the authority of the laws is established: "These laws were made known in ancient times to King Mangrai, (who) was descended in the direct line from.... Then King Mangrai promulgated these laws so that all ... may know what is right and what is wrong."

---

2 *Mangraisat,* ed. Dr. Prasert na Nagara [Bangkok: Cremation of *luang* Hotrakittayanuphat (Asa Hotrakit), 1971]; A.B. Griswold and Prasert na Nagara, "Epigraphic and Historical Studies No. 17: The 'Judgements of King Mang Ray,'" *Journal of the Siam Society* 65, part 1 (Jan. 1977), 137-60.

(ii) Decimal organization of society (Art. 1)—Society is organized in groups of ten, with a hierarchy of officials controlling groups of ten, fifty, a hundred, a thousand, and ten thousand.

(iii) Conduct in wartime (Arts. 2-7)—A series of articles follow that deal, first, with desertions in battle, and severe punishments are prescribed both for inferiors deserting their superiors, and for superiors deserting their inferiors. The section on desertion also includes a "later amendment" (Art. 4) moderating the prescribed punishments. The three remaining articles, in effect, link military performance and civilian life: The property and families of those who die in battle are not forfeited to the king, "because those who volunteer for the King's service do so in order to protect their property and their family. If anyone dies fighting for the King, let his family not suffer for it" (Art. 5). Similarly, those who demonstrate prowess in warfare are rewarded: "If anyone performs an outstanding service for his lord, let him receive an outstanding reward for it, so that others may be led to follow his example" (Art. 6).

(iv) Inheritance (Art. 8)—One long article on inheritance accomplishes the transition from military to civilian life. This applies only to royal officers, and not to the common people. Disposition of property by the will of the deceased is respected, and only in cases of intestacy does the king take half the deceased's property.

(v) Compulsory labor service (corvée; Art. 9)—Freeman are required to devote up to half their time to labor in the service of the king: "Ten days in the King's service, followed by ten days working at home, is in accord with ancient Dharma."

(vi) Investment credit (Arts. 10-11)—Two clauses that at first glance appear to be unrelated occur in the middle of the text; the first allowing a "citizen" ("freeman" might be a better translation of *phrai*) to borrow "money for investment from the lord who is his master" for three years without interest; and the second providing that "land brought under cultivation by a citizen shall be exempt from taxation for three years." Both articles, of course, have in common the generous policy of (apparently) encouraging productive investment by what amounts to a tax subsidy.

(vii) Slavery (Arts. 12-14)—The following three articles all contribute to actively discouraging or at least curbing the abuses of slavery: Article 12 forbids accepting debtors, litigants, thieves, and deserters as slaves; Article 13 contradictorily indicates that bankrupts became slaves and allows such wastrels to inherit only when specifically granted bequests and not in cases of intestacy; and Article 14 provides that the children of unions between the king's slaves and freemen should be freemen. This last article closes with the assertion that "Citizens [i.e., Freemen] are rare and should not be wasted [by allowing them to become slaves]."

(viii) Two kinds of lords (Art. 15)—The text here explains the differences between good and bad rulers, between Dharma lords and Mara lords, in terms of their adherence to Buddhist morality. These distinctions seem to apply equally to kings and to their officers, and kings are warned not to allow Mara (evil) lords to rise to power, "for he is like a poisonous growth in the midst of the kingdom, and if shoots or branches sprout from it, the kingdom will be harmed."

(ix) Criminal law (Arts. 16-18)—Three articles deal with the most serious felonies: Article 16 specifies conditions under which homicide may be considered legitimate; Article 17 lists twelve crimes that "should be punished by execution;" and Article 18 prescribes three kinds of punishment for felonies: execution, mutilation, and slavery or exile.

(x) Administration of justice (Arts. 19-22)—The final four articles all cover aspects of the administration of justice: Article 19 advises judges on the factors to take into consideration when rendering a judgment; Article 20 provides grounds for appeal by specifying wrong judgments, and by implication provides standards of judicial conduct; Article 21 lays down what amounts to a statute of limitations (twenty years); and Article 22 lists sixteen situations that give rise to litigation, from borrowing money or things to disputing ownership.

(xi) Peroration—The text as defined by Griswold and Prasert closes with what they call a peroration, which is worth reproducing in full: "Those who desire to administer a district for the King in such a way as to make it flourish, and to make the people live peacefully in every village, should act in accordance with these laws. All these words are [taken from] the ancient Rajasastra for ruling the country according to the royal tradition passed down by the many Kings who ruled in conformity with the Dasarajadhamma from ancient times to the present day."

Kirsch has a good deal to say concerning the social implications of these provisions of the ancient laws of Lan Na from the perspective of the anthropologist.[3] I should like, instead, to set them in two of their contexts: in the context of Southeast Asian and/or Buddhist legal tradition, and in the context of the legal traditions specific to northern Thailand or Lan Na.

First, if one considers this version of the *Mangraisat* in the context of Buddhist, Indic law the first and perhaps most striking thing is how little of the formal Indic legal tradition comes through in the text. Only two of its sections bear close resemblance to the Dharmasastra tradition: the articles detailing the fourteen causes of contention giving rise to litigation and the article on judgments that may be set aside—typical instances of the Indic legal style—as well as the general structure of the text as a whole.

Many will recall the legends respecting the origins of human government that are widespread in the Indic tradition, all of which generally begin with some "golden age" in the distant past, move to the decline of human society into chaos and lawlessness, and then to the creation of kings to restore order to the world. There are various such tales in the Indic tradition, in the Laws of Manu and in various Buddhist sources, for example.[4] It seems to me that the underlying logic of the *Mangraisat* falls into this pattern. It begins with a legendary history, and by implication the laws of the text spring from the preamble. But, even more interesting, perhaps, is the way in which the whole text seems to

---

[3] A. Thomas Kirsch, "Cosmology and Ecology as Factors in Interpreting Early Thai Social Organization," *Journal of Southeast Asian Studies* 15:2 (September 1984), 253-265.

[4] See, for example, the two excerpts from the *Digha Nikaya* and one from the *Mahabharata* in *Sources of Indian Tradition*, ed. Wm. Theodore de Bary (New York: Columbia University Press, 1958), I:129-33, 133-39, and 137-39.

pivot around Article 15, the article which distinguishes between "good" and "bad" rulers— between Dharma lords and Mara lords. In a sense the first half of the text speaks of a real, here-and-now, virtually "given" social and political world, structured by the exigencies of practical life in the uplands of interior Southeast Asia, while the latter half of the text is concerned with eternal verities, with the principles of justice and their application to the real world. If the details of the code only now and then resonate with the Indic texts, the structure of the code is a familiar one in Buddhist circles. The text would bear careful comparison both with other Southeast Asian (Buddhist and non-Buddhist) legal codes and with the classical texts of the Indian tradition. Such an examination would, I think, clarify questions of both legal and, especially, social evolution in the region.

When the *Mangraisat* is set in the context of Lan Na legal works, we immediately confront serious problems of dating and textual comparability that go far beyond what we can now accomplish. Griswold and Prasert did not have at their disposal the very considerable body of Lan Na legal texts that have come to light in recent years, much of which bears directly upon the *Mangraisat*. For the most part, these are texts that have been issued in Thai transliteration by Sommai Premchit from a major, large-scale project run out of the Department of Sociology and Anthropology of the Faculty of Social Sciences of Chiang Mai University, beginning in 1974. Even an unsystematic perusal of some of the publications of that project suggests the existence of a rich context within which Griswold and Prasert's *Mangraisat* may be studied.

At least for our present purposes, the most interesting of the texts transcribed by Sommai would appear to be the first, consisting of an undated manuscript of the *Mangraisat* from Wat Mün Ngœn Kòng in Chiang Mai.[5] This text includes more than half of the articles of the Griswold and Prasert version, excluding Articles 3-4, 7, 10, 13, 16, and 18-20. What is even more interesting,

_____

[5] *Mangraisat,* transcribed by Sommai Premchit in collaboration with Puangkam Tuikheo (Chiang Mai: Transliteration Series I, 1975).

however, is that the Wat Mün Ngœn Kòng manuscript is consistently much "simpler" than the Griswold and Prasert version. Take, for example, the equivalent of Article 1, describing the decimal organization of society.[6] The Wat Mün Ngœn Kòng text excludes the officers whose titles Griswold and Prasert translate as "Foreman," and simply describe an uncomplicated division of society into groups of ten, fifty, one hundred,. a thousand, ten thousand, and a hundred thousand. All the clauses that occur in both versions are shorter and "simpler" in the Wat Mün Ngœn Kòng version. Though the text itself is undated, it is reasonable to assume that the Wat Mün Ngœn Kòng manuscript is older than the Griswold and Prasert text. Careful comparison of the two versions should shed considerable light on both of them, no less than on the evolution of Lan Na society, at least in terms allowed by its laws.

There are. moreover, other legal texts issued by the Chiang Mai project in recent years that will repay careful study. At least two others appear to be versions, whole or fragmentary, of the *Mangraisat,*[7] while others appear to be closer to versions of classical Indic legal texts, or collections of cases, or versions of laws imported from elsewhere in the Tai world.[8] For now, allow me to make three observations that arise from the comparison of "earlier" and "later" versions of the *Mangraisat.*

First, comparison of the two versions of Article 1 suggests that the Lan Na social organization was complexifying vertically, but from the top down, as higher officers were given their assistants. It might have been more logical to have done what Ayudhya did with the *sakdi na* system, and create intermediary ranks—of twenty or

---

[6] See Appendix.

[7] *Kotmai Lan Na. Lanna Custom Law,* and *Kotmai Lan Na: Lanna Custom Law,* transliterated by Sommai Premchit (Chiang Mai: Transliteration Series 2 and 3, 1975). To those we should now add *The Laws of King Mangrai (Mangrayathammasart), The Wat Chang Kham, Nan Manuscript from the Richard Davis Collection,* tr. and ed., Aroonrut Wichienkeeo and Gehan Wijeyewardene (Canberra, 1986).

[8] *Awahan 25, Kotmai Lan Na: 25 Characteristics of Stealing, Lanna Custom Law, Thammasat chaofa Hariphunchai: Chao Pha Haribhunjayaûs Dharmashastra,* and *Kotmai khosarat: Kosarat Customary Law,* transliterated by Sommai Premchit (Chiang Mai: Transliteration Series 6, 14, 16, 1975-77).

thirty, for example; but the Lan Na system simply gives the various officers assistants. Was this a response to their need for help, or does it rather reflect the growth of a class of *cao* needing positions?

Second, it is worth noting that the Lan Na legal texts we have do not indicate the presence in that society of any substantial amount of functional differentiation, save on what we might call a class basis. There seems little differentiation made between civil and military roles, and officers are assigned no specialized roles.

Third, at least implicitly comparing the earlier *Mangraisat* text with the *Three Seals Laws* of 1805, I am struck by the apparent absence of any sense of institutions in the earlier text. The earlier text gives us little sense of the existence of a "state," but a very strong sense of the existence of a "king-dom" in the literal sense of that word. We might even go further to suggest that even the king is only intermittently "present" in the world of the text; for passages referring to persons in authority seem almost deliberately to leave it ambiguously unclear as to whether the king or others are intended.

In short, we appear to have in "The Judgments of King Mangrai" elements of a picture of an early Tai society and polity that seems relatively more "evolved," more complex, than the "tribal" Tai communities we associate with earlier centuries; and perhaps also somewhat more hierarchically structured than the Sukhothai depicted in King Ramkhamhaeng's inscription. At the same time, it is considerably less elaborate and bureaucratic than the picture we generally have of even early Ayudhya society. Just the differences noted between the (presumably) earlier and later texts of the *Mangraisat* suggest that there is much to be learned here about the evolution of early Tai societies in an increasingly hierarchical and differentiated direction.

Obviously, early Tai legal texts are an extremely important historical source for the analysis of social and political change. Their use is not without serious difficulties of language, and of chronology; but these are not insurmountable. And until we can range more widely through the texts of the early Tai world we cannot hope fully to understand the full significance of why Ayudhya's rulers chose one form of political and social organization while their "country cousins" in Lan Na and Laos chose others.

APPENDIX

Article 1 Compared

1800 Version *(Griswold & Prasert)*	*Wat Mün Ngœn Kong Ms.*
For every ten citizens let there be one Nay Sip, and one Foreman to act as intermediary and make known the tasks assigned. For each five Nay Sip, let there be one Nay Ha-sip [and two Foremen], one for the left side and one for the right side. For two Nay Ha-sip let there be one Nay Roy. For ten Nay Roy, let there be one Cau Ban. For ten Cau Ban let there be one Cau Hmün. For ten Cau Hmün, let there be one Cau Sen. Let the country be administered in this way so as not to inconvenience the King.	For every ten citizens let there be one Nay Sip. For each five Nay Sip, let there be one Nay Ha-sip. For two Nay Ha-sip let there be one Nay Roy. For ten Nay Roy, let there be one Cau Ban. For ten Cau Ban let there be one Cau Hmün. For ten Cau Hmün, let there be one Cau Sen.

THE THAI "PALATINE LAW" AND MALACCA*

The Thai "Palatine Law" (*Kot Monthianban*) invariably figures in any discussion of the early history of Malacca. Its ostensible date, Culasakaraja 720 or AD 1358, has long puzzled scholars who rightly but uncertainly have felt it necessary to dismiss on external grounds its inclusion of Malacca and other peninsular states in its list of the tributaries of the Empire of Ayudhya.[1] As a result, however, not only has the law been held as irrelevant to the study of the history of the Malay Peninsula in the fourteenth century, but it also has been neglected in considering the fifteenth century, primarily because of the difficulty in dating it. The recent chronological research of Phiphat Sukkhathit makes possible a fresh examination of this law as a piece of historical evidence in its own right and allows a more plausible date to be assigned to it.[2]

---

*Journal of the Siam Society, 55:2 (July 1967), 279-286.

The following abbreviations are employed:

KTSD = Lingat, R. (ed), *Kotmai tra sam duang* [Laws of the Three Seals], 5 vols, Bangkok 1962. Identical to Thammasat University edition of 1938.

Bradley = Bradley, D.B. (ed.), *Rüang kotmai müang Thai* [The Laws of Siam], 10th ed., 2 vols., Bangkok 1896.

Ratburi = Prince Ratburi Direkrit (ed.), *Kotmai* [Laws], 2nd ed., 2 vols., Bangkok 1901.

[1] See, for example, Paul Wheatley, *The Golden Khersonese* (Kuala Lumpur 1961), pp. 301, 307; and G. Cœdès, *Les états hindouises d'Indochine et d'Indonesie* (Paris 1964), p. 266.

[2] Phiphat Sukkhathit, "Sakkarat Culamani," .*Sinlapakòn* 6:5 (Jan. 1963), 47-57; and "Kannap pi nai phutthasakarat (Counting the Years of the Buddhist Era)," *Sinlapakòn* 7:1 (May 1963), 48-58.

The "Palatine Law" is a lengthy piece of legislation framed primarily to regulate the royal succession and the position and status of the royal family in old Thai society. Only two brief sections need concern us here: the preamble of the law (Clause 1), which bears upon its date; and its first substantive clause (Clause 2), the list of tributary states.

TEXT[3]

1

ศุภมัศดุศักราช ๗๒๐ วันเสาเดือนห้าขึ้นหกค่ำ ชวดนักสัตวศก สมเด็จพระเจ้ารามาธิบดี บรมไตรโลกนารถ มหามงกุฎเทพมนุษ วิสุทธิสุริยวงษองคพุทธางกูรบรมบพิตร พระพุทธเจ้าอยู่หัว ฯลฯ

2

ฝ่ายกระษัตรแต่ได้ถวายดอกไม้ทองเงินทังนั้น ๒๐ เมือง คือ เมืองนครหลวง เมืองศรีสัตนาคณหุต เมืองเชียงใหม่ เมืองตองอู เมืองเชียงไกร เมืองเชียงกราน เมืองเชียงแสน เมืองเชียงรุ้ง เมือง เชียงราย เมืองแสนหวี เมืองเขมราช เมืองแพร่ เมืองน่าน เมืองใต้ทอง เมืองโคตรบอง เมืองเรวแกว ๑๖ เมืองนี้ฝ่ายเหนือ เมืองฝ่ายใต้ เมืองอุยองตะหนะ เมืองมลากา เมืองมลายู เมืองวรวารี ๔ เมืองเข้ากัน ๒๐ เมือง ถวายดอกไม้ทองเงิน

พญามหานคร แต่ได้ถือน้ำพระพัท ๘ เมือง คือ เมืองพิศณุโลก เมืองสัชนาไล เมืองศุโขไท เมืองกำแพงเพช เมืองนครศรีธรรมราช เมืองนครราชสีมา เมืองตนาวศรี เมืองทวาย

---

[3] Following KTSD vol. 1, pp. 69-70.

TRANSLATION

Clause 1

Auspicious moment, 720 of the era; on Saturday, the sixth day of the waxing moon of the fifth month in the year of the Rat, King Ramathibòdi Bòrommatrailokkanât ...

Clause 2

Altogether, twenty towns (*müang*) send the gold and silver flowers to the King: Nakhòn Luang, Sri Sattanâkkhanahut, Chiang Mai, Tòng U, Chiang Krai, Chiang Kran, Chiang Sæn, Chiang Rung, Chiang Rai, Hsenwi, Khemmarat, Phræ, Nan, Tai Thòng, Khotrabòng, and Reo Kæo, these sixteen in the north; and, in the south, Ujong Tanah, Malacca, Malayu and Varavari four towns; altogether twenty towns which send the gold and silver flowers.

There are eight rulers of great cities (*mahanakhòn*) who bear only the water of allegiance: Phitsanulok, Satchanalai, Sukhothai, Kamphængphet, Nakhòn Si Thammarat, Nakhòn Ratchasima, Tenasserim, and Tavoy.

The Date of the Law

Four elements in the law's preamble have a bearing upon its date: (1) the year, 720, of an unspecified era; (2) the cyclical Year of the Rat; (3) the day on which the law was promulgated, expressed in terms of the lunar calendar; and (4) the name of the king who ordered its promulgation, Ramathibòdi Bòrommatrailokkanât. The name of the king alone would appear to point to the reign of King Trailok (AD 1448-1488); but there is one section of the "Law on Rebellion" which includes his name in terms almost identical to those of this law, and which dates unmistakably from the year A.D. 1434.[4] While this is the only such case, it is sufficiently an exception to urge the advisability of relying primarily upon other elements of the law in determining its date.

There were four distinct dating systems employed in the laws of the Ayudhya period: (1) Culasakkarat, the Lesser Era (+ 638

---

[4] KTSD vol. 4 p. 132 (Phra aiyakan krabot sük, Clause 15).

= AD); (2) Mahasakkarat, the Greater Era (+ 78 = AD); (3) Phutthasakkarat, the Buddhist Era (−543 = AD);[5] and (4) Culamanisakkarat, Culamani Era, or, as Prince Damrong termed it, Sakkarat Kotmai, "Legal Era" (+ 188 = A.D.).[6] Faced with a law or inscription of the Ayudhya period bearing a date between 712 and 1129, one's most ready inclination is to assume that the date is expressed in the Lesser Era. With the "Palatine Law," this temptation is nearly irresistible, as conversion yields a date of A.D. 1358, eight years after the founding of a new dynasty at Ayudhya and at a time when one would expect such a law as this to be framed. The 1358 date, however, cannot be correct, as 1358 was the Year of the Dog and not the Year of the Rat.[7] One may take it as a cardinal rule that, however much scribes and copyists may confuse dates, the animal cyclical years are almost never incorrect. As the law's date yields no tenable dales by conversion from any of the other eras,[8] one is forced to assume either that the figure given was miscopied, or that it was incorrectly converted from another era to 720 of the Lesser Era.

Prince Damrong, in his study of the Thai laws, took the last alternative and suggested that the date should read 820, i.e., A.D. 1458;[9] but 820 was a Year of the Tiger. In cases where a miscopied digit is suspected, the likelihood is that the animal year and final digit are correct, the latter because it must coincide with the correct cyclical year of the decade (in this case, the tenth year). The "Palatine

---

[5] Until early in the seventeenth century, Buddhist Era was expressed in Thailand in the Sinhalese manner, in terms of current rather than expired years. Phiphat, "Kan nap pi," p. 48.

[6] See Prince Damrong Rajanubhab (ed.), *Royal Autograph Edition*, vol. 1 p. 641 (Bangkok 1962); and, especially, Phiphat, "Sakkarat culamani," op. cit.

[7] Established by means of the Luang Prasœt version of the Royal Chronicles of Ayudhya (an English translation of which, by O. Frankfurter, appears in *Journal of the Siam Society* 6:3 (1909), 1-21); and the inscriptions, G. Cœdès, *Recueil des inscriptions du Siam*, I; and Thailand, Office of the Prime Minister, Commission for the Publication of Historical, Cultural, and Archeological Records (comps.), *Prachum sila cârük*, 3 (Bangkok, 1965).

[8] Read with an assumed thousand digit as Mahasakkarat 1720, it becomes AD 1798, Year of the Horse; as Buddhist Era 1720 it becomes AD 1177; and as Culamani Era 1720 it becomes AD 1908.

[9] *Royal Autograph Edition*, I, 643.

Law," then, on this test, probably was framed in 710, 770, 830 ... of the Lesser Era, all of which were years of the Rat. Of these, only 830 (A.D. 1468) falls within the reign of King Trailok.

Similarly, in the event of incorrect conversion from one era to another, the year A.D. 1468 also is indicated. First, the Palatine Law bears by far the lowest-numbered date of almost fifty pre-eighteenth century Thai laws. The next nearest is 796, the law already mentioned of AD 1434; while the next after it are two laws of 955 (BE 1955 ?), each mentioning a different year of the animal cycle, neither of which corresponds to the correct animal year.[10] The possibility of an incorrect conversion is further strengthened by the fact that the only other laws known definitely to date from the reign of King Trailok are both dated 129X in an unspecified era.[11] If the "Palatine Law" dated from the reign of King Trailok, one would expect it to bear a date of ca. 1300 in the same era. Of six possible misconversions,[12] only one is reasonable: that a scribe, assuming a date of 1280 to be expressed in Mahasakaraja, converted it to Culasakaraja by subtracting 560 to obtain CS 720; when the date actually was expressed in Culamanisakkarat, and he should have subtracted 450 to obtain a date of CS 830, AD 1468. The likelihood that this indeed occurred is increased by the fact that the Culamani Era was imperfectly known in the nineteenth century when the present collection of old Thai laws was compiled, and only recently has been identified and conclusively dated.[13]

Both possibilities, then—the possibility of misread digits and the possibility of misconversion from one era to another— suggest the same year, CS 830 or AD 1468/69, as the date of the "Palatine Law."

---

[10] KTSD, vol I p. 197 (Phrommasak); and IV, 155 (Krabot sük, Clause 68).

[11] KTSD vol I p. 219 (Phra aiyakan tamnæng na phonlarüan, Clause 1), and 316 (Phra aiyakan tamnæng na thahan huamüang, Clause 30).

[12] The two permutations of Buddhist Era yield Lesser Era 1341 (by Greater Era rules) or 1451 (by Legal Era rules); the two permutations of Legal Era yield Lesser Era -11 (by Buddhist Era rules) or 610 (by Greater Era rules); and the other Greater Era permutation yields Lesser Era 99 by Buddhist Era rules.

[13] Phiphat, "Sakkarat Culamani," *op. cit.*

An empirical check on the accuracy of this date is possible through reference to the weekday, Saturday, on which the law is said to have been promulgated. The Burmese, Lao, and Cambodian chronological systems all prescribe Tuesday for the sixth day of the waxing moon of the fifth month in the year in question, a discrepancy of three days; but they also miss by three days the correct weekday of the Wat Culamani inscription of 1465.[14] If the date of the 1465 inscription is used as a basis for calculation of the weekday of the sixth of the waxing moon of the fifth month three years later, the result is the expected Saturday. Thus the empirical consistency between the inscription and the law lends certainty to a date of mid-April, AD 1468, for the "Palatine Law."[15]

The Tributary States

Of the twenty tributary states mentioned in Clause 2, most are readily identifiable, and the list as a whole fits much more readily into the context of fifteenth century Southeast Asian history than into either the preceding or succeeding centuries. The sixteen northern tributaries were a product of the wars begun in the reign of King Bòrommaracha I (1370-1388) which continued through much of the fifteenth century. By the middle of the sixteenth century, however, almost all of them had fallen to the Burmese. Chiang Mai, Chiang Sæn, Chiang Rai, Phræ, and Nan are present-day provincial centers in North Thailand, while Hsenwi in the Burmese Shan States and Chiang Rung (Keng Hung) in Yunnan are readily identifiable. The remainder require some explanation.

Nakhòn Luang: This term is used in the chronicles in the fourteenth and fifteenth centuries to refer to Angkor, the date of

---

[14] A.M.B. Irwin, *The Burmese & Arakanese Calendars* (Rangoon, 1909); Tiao Maha Upahat Phetsarath, "The Laotian Calendar," in René de Berval (ed), *Kingdom of Laos* (Saigon, 1959), pp. 97-125; and F.G. Faraut, *Astronomie cambodgienne* (Phnom Penh, 1910). The Wat Culamani inscription is published in *Prachum phongsawadan* (Collected Chronicles), I (Bangkok: Progress Bookstore, 1963), pp. 139-42.

[15] The only available tables for conversion to the Julian calendar are those for the Hindu and Chinese calendars, neither of which fit the Indochina cases.

the first capture of which has now been firmly established as 1369 by O.W. Wolters.[16] Its inclusion among the northern tributaries is no more unusual then the inclusion of some eastern provinces among those administered by the Department of the North (Krom Mahatthai) in the latter portion of the Ayudhya and in the Bangkok period.

Sri Sattanakhanahut: Luang Prabang, capital of the Lao kingdom of Lan Xang until 1560.

Tòng U: Either Toungoo in Burma, or, possibly, Tang Au, an old town on the Mekong River about twenty-five miles north of Chiang Sæn.[17]

Chiang Krai and Chiang Kran: Two paired towns, mentioned in the Luang Prasœt version of the Royal Chronicles under the date Culasakkarat 900 (1538). Wood reads the two as a single town, Gyaing, in the Moulmein district of Burma, which was tributary to Siam in the fifteenth and early sixteenth centuries.[18]

Khemmarat: The name used in the old Pali-Thai chronicles for Chiang Tung, or Keng Tung, in the Burmese Shan States.[19]

Tai Thòng: ?

Khotrabòng: Probably Nakhòn Phanom in Northeast Thailand.[20]

---

[16] O.W. Wolters, "The Khmer King at Basan (1371-3) and the Restoration of the Cambodian Chronology During the Fourteenth and Fifteenth centuries," *Asia Major* new series, vol 12 pt 1, 1966 pp. 14-89.

[17] L. Sternstein, "An Historical Atlas of Thailand'," *Journal of the Siam Society* 52:1 (1964), map 2.

[18] See Prince Damrong Rajanubhab, "Our Wars with the Burmese: A Work in Thai Language by Prince Damrong and Translated (by) U Aung Thein (a) Phra Phraison Salarak," *Journal of the Siam Society* 38:2 (1955), 129-131; and W.A.R. Wood, *A History of Siam* (Bangkok, 1959), p. 102.

[19] Phraya Prachakitkòracak, *Phongsawadan Yonok* [Chronicle of Yonok] (Bangkok, 1961); earlier edition followed by C. Notton, *Annales du Siam* I (Paris, 1926), pp. 143-44 n.5; and III (Paris, 1932), p. 77.

[20] See Prince Damrong Rajanubhab and Luang Boribal Buribhand, *Rüang borankhadi* (Bangkok, 1959), pp. 122-26; and Phraya Anuman Rajadhon and Prince Naris, *Banthük rüang khwamru tangtang*, III (Bangkok, 1963), pp. 9-12.

Reo Kæo. Possibly a town in the region of Ubon?[21]
As for the four southern vassals, only Malacca's identification
is both clear and reasonable, the chronicles recording a Thai
attack on Malacca and the lower peninsula in Culasakkarat 817
(AD 1455/56).[22] In the course of this expedition the enlistment
of tributaries might be expected, but there is no indication of
whom they may have been, outside this reference in the 1468
"Palatine Law:" Ujong Tanah, Malayu, and Varavari. Johore
seems indicated by the first. Gerini long ago suggested Muar for
Varavari; and "the district on and about the Malayu river,
immediately adjoining Johore on the West" for Malayu;[23] and
Cœdes has been able to carry their identifications no further.[24] At
least the establishing of the later date of 1468 for the "Palatine
Law" removes the conflict of claims between it and the
Nagarakrtagama. It would be hoped that the resolution of this
conflict of evidence might lead to a closer examination of what
may now be viewed as two mutually valid claims of peninsular
territory separated by a century.

---

[21] In conversation at the Fifth International Conference of Thai Studies
(London, July 1993), Geoff Wade urged me to consider the possibility that this
is a rendering of Ryukyu. This seemed far-fetched when he mentioned it; but
a paper written by Leonard Blussé and Zhuang Guoto for the same conference
notes that Chinese sources place a mission from Siam to Ryukyu in 1406, the
purpose of the mission being "to forge friendly relations." Ryukyu may not be
so far-fetched after all!

[22] Luang Prasœt Version. The argument presented by G.E. Marrison,
"The Siamese Wars with Malacca During the Reign of Muzaffar Shah," *Journal
of the Malayan Branch of the Royal Asiatic Society* 22:1 (1949), 61-66, remains
unconvincing.

[23] G.E. Gerini, "Historical Retrospect of Junkceylon Island," *Journal of
the Siam Society* 2:2 (1905), 11. C.O. Blagden, "Antiquity of Malacca,"
Journal of the Straits Branch of the Royal Asiatic Society 57 (1910), 189-90,
expressed his dissatisfaction with these identifications, but could propose no
alternatives.

[24] Cœdès, *Les états*, pp. 266-67 and 439.

A PERSIAN MISSION TO SIAM
IN THE REIGN OF KING NARAI*

Some years ago, intrigued by comments I had made about the origins of the Bunnag family, one of my students suggested she might study the Persian language and investigate Thai relations with Persia in the seventeenth century. My response must have carried with it a hint of ridicule, for she never mentioned the subject again. I am now embarrassed to have to tell her that the study of Persian would have repaid her efforts, for John O'Kane has brought to light a previously-unsuspected, major source for the history of Siam with his translation of *The Ship of Sulaiman*, published in the impressive series of English, French, and Italian translations in the "Persian Heritage Series" edited by Ehsan Yar-Shater of Columbia University.

The *Safina'i Sulaimâni* was written by ibn Muhammad Ibrahim, secretary of a mission sent by Shah Sulaiman the Safavid (1666-94) to King Narai in 1685. The work must have been written shortly after the mission's return to Persia in May, 1688. O'Kane says virtually nothing about the original manuscript bearing on its provenance, save that "it has been sitting in the British Museum for many years now." In a fourteen-page Translator's Preface he presents the work primarily as an example of Persian literature. Although written as an official report, it is a work of considerable imagination, contrived and stylized, and

* Review article; *Journal of the Siam Society* 62:1 (January 1974), 151-157. The review is of ibn Muhammad Ibrahim, *The Ship of Sulaiman*, Translated from the Persian by John O'Kane (Persian Heritage Series, No. 11; London: Routledge & Kegan Paul, and New York: Columbia University Press, 1972). x, 250 pp. Reprinted by permission of The Siam Society.

littered with cliché. This Preface succeeds remarkably well at conveying to the reader some understanding of a style that might easily be taken as eccentric, but which in fact is fairly typical of the official style of a cultivated man of the author's day.

The work is divided into four main parts or "jewels," preceded by an introduction in which the author praises God and his ruler and outlines the background to the mission. Here he explains that King Narai sent a certain Haji Salim Mazandarani as an envoy to Iran in 1682, to which the 1685 mission was the Persian response.

Part I, the "First Jewel," describes the early portion of the mission's journey, from Bandar 'Abbas on the Persian Gulf on 27 June 1685 through their short stay in India. Of some interest here are the author's comments on his contacts with Europeans in India.

Part II, the "Second Jewel," begins with the mission's departure from India on 16 September 1685. The mission then traversed the Bay of Bengal to Siamese Tenasserim, where they landed at Mergui and travelled by way of Tenasserim town, Jalang (in the headwaters of the Tenasserim River?), Paj Purî (Phetburi), Sûhân (Suphanburi?), and Shahr Nâv (Ayudhya) to Lubû (Lopburi), where the mission was received by King Narai. The mission was entertained in Lopburi for some time, hunting elephant and tiger, and then followed the king back to Ayudhya. Remaining quite a considerable space of time there, the envoys finally took their leave of the king in formal audience and sailed for their return home on 18 January 1687.

Part III, the "Third Jewel," is an extremely interesting attempt at "recording some facts about the local conditions." In particular, the author recounts what had been related to him as recent Siamese history. He gives a brief account of "The war between Siam and Paigu [Pegu]," and writes at some length about the role of the Iranian community in Siam in the seventeenth century. He ascribes to them a major role in bringing King Narai to the throne on a date he gives equivalent to 17 October 1657.[1] Two Persians are

---

[1] The dates given by the *Royal Autograph Chronicle* of Ayudhya for Naraiûs "victory over his enemies" and invitation to become king are, respectively, equivalent to 29 October and 4 November 1657.

mentioned as having held the office of "prime minister" subsequently filled by Constantine Phaulkon: 'Abdu'r-Razzâq of Gîlân and Âqâ Muhammad Astarâbâdî. The latter, long in favor with King Narai, introduced into the court an Iranian Guard of 200 men apparently similar to the Japanese Guard of Ekathotsarot's reign and to the French of 1688. After discussing briefly the rise of Phaulkon, he moves through a long series of desultory comments about life in Siam, and particularly on Buddhist religious belief and practice, the legal system, the character and religious faith of King Narai, marriage, debt bondage, and various festivals. He includes nearly four pages on the Macassarese and their revolt of 1686, and has an even longer section on court administrative procedure, the income and expenses of the Crown, and trade in various commodities.

Part IV, the "Fourth Jewel," has very little to do with Siam or the Iranian mission. It is a miscellaneous collection of information on winds and tides, various forms of animal life, notes on Ceylon, Aceh, the Andaman and Nicobar Islands, Spanish Manila, Japan and Dutch activities there, Pegu, and China. The last portion of this section, however, details the mission's return journey from Siam, beginning with their embarcation aboard a Surat vessel on 21 December 1686. The mission sailed via Patani and Malacca to Cochin, and eventually returned to Bandar 'Abbas on 14 May 1688.

A short final section entitled "The Case of Abu'l-Hasan and the Fall of Haidarabad" briefly recounts "The latest news from India."

The audience for which *The Ship of Sulaiman* was intended may have read it in several different ways. Although formally written as an official report of the mission, it is little more useful in that regard than John Crawfurd's *Journal of an Embassy from the Governor-General of India to the Courts of Siam and Cochin China,* for the author's account of official business takes second place to his description of unfamiliar peoples and places. His account is written more as an expression and affirmation of his own society's Islamic religious beliefs and values. Most of all, however, it must have been read for its style, for its inventive metaphor, for its learned borrowings from Islamic, Persian, and Indian literature, and for its incessant cleverness. It is not, perhaps, a style with which most English readers will at first be comfortable, but as one proceeds through the book it assumes a weight and form that bring its author alive.

The importance of *The Ship of Sulaiman* to those interested in Thai history is considerable. Its evidence bears on three main themes: the foreign policy of King Narai, the Persian community in Siam, and the rise and fortunes of the Bunnag family in the seventeenth century.

The connection with Persia is treated only in passing in the conventional accounts of King Narai's reign, and much of its significance often is lost in general references to "the Moors." *The Ship of Sulaiman* expands upon, and renders more concrete, vague references in such accounts as that of Père de Béze, which mentions Phaulkon's supervision of a mission to Persia at some unspecified date,[2] which on the evidence of the Persian account must have taken place in 1682. Even cursory examination of the history of the Persian mission of 1685-87 suggests that it might be useful to consider Narai's foreign policy within an international framework much broader than the Thai-French-Dutch-English pattern within which it usually is viewed.

Muhammad Ibrahim's frequent references to the Persian community in old Siam are a real eye-opener in many ways. He mentions the presence of Persians wherever he went in Siam, beginning with high public officials in the Tenasserim province, Phetburi, and Suphanburi, and including numerous merchants and officials including the highest officials in the kingdom. He explains that "From the time merchants first arrived until just before the present king came to power, about thirty Iranians had settled in Siam due to the great profits to be made in trade" (p. 94), and later notes that 200 Iranians were recruited in India for service in the royal bodyguard. The community subsequently was racked with dissension and lost permanently its grip on

---

[2] E.W. Hutchinson, *1688 Revolution in Siam: The Memoir of Father de Beze, s.j.* (Hong Kong, 1968), pp. 11-12.

public affairs when Phaulkon succeeded to the office of prime minister previously held by three successive Iranians. The significance of Muhammad Ibrahim's numerous references to the Iranian community in Siam is that they enable one to begin to see better, in ways not previously possible, some of the details of Ayudhya's social and economic structure, particularly as that structure incorporated immigrant communities. His account is the first we have had from within any Muslim community of Ayudhya, and is of assistance not least in enabling us to see how Dutch and English traders of the time were treated like other Asian traders.

Finally, material contained in *The Ship of Sulaiman* provides important information that goes a long way towards solving the mystery of the origins and early history of the Bunnag family, a noble family powerful in the affairs of the kingdom of Siam for more than three centuries.[3] At the same time, it provides startling confirmation of the validity of some of the historical work of the much-maligned K. S. R. Kulap.[4]

Of the Persians specifically mentioned by Muhammad Ibrah; m, there are the following individuals:

(1) Haji Salîm Mâzandrânî, Siamese king's envoy to Persia (1682), pp. 20, 44, 46, 53, 104-5

(2) (unnamed), former governor of Tenasserim or Mergui (?), p. 46

(3) Muhammad Sâdiq, son of (2), pp. 46-47

(4) Sayyid Mâzandarânî, governor of Phetburi, p. 50

(5) Rajah Chelebî, "from among the people of Rum" (i.e., Anatolia), rajah of Suphanburi, pp. 50-51

(6) Khwâja Hasan 'Alî, from Khurâsân, "presently holds the ministerial post which Âqâ Muhammad held and as such is the head of the Iranian community in Siam," pp. 55, 69, 74-75, 144 (?)

---

[3] See D.K. Wyatt; "Family Politics in Nineteenth Century Thailand," *Journal of Southeast Asian History IX:* 2 (September 1968), esp. pp. 211-12, 214.

[4] See Craig J. Reynolds, "The Case of K.S.R. Kulap: A Challenge to Royal Historical Writing in Late Nineteenth Century Thailand" *Journal of the Siam Society* 61: 2 (July 1973). pp. 63-90.

(7) Âqâ Muhammad Astarâbâdî, [see quotation above under (6)]: originally from Astarâbâd, settled in Siam to trade, became minister (ca. 1660 ?), fell out of favor; "has been dead for a while now" (p. 101); Phaulkon was hired when he was still in office (p. 103); cf. pp. 55, 58, 59, 77, 98, 100-103, 126, 151, 218

(8) 'Abdu'r-Razzaq, "whose family is from Gîlân," made prime minister by King Narai in 1657, continued in office several years, then was imprisoned and died; pp. 97-98

(9) Chû Chî, and (10) Chû Kîâ, sons of (8), sent into exile; pp. 101-102

(11) (unnamed) prime minister, originally from Shûshtar, lineage traced to the Mullâ Hasan 'Alî of Shûshtar, assassinated, shortly after appointment as premier; pp. 102-103

(12) Sayyid Dardmandî, poet from Khurâsân, commissioned by Narai to present a written summary of the Shâhnâma; p. 127.

The conventional accounts of Bunnag genealogy mention none of these individuals.[5] The only detailed information on Bunnag genealogy in this period is provided in a rare book compiled by K.S.R. Kulap in the early years of the current century.[6] On the basis of this, the following genealogical chart may be constructed:

The only firm correspondence between the list of individuals mentioned in *The Ship of Sulaiman* and the genealogy provided by K.S.R. Kulap is between the former's (7) and the latter's (D)—Aqa Muhammad (which Kulap spells as 'Akamahamat). Several other tentative identifications might also be put forward:

(2) the former governor of Mergui or Tenasserim may be Kulap's (F), although we might expect that individual's descent from Aqa Muhammad would have been mentioned;

---

[5] Phraya Cularatchamontri, *Cotmaihet prathom wongsakun Bunnak* [Documents on the Origins of the Bunnag Family](Bangkok, 1939); Caophraya Thiphakòrawong, *Sakun Chek Amat* [The Lineage of Sheik Ahmad](*Lamdap sakun kao bang sakun* pt. 3; Bangkok, 1930).

[6] K.S.R. Kulap, *Mahamukkhamattayanukunlawong lem 1 wa duai lamdap wongtrakun khunnang Thai thang sin nai phandin Sayam* [Great Official Families, volume 1, all the Thai noble families in the land of Siam](Bangkok, 1905).

(6) apparently refers to the position of *phraya* Cularatchamontri, head of the Right-hand Department of the Phrakhlang *(krom tha khwa)*, a post consistently held by Bunnags in the nineteenth century. This might be Kulap's (G); and

(8) might be identified with Kulap's (C), although the latter's dates are suspicious.

Even if only the identification of Aqa Muhammad holds, this is sufficient cause for us to take most seriously the enormous quantity of genealogical and historical information published around the turn of the century by K.S.R. Kulap which, among other things, includes extensive discussion of Chinese commercial families in Ayudhya early in the eighteenth century.

There are many small points on which O'Kane's translation of *The Ship of Sulaiman* might be criticized. Notes on Siamese aspects of the book are wholly inadequate, especially in the failure to identify relatively simple toponyms and Thai words (e.g., *mahalak/mahatlek, salah lakun/sala lukkhun, kurum kan/ kromkan, kawam/khwam, vam pra/wan phra*). The index is incomplete: it lists, for example, only four of the nine or ten references to Aqa Muhammad. And a fuller account of the origins and provenance of the British Museum manuscript would have been appreciated. These are, however, only minor faults.

The Ship of Sulaiman deserves to be included among the most important primary sources for the history of Siam in the reign of King Narai. It is particularly welcome because it should serve to open up new avenues of inquiry that have previously been neglected.

EARLY ANCESTORS OF THE BUNNAG FAMILY

Merchant family of Ma-ngon Muslims,
of Müang Kunî

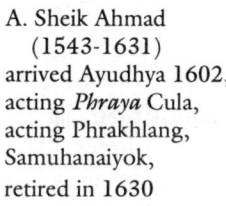

A. Sheik Ahmad
(1543-1631)
arrived Ayudhya 1602,
acting *Phraya* Cula,
acting Phrakhlang,
Samuhanaiyok,
retired in 1630

B. Muhammad Said

C. *Caophraya* Aphairacha (Chün)
(? 1600-1670) acting *phraya*
Cula 1624-30 under title *phraya*
Wòrachetphakdî; Samuhanaiyok
from 1630

D. Âkâ Muhammad
phraya Sî Naowarat of Central
Phrakhlang Department *(krom
tha klang)* in reign of Narai

E. *caophraya* Chamnan-
phakdî (Sombun,
1630- c. 1683);
palace official under
Narai; Samuhanaiyok
1670-1683

F. *caophraya* Sî Chaihân-
narong (Yî); *phra* Anu-
rakracha in Narai's
reign; ca. 1689 made
caophraya and governor
of Tenasserim; rebelled

G. *phraya* Cula (Kaeo)
in reign of Narai

FAMILY POLITICS IN SEVENTEENTH- AND EIGHTEENTH-CENTURY SIAM[*]

One of the most difficult of the historiographical problems that bedevil the work of historians of premodern Siam is the almost exclusively royal-centered quality of his sources. The chronicles in particular focus heavily upon the doings of kings and rarely give much attention to other, less-exalted individuals and groups. The apparent lack of information, or the historian's neglect of such information as does occur, has made it difficult to assess accurately the political, social, and economic dimensions of Thai history, particularly in the Ayudhya period. Until we begin to get beneath the surface of that history, figuratively to dig behind and beneath the throne, we cannot approach a true understanding of Ayudhya's history.

In the face of somewhat intractable and opaque sources, I began some years ago to attack a comparable problem in the history of Siam in the nineteenth century by looking at "Family Politics in Nineteenth Century Thailand."[1] Utilizing mainly genealogical sources, and applying what have come to be known as prosopographical techniques in a very rudimentary manner, I was interested in exploring the family relationships that seemed to me to undergird politics (and economics) in the Bangkok period

[*] Published in, *Papers from a Conference on Thai Studies in Honor of William J. Gedney,* ed. Robert J. Bickner, Thomas J. Hudak, and Patcharin Peyasantiwong (Ann Arbor: Center for South and Southeast Asian Studies, The University of Michigan, 1986; Michigan Papers on South and Southeast Asia, 25), pp. 257-265. Reprinted with the permission of the Center for South and Southeast Asian Studies, The University of Michigan.

[1] David K. Wyatt, "Family Politics in Nineteenth Century Thailand," *Journal of Southeast Asian History* 9, no. 2 (September 1968): 208-28.

(1782-present). I focused particularly on the rise of the Bunnag family and its domination over the politics of the reigns of kings Mongkut and Chulalongkorn. It was not until a year or so after I had published that article that I began to find additional information on the ministerial families, that is, the leading noble families, of the late Ayudhya period (about 1610-1767). The most important source of new information was a large volume entitled *Mahamukkhamattayanukunlawong,* roughly translated as "History of the Great Ministerial Families," by that enigmatic amateur man of letters of the late nineteenth century K.S.R. Kulap (Kulap Kritsananon).[2] In nearly eight hundred typographically florid pages, Kulap provides many details about the important ministerial families of Ayudhya and Bangkok, including a great deal of material concerned with these families in the seventeenth and eighteenth centuries. However, Kulap's unreliability is well known, and it would have been foolish for me to have accepted his information uncritically, without external, independent corroboration.[3] Accordingly, for some years I was loath to carry this line of research further.

Within the past year I have been drawn back to this problem, owing mainly to difficulties I have been having in writing the history of Siam in the seventeenth and eighteenth centuries. In trying to get away from an exclusively court-centered, royal-centered history and understand the politics—in the broadest sense of that word—of the Kingdom of Ayudhya, it has been necessary to try to identify other groups and individuals and to assess their role in that society. The desirability of doing so becomes immediately apparent when one considers the politics of the succession to the throne of the kingdom. Note that from 1610 to the fall of Ayudhya in 1767 virtually every succession

---

[2] K.S.R. Kulap, *Mahamukkhamattayanukunlawong lem nüng, wa duai lamdap wong trakun khunnang Thai thang sin nai phæn din Sayam* [Mahamukkhamattayanukunlawong volume one, genealogies of all the Thai noble families in the kingdom of Siam] (Bangkok: Sayam Praphet, 1905).

[3] Craig J. Reynolds, "The Case of K.S.R. Kulap: A Challenge to Royal Historical Writing in Late Nineteenth Century Thailand," *Journal of the Siam Society* 61, no.2 (July 1973):63-90.

to the throne was contested; and in no case could a king come to the throne without some support from the nobles *(khunnang)*, the officials of the capital, and, to a certain extent, the provinces. Who were these people? Were they simply a random, constantly changing collection of individuals? Or did they have group or family identities extending over several generations? On what was their power based? How did their situations, and their power, change over time? And what were their relationships to the families that came to power in the Bangkok period?

In trying to answer such questions, l have had to return to Kulap's book, supported now by limited external, independent corroboration of some of his data. Without going into the full details, let me briefly summarize two examples. First, as I explained in a review article a few years ago, some of Kulap's information concerning the early history of the ancestors of the Bunnag family in the seventeenth century are confirmed by a Persian account of a mission to Siam in 1685, which explicitly mentions several individuals also mentioned by Kulap.[4] Second, Kulap presents an exceedingly detailed account of a certain Chinese family that began trading to Siam in the reign of King Thai Sa (reigned 1709-33), from whom are descended a number of high officials in the Phrakhlang ministry, including a certain Caophraya Phrakhlang (Chim). This latter individual turns up by full name both in the Ayudhya chronicles and in the genealogy of a family into which he married.[5] Such reassurances as these have led me to look again at Kulap's book, and to consider again the "family politics" of a later Ayudhya period.

---

[4] See the preceding article in this collection.

[5] Kulap, *Mahamukkhamattayanukunlawong,* circa p. 289; *Phraratcha-phongsawadan chabap Phraratchahatlekha* [Royal chronicles, royal autograph edition] (Bangkok: Khlang Witthaya, 1973), vol. 2, pp. 235-36; Khun Siriwatthana-anathòn (Phon Siriwatthanakun), "Rüang chüa sai Phra Maharatchakhru Siriwatthana" [Concerning the line of Phra Maharatchakhru Siriwatthana], in *Thiralük nai kanrap phraratchathan phlœng sop nangsao Phròm Siriwatthanakun* [Memorial volume on the occasion of the royal-sponsored cremation of Miss Phrom Siriwatthanakun] (Bangkok, 1966), 20, among many other sources.

I will not trouble you now with tedious genealogical details, many of which are represented in the accompanying chart and table. Let me instead draw your attention to four themes that now seem to me to emerge out of this information culled from Kulap and similar sources, all of which seem to underline strong continuities in Siamese history.

First, l am struck by the ethnic diversity of Ayudhya's nobles. There are four major ministerial families—that is, families whose members rose to the rank of *caophraya* (roughly, "minister of state") in at least two generations—and all four of them are non-Thai in origin. The Persian (or Arabo-Persian) origins of the Bunnag and related families are well known. Down to the end of the Ayudhya period they produced at least five *caophraya*, and their daughters married two others. A second family I have referred to elsewhere as the "Brahman" family was descended from Brahmans who came from India. They are the ancestors of the Singhaseni, Cantharotwong, Buranasiri, Thòng-In, and Siriwatthanakun families, among others, and they accounted for seven *caophraya* and another by marriage. A third family, notable for two *Caophraya* Phrakhlang (Lek and Pan) of Narai's and Phetracha's reigns, was of Mon origin, and from them descended the kings of the Cakri dynasty. A fourth, the Chinese family mentioned above, included at least three *caophraya*, and they also are included among the ancestors of the Cakri kings. All four of these families, then, are of foreign origin. All four were at least initially involved to some degree with the Phrakhlang ministry (the government office that dealt with foreign trade), and particularly with branches of the Phrakhlang that had special responsibility for foreign trading communities resident in Siam. Indeed, the "Persian" and "Chinese" families continued to control at least portions (the Krom Tha Khwa and Krom Tha Sai, respectively) of the Phrakhlang's responsibilities and perquisites down to the nineteenth century. This particular phenomenon compels some modification of the accepted characterization of the premodern Siamese bureaucracy as being founded primarily on the control of manpower, for to at least some limited degree these families' power was based not on manpower but on commerce and money. I am especially struck by the extent to which the members of these families, and of families like them with roots in resident foreign communities, frequently played important roles in succession disputes, not least of all the so-called Siamese Revolution of 1688, which put King Phetracha on the throne. Their durable prominence over a long period of time compels a reconsideration of the "dynastic" politics of the late Ayudhya period.

Second, if we recognize that long-standing noble families were prominent in court politics over generations, we need to consider to what extent royal policies were framed in response or reaction to them. Busakorn Lailert has moved in this direction with her treatment of the dynasty founded by Phetracha, and has interpreted the furnishing of princes with direct control over manpower (through personal *krom*) as royal attempts to counter noble power.[6] In a recent paper, Nidhi Aeusrivongse has done the same with respect to the reign of King Narai and those of some of his predecessors.[7] Nidhi draws a useful distinction between the "administrative" bureaucracy and the "skilled" or "professional" bureaucracy, the latter being almost exclusively of foreign origin. He outlines the competition between the interests of the two, and royal attempts to manipulate the differences between them. In short, our appreciation of the politics of Ayudhya has begun to widen by looking not just at kings and their quarrelsome heirs but at the main interest groups at court.

Third, the chief noble families of the late Ayudhya period demonstrate considerable continuity and strength. Generation after generation, their members held high office. Moreover, when there were no sons to succeed their fathers in office, their daughters married into powerful "outside" families that had risen

---

[6] Busakorn Lailert, "The Ban Phlu Luang Dynasty 1688-1767: A Study of the Thai Monarchy During the Closing Years of the Ayuthya Period," Ph.D. diss., University of London, 1972.

[7] Nidhi Aeusrivongse. *Kanmüang Thai samai Phra Narai* [Thai politics in the time of Phra Narai] (Bangkok: Sathaban Thai Khadi Süksa,1980).

to high office. The data suggest the existence of at least the core of a cohesive nobility, a group with traditions of power and service to the crown, who competed among themselves but at the same time could maximize their power as a group vis-à-vis both the king and upwardly mobile "outsiders."

Finally, it is perhaps most intriguing that all four of the main families with which we have been concerned intermarried with the Chakri family *before 1782* when Rama I ascended the throne of Siam. The implications of this fact may prove to be of paramount significance, for it suggests that the Bangkok monarchy was well rooted in the nobility of late Ayudhya in a way that none of its predecessors were. No wonder, then, that the Bangkok kings seem to have had a much closer working relationship with their nobles than the Ayudhya kings had, nor that the same families that were prominent in the late Ayudhya period continued to gain in power under the Bangkok monarchy.

What comes out of a mass of genealogical data and snippets of bare facts about individuals is a picture of at least the elite of Ayudhya society that is at some variance with the images with which we heretofore have been presented. It is a fuzzy, indistinct picture still, and I do not mean to suggest that K.S.R. Kulap, like some magic Rosetta Stone, has managed to clear up a previously unsolved mystery. We have, however, at least an outline map of some of the directions in which we now can go. Surely, hidden away in other neglected books and manuscripts are additional details that may help bring this picture into focus and lead us towards a better appreciation of the dynamics of earlier Siamese history.

TABLE SHOWING KNOWN/NAMED MINISTERS OF THE LATE AYUDHYA PERIOD, 1610-1767

REIGN	MAHATTHAI	KALAHOM
Song Tham (1610-28)	1. C. Bòwònnaiyok (Sheik Ahmad, 1543-1631)	21. Òkphra Kalahom (1612-28) 22. ... Kalahom Suriyawong (1628-29)
Prasat Thòng (1629-56)	2. C. Aphairacha (Chün) (1600-1670)	
Narai (1656-88)	3. C. Chamnanphakdi (Sombun) (1630-85?) 4. Constant Phaulkon (1685-88)	32. C. Kosa ... (Lek)
Phetracha (1688-1703)		
Su'a (1703-09)		
Thai Sa (1709-33)	5. C. Chakri (Rongkhòng)	23. C. Rattanathibet (Khun Nen, 17_-33)
	6. Phra Ratchasongkhram	
	7 . ? C. Phetphichai (Cai)	
Bòrommakot (1733-58)	8. C. Aphaimontri (Carun) (1733-42) 9. C. Ratchaphakdi (Sawang) (1742-55) 10. C. Inthara'aphai (Arun) or C. Aphairacha (Ban Patu Cin) (1755-58)	24. Phra Ratchasong- khram (1733-55) 25. C. Mahasena (Khlòng Klaep) (1755-58?)
Uthumphòn (1758)		26. ?C. Aphaimontri (1758?-60)
Suriyamarin	11. ?C. Chakri (Khrut)	27. C. Mahasena (Sen or Sep), acting

PHRAKHLANG	YOMMARAT	OTHERS
31. Phraya Thai Nam		
33. C. Kosa ... (Pan) (168_-1700)	41. Phraya Yommarat (Sang)(16__-88)	
34. C. Phrakhlang (1700-)		51. C. Thamma
		54. C.Phitsanulok (Mek)
		55. C. Mahasombat (Phon)
35. C. Kosa ... (Cin) (Ong Heng Chuan?)	42. C. Yommarat (Phun)	
36. C. Chamnanborirak (O) (1733-54)		52. C. Thamma (Khun Thòng) 56. C. Narenthara (Bunkœt)
37. C.Phrakhlang(Chim) (1754-)	43. C. Yommarat (Cham)(17 -60)	57. C. Surinphakdi (Bunmi) 53. P. Rattana- thibet (acting)
38. C. Kosa ...	44. C. Yommarat	

Note: There surely are many others who held the offices listed, whose names and dates cannot be ascertained from present sources. Those included are those known from historical sources as distinctive individuals.

C. = Caophraya   P. = Phraya

SCHEMATIC CHART SHOWING FAMILY
RELATIONSHIPS AMONG
THE MINISTERS OF THE LATE AYUDHYA PERIOD,
1610- 1767

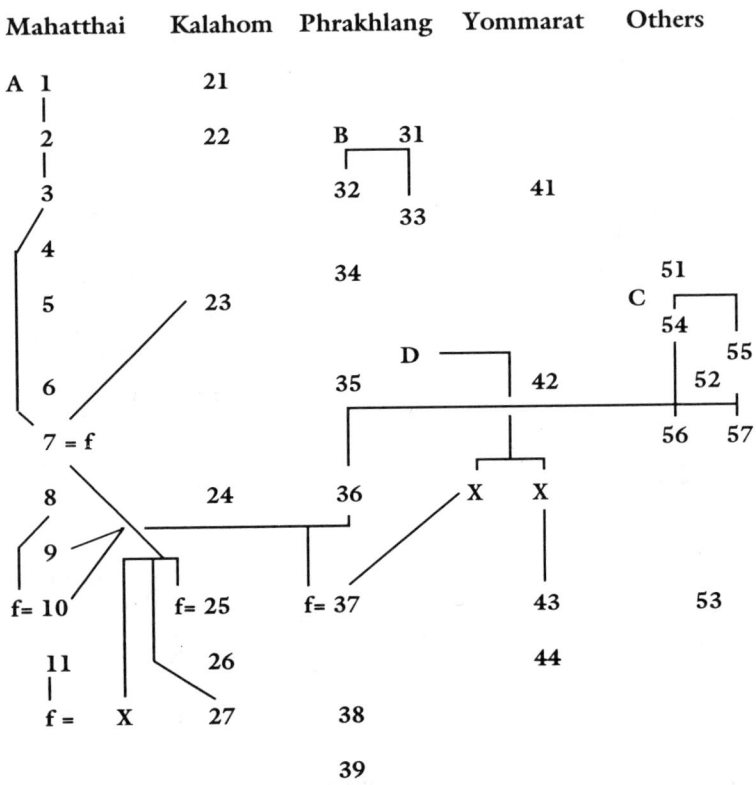

| Mahatthai | Kalahom | Phrakhlang | Yommarat | Others |

Key   f = daughter
       A = the "Persian" line
       B = the "Mon" line
       C = the "Brahman" line
       D = the "Chinese" line

FAMILY POLITICS
IN NINETEENTH-CENTURY THAILAND*

One of the most arresting periods in modern Thai history is the latter half of the nineteenth century, when a process of social and political development begun in the previous century reached its fruition when a single bureaucratic family obtained a virtual monopoly on high state office in the reign of King Mongkut (1851-68) and the first half of the reign of King Chulalongkorn (1868-1910). This situation had profound effects on the course of modern Thai history; and its study enlightens our understanding of Thailand's foreign relations and of the course of reform and modernization in a period when the successful conduct of these was crucially vital to the survival of the Kingdom.

The origins and growth of one-family dominance in nineteenth century Thai politics are not readily susceptible to study. Family names are essentially a twentieth-century innovation, and nineteenth century documents rarely reveal even the personal names of government officials who were known only by their titles. However, it is obvious both from the comments of such foreign observers as Captain Henry Burney

---

* *Journal of Southeast Asian History* 9:2 (September 1968), 208-228. Reprinted with permission of the Department of History, National University of Singapore. This essay was written for presentation to a seminar at the London School of Economics and Political Science in March, 1966; and since has been presented at the University of Malaya in Kuala Lumpur, the University of Michigan, St. Anthony's College of Oxford, and the School of Oriental and African Studies. The comments and suggestions of those present on those occasions I have found extremely useful and I acknowledge gratefully their assistance and stimulation.

and Sir John Bowring, and from the expressed concerns of Thai kings from Rama III to Chulalongkorn, that family relationships among the royalty and nobility were of considerable importance politically. The availability of three general types of sources makes possible a preliminary analysis of nineteenth-century Thai politics and the family relationships which undergirded them. First, there are a number of genealogical compilations, most of which were compiled early in the current century. Important among these are a collection of genealogies of major noble families begun by Phraya Rattanakun (Camrat Rattanakun) in 1920,[1] the official genealogy of the royal family,[2] and the genealogies of the families of the mothers of the Bangkok kings.[3] Second, there are available a large number of biographies of individuals, including both high government officials and members of the royal family, of which the most important is the collection of biographies of ministers of state (*caophraya*) compiled by Prince Sommot Amòraphan.[4] Finally, there are numerous valuable references to the family relationships of nineteenth-century officials in the standard chronicles of the first five reigns of the Bangkok period, in published collections of documents, and in such Western-language sources as *The Burney Papers* and Sir John Bowring's *The Kingdom and People of Siam*. From these and other such sources it is possible to construct an analysis of the origins, structure, and behavior of an important segment of the political and social elite of nineteenth century Thailand and to trace its development from the seventeenth century to the end of the nineteenth.

---

[1] Phraya Rattanakun et al. (comps.) *Lamdap sakun kao bang sakun* (Genealogies of some Old Families) (4 vols.; Bangkok, 1920-1937).

[2] Yim Panthayangkun (comp.), *Ratchasakunwong* (Royal Genealogy) (7th rev. ed.: Bangkok, 1964).

[3] Thailand, Fine Arts Dept. (comps.), *Lamdap rachinikun bang chang* (Genealogy of the Royal Maternal Line çBang Changé) (new ed.; Bangkok, 1958); Prince Phanurangsi Sawangwong (comp.), *Rachinikun ratchakan thi 3* (The Royal Maternal Line of King Rama III) (Bangkok, 1928), and *Rachinikun ratchakan thi 5* (The Royal Matetnal Line of King Rama V) (Bangkok, 1933).

[4] Prince Sommot Amòraphan and Prince Damrong Rajanubhab, *Ruang tang caophraya krung rattanakosin* (On Appointments to the Rank of Caophraya in the Bangkok Period) (2nd ed.; Bangkok, 1931).

The Framework

As a framework within which to set the analysis which follows, it would be well to set forth here two general features of pre-modern Thai social and political life.[5] First, the Thai political system was based upon, and the social system revolved around, a monarchy which in theory was absolute. The throne was occupied by a member of a royal family which was polygamous to a high degree and hereditary in a modified sense, following the "declining descent rule" by which status within the royal family diminished by one degree in each generation, until the fifth-generation descendants of kings were simple commoners.[6] Succession to the throne could be highly flexible. Sons of the king by a queen were in a more favorable position to succeed to the throne than their brothers born of concubines, but the latter could and did succeed to the throne, as Rama III did in 1824. Attempting to secure the succession, Uparajas (or so-called "Second Kings") were appointed by each of the first five monarchs of the Bangkok line, but in each case they died before the king. In any case, succession to the throne could follow only upon election by the consensus of a combined council composed of senior members of the royal family and the bureaucracy. Generally, succession did not pose such serious political problems as it did at the same time in Burma.

The second dominant feature of the social and political structure was a bureaucratic, semi-hereditary nobility appointed by the king, who could appoint and remove its members at will, at least in theory. This was an administrative class, rigidly graded by rank and dignity, entrance into the upper levels of which was restricted by both law and convention to the sons of the upper nobility who had passed through a period of service as pages at Court or in the establishments of the princes.[7] These young men

---

[5] On this general subject, see H. G. Quaritch Wales, *Ancient Siamese Government and Administration* (London, 1934; New York, 1965), pp. 14-131.

[6] See Mary R. Haas, "The Declining Descent Rule for Rank in Thailand: A Correction," *American Anthropologist* 53 (1951), 585-87.

[7] Extremely useful on this subject is M.R.W. Akin Rabibhadana, *The Organization of Thai Society in the Early Bangkok Period, 1782-1873* (Ithaca: Cornell University Southeast Asia Program, 1969; Data Paper 74).

were subject to no educational qualifications, but they appear to have had to submit to practical tests of their ability in order to reach high administrative positions, and it is this factor which modified the otherwise hereditary bias of the nobility.

The bulk of the higher ranks of the nobility was concentrated in the capital, in the six major departments of government, each of which was headed by a *caophraya*, a noble of the highest rank. Although each of the six departments originally had been defined functionally, the functional distinctions between them had broken down by the eighteenth century, to the extent that three, the Mahatthai, Kalahom, and Phrakhlang (originally ministries of civil administration, military administration, and finance, respectively), each governed provinces, collected taxes, and maintained law and order in a section of the country. Each, however, still retained some measure of its original functions. The Kalahom, the "Ministry of the Southern Provinces," retained many of its military functions, and the Phrakhlang (sometimes rendered as the "Ministry of Finance") retained control over the conduct of foreign trade and foreign relations, as well as some of its treasury functions; while the Mahatthai extended its civil administration only over the provinces of the North and East. Each of these three ministries was in many ways a completely developed government in itself for the provinces which it controlled. The other three, the departments of the Palace, Lands, and the Capital, maintained their old functions of supervising the royal household, promoting agriculture and collecting the land tax, and keeping law and order in the immediate vicinity of the capital, respectively. These latter three departments were in a distinctly weaker position in the government, and the patterns of promotion in the administration indicate that they were used as stepping stones to real political power in the three major ministries.[8]

There were also a number of subsidiary departments of government attached either to the major ministries or directly to the King, but only one is of major significance: the Royal Pages'

---

[8] Note in the accompanying appendix those individuals in these three ministries who were later promoted to the other three ministries.

Department (*krom mahatlek*), whose officers held lesser ranks and dignity than their equals in other departments but who, because of their proximity to the king and their control over access to him, enjoyed an influence greater than their ranks would indicate. Another large and important element in the capital nobility was the establishment of the Uparaja, modeled on that of the king. The status of the officers of the Uparaja depended on the political position of the heir-apparent whom they served. It undoubtedly is significant that the Uparaja's administration was headed by a *caophraya* only in the first, second, and fourth reigns of the Bangkok period. Of all avenues of advancement, the service of the Front Palace was least secure, as it was liable to be disbanded on the death of the Uparaja unless a successor were named. Finally, there was a large provincial nobility composed of the governors and ruling princes of Siam's provinces and tributary states. Very few of these enjoyed any position of importance or participated meaningfully in national political life, with perhaps two exceptions, the ruling families of Nakhòn Si Thammarat (Ligor) in the South and of Nakhòn Ratchasima (Khorat) in the North-East, both for very special reasons and during a limited period of time.[9]

If one were to list the members of the highest level of this bureaucratic and political élite, it would include six *caophraya* who headed the main departments of government, the chief of the Uparaja's ministers, and perhaps the four *cangwang* or heads of the Royal Pages' Department. It was these men who stood at the top of the social and political system, their positions secured by a nexus of values, attitudes, and behavioral patterns. It was in their hands that administrative power was concentrated. Their positions were coveted by every member of the bureaucracy, for whom the attainment of the rank of *caophraya* was the crowning ambition in life; and this ambition was sanctioned by a society which identified personal power with personal merit in the Buddhist

---

[9] The ruling family of Nakhòn Si Thammarat was very closely connected with the royal family (see *Lamdap sakun kao*, I, 1-12, and IV, 1-10) and that of Nakhòn Ratchasima with the Singhaseni family (see *Lamdap sakun kao*, I, *s.v. Singhaseni*), and these relationships certainly contributed to their prominence.s

sense and gave to personal political and bureaucratic advancement an aura of religious attainment.[10]

The New Siam of Rama I

During the last dynasty of the Kingdom of Ayudhya, which in six reigns ruled from 1688 to 1767, there were at least two outstanding families of nobles, both of non-Thai origins and both of which first came to prominence in the seventeenth century. One of these, said to have descended from a Brahman at the court of King Prasat Thong (1630-56), provided the service of the king with seven *caophraya* in the later years of the dynasty (Chart I).[11] The other family, descended from a Persian Gulf merchant who came to Siam early in the seventeenth century, included *caophraya* in five successive generations down to the fall of Ayudhya, the last generation including the Kalahom and another by marriage (Chart II).[12] Noticeable particularly in the latter, the Bunnag, family is a high degree of official continuity: members of the family served as *samuhanaiyok* (Minister of the North, *Mahatthai*) in four successive generations. In addition, they seem to have maintained a base in that department (the *krom tha khwa*) of the Phrakhlang which dealt with Indian, Arab, and Malay merchants.[13] In the present imperfect state of knowledge about the later history of Ayudhya it is impossible to gauge the significance of this official continuity. The limited information available on these two families would suggest that the administrative empires of individual families were restricted to

---

[10] See Lucien M. Hanks, Jr., "Merit and Power in the Thai Social Order," *American Anthropologist* 64:6 (1962), 1247-61.

[11] This chart is based on *Lamdap sakun kao*, 1, 28-29; and on Thailand, Fine Arts Dept. (comps.), *Phongsawadan müang songkhla læ phatthalung* (Chronicles of Phatthalung and Songkhla) (Bangkok, 1962), charts.

[12] The main source on the early history of the Bunnag family is Caophraya Thiphakorawong (Kham Bunnag), "Sakun Shek ahamat," *Lamdap sakun kao*, III (Bangkok, 1930), esp. pp. 21-23.

[13] Many of the individuals who held the titles of *Phraya* Cularatchamontri and *Luang* Ratchasethi (director and deputy director) in that department were Bunnags. See *Lamdap sakun kao*, III.

single ministries and departments until the last two decades of the Kingdom of Ayudhya, when there werethree *caophraya* in a single generation of the "Brahman" family—presumably spread over three ministries—and when the Bunnag family moved from the *mahatthai* to the *kalahom* both directly and by marriage. It would be tempting to interpret these developments as a shift in the balance of power in favor of the established noble families and against the king; but the contrary interpretation is equally tenable. Whatever the case, both these families do appear to have retained very considerable strength to the end of the Ayudhya period.

When the Burmese captured and sacked Ayudhya in 1767 they shocked severely the old Thai state and administration. The old royal family was all but extinguished, and centuries-old institutions were destroyed. The nation's savior was a man on horseback, the half-Chinese adopted son of the last *caophraya* Cakri (the *samuhanaiyok*) of the Ayudhya period. He was a superlative general who rallied around him all who could heed his call and recognize his merit, and welded together again the fragments of the old state.

The men he gathered around him were a mixed group, the composition of which was determined partly by the heavy toll the Burmese had taken among the skilled men of the old order, and partly by the handicap under which he labored, being half-Chinese and without a clear, legitimate status. Part of his entourage was composed of young men of his own generation and similar social status who attained supreme power perhaps a generation earlier than they might otherwise have expected. Another strong element at his Court was made up of men of obscure origins who had earned their positions through deeds in battle. Easily the most prominent among his servants as King was his Caophraya Cakri, the son of a middle-echelon official and a boyhood friend of the king.[14] The king, generally known in the West as Taksin, ruled for fifteen years, and gradually revealed himself to be much more

---

[14] See *Phraya* Komarakunmontri, *Prawat caophraya mahasena (bunnak)* (The Life of Caophraya Mahasena, Bunnag) (Bangkok, 1961), pp. 1-6, for an account of the boyhood friendship of Taksin, Rama I, and Bunnag.

proficient in the arts of warfare than in those of government and politics. His overthrow in 1782 in favor of his Caophraya Cakri is commonly attributed to his madness, important not so much for the form which it took (pretensions to divinity, and arbitrary and despotic acts) as for the effect which it had of alienating the elite by depriving them of the stability and orthodox order so desperately required in this time of troubles.

In appointing his ministers in 1782, King Rama I retained only two of Taksin's five ministers (he being himself the sixth).[15] One of the two he retained was in a skilled position, the Ministry of the Palace, and this minister was descended from a family which had served in that ministry during the Ayudhya period.[16] The other was a man of unknown origins who had risen to power in the warfare of the 1770s. The remaining four all had held second-level positions or less under Taksin: and two were descendants of old official families while two were of obscure origins. Noteworthy is the prominence he gave to the old families of the Ayudhya period. The new *kalahom*, Caophraya Mahasena (Pli), was the son of the last *kalahom* of the Ayudhya period by a Bunnag mother; and the new Minister of Lands, Caophraya Phonlathep (Pin Singhaseni), was a direct descendent of the old "Brahman" family. With these men, with whom he had worked closely and directly prior to 1782, King Rama I must at least initially have been little more than a first among equals. In the first years of the reign he appears to have maintained his advantage at least partly by rigorous use of his powers of appointment and dismissal. Contrary to usual practice, only three of his first six ministerial appointees died in office, while the other three were dismissed for demonstrable incompetence within three years of the beginning of the reign.

It was in 1785 that a ministerial shake-up brought to power the direct male line of the Bunnag family with the appointment to

---

[15] Sommot and Damrong, *Rüang tang caophraya*, pp. 1-19, give short biographies of all the *caophraya* of the First Reign.

[16] *Caophraya* Thiphakorawong (Kham), *Phraratchaphongsawadan krung rattanakosin ratchakan thi 1* (Royal Chronicles of the First Reign of the Bangkok Period)(combined ed.; Bangkok, 1962), p. 21.

CHART I

THE "BRAHMAN" FAMILY

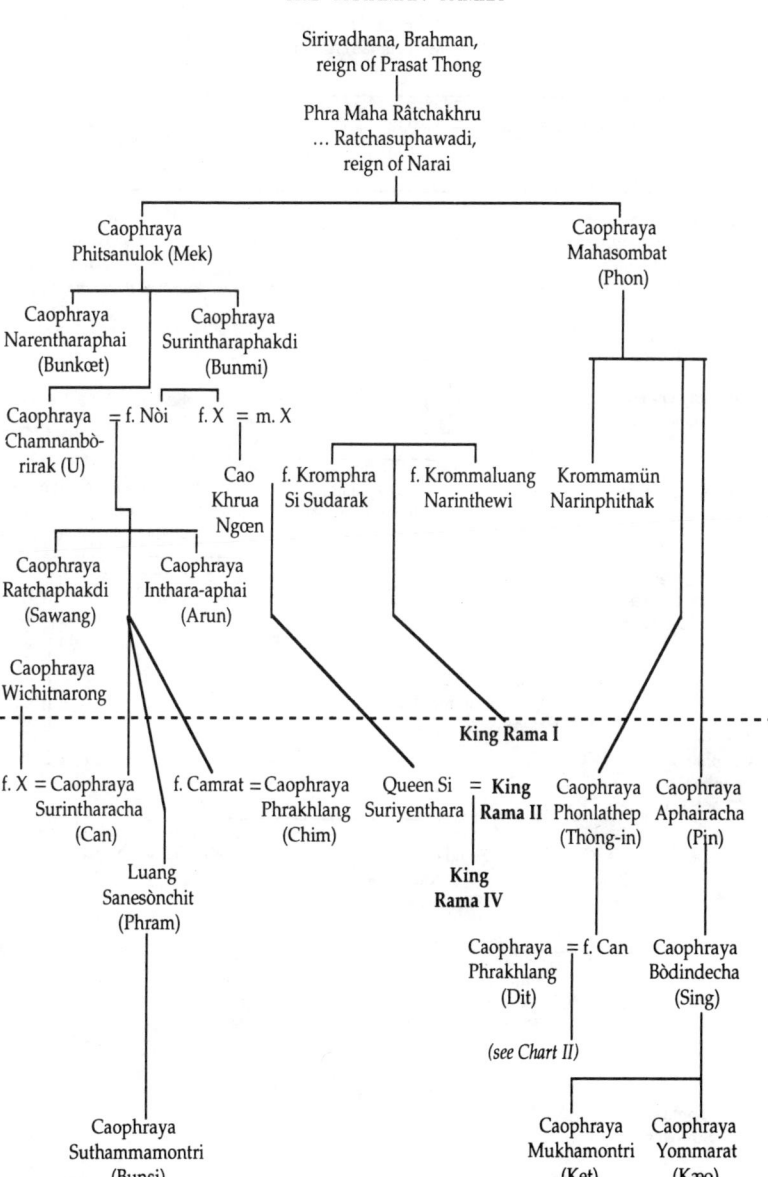

Sirivadhana, Brahman,
reign of Prasat Thong

Phra Maha Râtchakhru
... Ratchasuphawadi,
reign of Narai

Caophraya
Phitsanulok (Mek)

Caophraya
Mahasombat
(Phon)

Caophraya
Narentharaphai
(Bunkœt)

Caophraya
Surintharaphakdi
(Bunmi)

Caophraya = f. Nòi
Chamnanbò-
rirak (U)

f. X = m. X

Cao   f. Kromphra   f. Krommaluang   Krommamün
Khrua   Si Sudarak   Narinthewi   Narinphithak
Ngœn

Caophraya
Ratchaphakdi
(Sawang)

Caophraya
Inthara-aphai
(Arun)

Caophraya
Wichitnarong

King Rama I

f. X = Caophraya
Surintharacha
(Can)

f. Camrat = Caophraya
Phrakhlang
(Chim)

Queen Si = King
Suriyenthara | Rama II

Caophraya
Phonlathep
(Thòng-in)

Caophraya
Aphairacha
(Pin)

Luang
Sanesònchit
(Phram)

King
Rama IV

Caophraya = f. Can
Phrakhlang
(Dit)

Caophraya
Bòdindecha
(Sing)

(see Chart II)

Caophraya
Suthammamontri
(Bunsi)

Caophraya
Mukhamontri
(Ket)

Caophraya
Yommarat
(Kæo)

CHART II

THE "BUNNAG" FAMILY

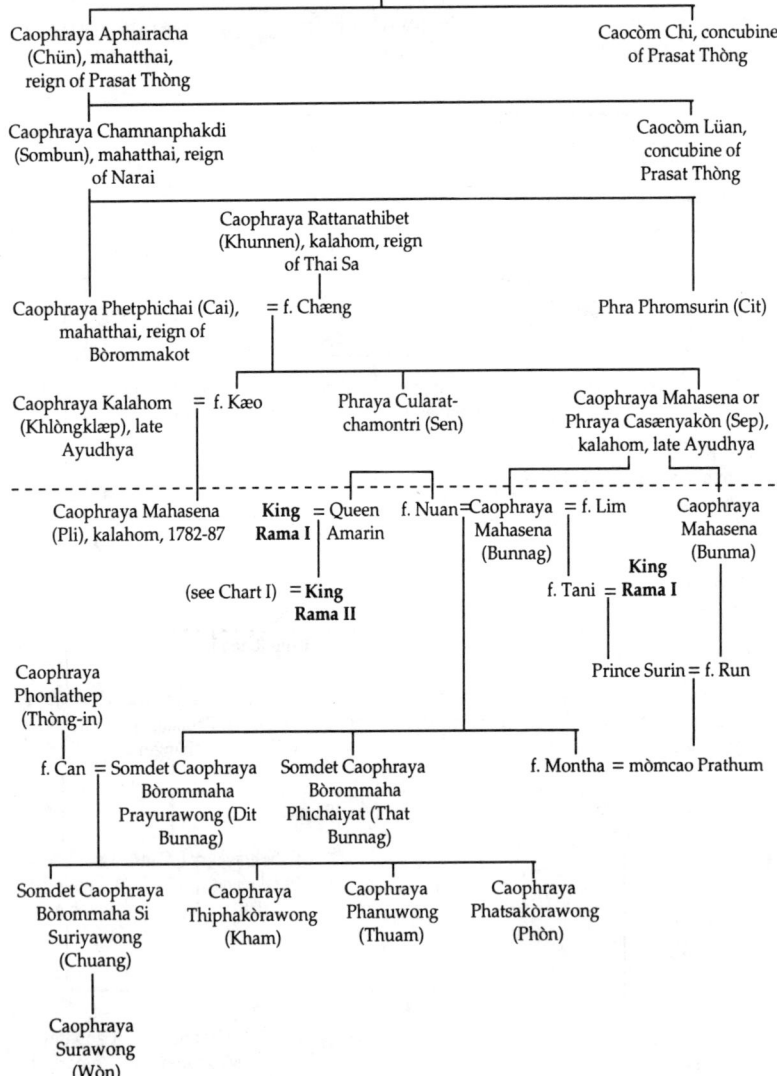

Caophraya Bòwònnayok
(Sheikh Mohammad/Ahmad),
mahatthai, reign of Prasat Thòng

Caophraya Aphairacha
(Chün), mahatthai,
reign of Prasat Thòng

Caocòm Chi, concubine
of Prasat Thòng

Caophraya Chamnanphakdi
(Sombun), mahatthai, reign
of Narai

Caocòm Lüan,
concubine of
Prasat Thòng

Caophraya Rattanathibet
(Khunnen), kalahom, reign
of Thai Sa

Caophraya Phetphichai (Cai),
mahatthai, reign of
Bòrommakot
= f. Chæng

Phra Phromsurin (Cit)

Caophraya Kalahom
(Khlòngklæp), late
Ayudhya
= f. Kæo

Phraya Cularat-
chamontri (Sen)

Caophraya Mahasena or
Phraya Casænyakòn (Sep),
kalahom, late Ayudhya

Caophraya Mahasena
(Pli), kalahom, 1782-87

King = Queen
Rama I | Amarin

f. Nuan=Caophraya = f. Lim
Mahasena
(Bunnag)

Caophraya
Mahasena
(Bunma)

(see Chart I) = **King**
Rama II

f. Tani = **King**
Rama I

Caophraya
Phonlathep
(Thòng-in)

Prince Surin = f. Run

f. Can = Somdet Caophraya
Bòrommaha
Prayurawong (Dit
Bunnag)

Somdet Caophraya
Bòrommaha
Phichaiyat (That
Bunnag)

f. Montha = mòmcao Prathum

Somdet Caophraya
Bòrommaha Si
Suriyawong
(Chuang)

Caophraya
Thiphakòrawong
(Kham)

Caophraya
Phanuwong
(Thuam)

Caophraya
Phatsakòrawong
(Phòn)

Caophraya
Surawong
(Wòn)

the Ministry of the Capital of a young man whose personal name was Bunnag. He and his half-brother Bunma were sons of Phraya Casænyakòn (Sep), who served as *kalahom* late in the Ayudhya period, and he was a boyhood friend of Rama I. Bunnag had refused to serve Taksin, but had maintained close relations with Rama I during the Thonburi period. After the death of his first wife (ca. 1775), Bunnag married a woman of the Bang Chang family named Nuan, who was the sister of the chief Queen of Rama I. Inasmuch as his sister-in-law was the chief Queen of Rama I and the mother of the future Rama II, and as he was a long-time loyal friend of the new king and had cared for Rama I's family when the Burmese overran Siam in 1767, Bunnag was in a highly-favored position, which he shared with his wife's relatives by virtue of their membership in the *rachinikun* (the family providing the royal family with the mother of a king).[17] On coming to the throne, King Rama I appointed Bunnag to the title of Phraya Uthaitham in the Department of Royal Apparel and Insignia, and Bunma as Phraya Takœng (position unidentified), while their first cousin, Caophraya Mahasena (Pli), became *kalahom*. Bunnag became *Caophraya* Yommarat (Minister of the Capital) in 1785; and then, on the death in battle of *Caophraya* Mahasena (Pli) in 1787, Bunnag succeeded him under the same title, and Bunma replaced Bunnag in the Ministry of the Capital. It was as though the reign of Taksin had not occurred: two members of the family had served as *kalahom* immediately prior to the fall of Ayudhya; and three members of the family succeeded each other as *kalahom* beginning in 1782, and they were to dominate that ministry until 1888.

In assessing the special position of the Bunnag family in the nineteenth century, it is clear that a combination of factors contributed to their extraordinary continuity of office. This was a family of very considerable abilities, possessed of a long tradition

---

[17] For a full explanation of the term *rachinikun*, see Prince Damrong Rajanubhab's introductory essay in *Lamdap rachinikun bang chang* pp. (3)-(8). There are obvious sociological and psychological reasons why maternal descent should be stressed in the royal family: among the fifty to eighty children of a single king, it was natural that individuals should be distinguished one from another by their maternity, as their paternity was common to all.

of public service. However, it was not the only family of ability or the sole repository of such traditions. Its position must have been strengthened by the fact that its unique marriage relationship with the royal family gave it a special claim for preferment; and it was able further to exploit this status by providing not only further concubines for the kings but also wives for the princes born of these unions. The advantage of the Bunnags in this particular mode of politicking was simply that they entered it early, before the dynasty had even begun its reign. They did not have to rely on the long-established stratagem of offering the king a concubine in the hope that she would please him, bear a son, and gain the promotion to chief queen's status which would bring their grandson to the throne. The reverse was the case, for Rama I had provided Bunnag with a wife.

As a matter of right, members of the *rachinikun* expected preferment in royal appointments. The efficacy of the claims of the Bunnags and the rest of the *rachinikun* Bang Chang was amply demonstrated by 1845, when it was found necessary to compile an official genealogy of the family in order to substantiate the claims its members were making for official positions.[18] For their own part, kings appeared to expect automatic support from the members of the family of their mothers.[19] Certainly family relationships among the nobility and royalty counted for a great deal on both sides. It was advantageous for nobles to seek for their daughters a place at Court, and generally desirable to marry them upwards on the social scale. The concubines of Rama I who bore him children included the daughters of two of his ministers, King Inthavong of Vientiane, and the governors of Nakhòn Si Thammarat and Phatthalung, as well as other women of less distinguished families. Thirty-nine different women bore children by Rama II. Five were of the family of his own mother (the *rachinikun* Bang Chang), and three were daughters of *caophraya*. His Queen, the mother of King Mongkut, was closely related to the "Brahman" line; and had Mongkut come to the

---

[18] Damrong's essay in *Lamdap ratchinikun bang chang,* pp. (3)-(6).

[19] See King Chulalongkorn, *Phraborommarachowat nai ratchakan thi 5* [Royal Advices of the Fifth Reign (Bangkok, 1960) p. 20.

throne in 1824 instead of 1851, one would have expected a more substantial improvement in the fortunes of his mother's relatives in the Singhaseni, Phumirat, and related families than eventually transpired.

Of all the official families established in the first years of the Bangkok period, it was the Bunnag family and the related *rachinikun* Bang Chang which most securely established and maintained a pre-eminent position in the life of the state. There were several families which numbered more than one *caophraya* of ministerial status among their members. Considering only the period down to about 1885, all but one of the families which reproduced themselves among the ranks of the *caophraya* had reached that rank by 1785. There were two members of the Sonthirat family, father and son; three members of the Bunyaratthaphan family, father, son, and grandson; three members of the Singhaseni family, father, son, and grandson;[20] and no less than nine members of the direct male line of the Bunnag family, not to mention at least another fourteen *caophraya* related to them by marriage.[21] More notable than the number of individuals is the continuity of their tenure in office. With none of the other families did sons directly succeed their fathers as *caophraya*; but the Bunnags and those directly related to them by marriage maintained unbroken control over the *kalahom* from 1782 to 1886, and over the Phrakhlang from 1822 to 1885 (except for a brief interlude late in the Fourth Reign). The Bunnags thereby had control over two of the three most powerful ministries, the ministry controlling the administration of the Southern and Western provinces, and the ministry which dealt with foreign trade and foreign affairs, administered much of the revenue system, and governed the Gulf provinces. In addition, the Ministry of Lands was controlled by affinal relatives of the Bunnags for all but thirty years of the period 1832-1874. Clearly critical is the question of how they were able to achieve and maintain such a dominant position.

---

[20] Not including another member of the family who served as the "prime minister" of the Uparaja in the Reign of King Mongkut, *Caophraya* Mukkhamontri (Ket Singhaseni).

[21] See the accompanying Appendix.

The Growth of One-Family Dominance

In pre-modern Thai society, a number of factors coincided to put a premium on the holding of administrative office. The service of the state and the king were enhanced with a prestige and honor which no other vocation could match; and the office was the single most socially acceptable source of wealth and power. Wealth and power were synonymous: an appointee automatically came into both upon his appointment to high office, and automatically lost both on his dismissal. The social and political demands placed on officeholders by the Crown, on the one hand, and by their subordinates, clients, and families, on the other, called forth a high rate of conspicuous consumption and expenditure, and it was very rare for an individual to have the opportunity, the wisdom, or the incentive to amass private wealth. It was, then, all important for an individual to maintain his bureaucratic position and for a family to maintain a steady flow of its members into the state service.

The sons of the elite did not begin their bureaucratic careers with equal advantages. To begin with, only the sons of nobles of the rank of *phra* or higher could gain easy entrance to the Royal Pages' Corps, failing which one had to gain the patronage of an official or prince of the highest level.[22] The period of service as Royal Pages was a period of sorting men out by their abilities. Some, even of lesser abilities, might have been able to gain appointment to minor positions in their fathers' departments; but they would find it difficult to reach high rank without showing considerable ability. Of the thirty-seven known sons of nine of the *caophraya* of King Rama I, six attained the rank of *caophraya*, twelve that of *phraya*, one *phra*, and five *luang*, while two sought careers in the Buddhist monkhood and another six remained in the Royal Pages' Corps. Eldest sons fared somewhat better than younger sons, as did sons by major wives as opposed to the sons of concubines, but not greatly so. Primogeniture was not the rule either in inheritance or in descent.

---

[22] See M.R.W. Akin, "Stratification and Mobility."

In the furtherance of their careers, these young men had a number of devices at hand. Fathers unquestionably did what they could to gain for their sons a favorable place in the Royal Pages' Corps or to draw the king's attention to them; and it was much easier to do this if one was married to the daughter of an officer of the Corps,[23] or held high office, or if one's daughter or sister was a favorite concubine of the king. Family relationships or economic power might be played upon to some advantage in manipulating a situation in one's favor.

The crucial point in the history of the Bunnag family's rise to power came early in the reign of King Rama II, when the direct male line of the family temporarily passed from ministerial rank with the death of *caophraya* Mahasena (Bunmi), who had succeeded his half-brother *Caophraya* Mahasena (Bunnag) as *kalahom* in 1809. The eldest and ablest of the next generation of Bunnags was by 1810 only twenty-two years of age—hardly old enough to succeed his uncle and father in the *kalahom*. Everything, however, was in his favor. This was the reign of his first cousin, the son of his mother's sister; and five of the six ministers at that time were his relatives. The Kalahom, Phrakhlang, and the Minister of the Palace were, like himself, relatives of the reigning king's mother, while the Minister of the Capital was a paternal cousin and his father-in-law was the Minister of Lands. One of the most prominent of the sons of King Rama I, Prince Surin, was his first cousin, the son of his sister.[24] In 1822 he was made Phrakhlang, and in that office dealt with the Crawfurd and Burney missions with considerable skill. He was offered the post of *kalahom* in 1824, but refused it on the grounds that he was too young for such high honor.[25] On again being offered the post of in 1830, he accepted, but obtained the king's consent to retain his position as Phrakhlang. Over the next twenty years, with the help of his younger brother (who harbored a strong resentment against him for not

---

[23] See, for example, *Phraya* Komarakun, *Caophraya Mahasena*, pp. 6-7.
[24] Prince Surin (1790-1830) was the 29th child of King Rama I. On him, see *The Burney Papers*, I (Bangkok, 1910), p. 25.
[25] *The Burney Papers*, I, p. 65.

relinquishing the Phrakhlang in his favor), *Caophraya* Phrakhlang (Dit Bunnag) controlled both ministries concurrently—a most unusual feat.

During the reign of King Rama III (1824–51), *Caophraya* Phrakhlang (Dit) built up an unassailable political position He filled both of his own ministries and the Royal Pages' Corps with members of his own family, and had no difficulty in doing so: he and his brother together brought forty-three sons into the world. At the same time, they restricted their marriage obligations to other families. Most daughters of the two brothers either went into the palace service or married their own first cousins.[26] *Caophraya* Phrakhlang (Dit) carefully built up his economic base both domestically in the Western provinces and through external trade, and he seems to have contracted an alliance of convenience with the growing Chinese community which was under his control as Phrakhlang.[27] He was primarily responsible for turning what might have been a fiscal disadvantage created by the Anglo-Siamese Treaty of 1826 into a system of farmed taxes and monopolies which was both personally and officially profitable His eldest son, Chuang, was one of that small group of well-placed Thai who, during the Third Reign, began to learn from the West. Chuang's interest was primarily practical and bound up with his family's interests in foreign trade, foreign relations, and military affairs; and from the West he learned English and modern techniques of shipbuilding, which he put to use in building modern vessels for his father's private and official trade.[28]

---

[26] Data from *Lamdap rachinikun bang chang*, pp. 11-22. Parallel-cousin marriage was quite common in the Bunnag and Singhaseni families by the latter half of the nineteenth century; see also *Lamdap sakun kao*, I.

[27] This is an inference from a great number of scattered sources, notably references to close relations between them in the Bowring journal; and from the structural probabilities stemming from the position of the two brothers in the Phrakhlang. Most of the new taxes which they introduced in the Third and Fourth Reigns depended on the participation of Chinese tax farmers; and, in addition, in order to make their official control over the Chinese community effective, they would have had to work through the Chinese secret societies. I am sure that they did so, but I am equally certain the concrete evidence on this point will be hard to find.

[28] Natthawut Sutthisongkhram, *Somdet caophraya borommaha si suriyawong*, vol. I (Bangkok, 1961), pp. 189-90.

The ties which linked the Bunnags to the forward-looking generation of Mongkut grew rapidly. By 1851, as Rama III lay on his deathbed, *Caophraya* Phrakhlang (Dit Bunnag) was admirably suited to play the role of kingmaker. The kingdom was acutely fearful of the threat of the West, and the Bunnags, who long had dealt with foreign traders and emissaries, were among the leaders of those who were confident that that threat could be contained and manipulated in their favor. They had formidable power and resources, and were closely associated with the most logical candidate for the throne, the prince-priest Mongkut who had been passed over for the succession in 1824 and who had spent much of the intervening quarter-century studying Western science, English, and Latin from the European and American missionaries resident in Bangkok. It was the Bunnags who were primarily responsible for raising Mongkut to the throne in 1851, presenting the rest of the government with a thinly-disguised fait accompli; and it was the Bunnags who were paid the price of that accession.[29] *Caophraya* Phrakhlang (Dit) and his brother, *Phraya* Si Phiphat (That Bunnag), were created *somdet caophraya* (viceroys) with almost unlimited powers by the grateful Mongkut, who also raised two of the Phrakhlang's sons to succeed their father as Kalahom and Phrakhlang. Of Mongkut's first twenty-one appointments made immediately on his accession, eight went to Bunnags, and another two to their sons-in-law.[30] A few months later, another affinal relative, the Minister of Lands *Caophraya* Phonlathep (Long Bun-long), gained his appointment by promising to pay the king 160,000 baht each year, a sum just sufficient to keep the small Privy Purse out of deficit.[31]

---

[29] Again, this is a tendentious point, but one which emerges strongly from a careful reading of the closing portions of the Third Reign Chronicle and the opening portion of the Fourth Reign Chronicle, both written by *Caophraya* Thiphakorawong (Kham Bunnag), a participant in these events.

[30] *Caophraya* Thiphakòrawong, *The Dynastic Chronicles, Bangkok Era, The Fourth Reign, B.E. 2394-1411*, tr. Chadin Flood, vol. I (Tokyo, 1965), pp. 62-69.

[31] King Chulalongkorn, *Phraratchahatlekha phrabat somdet phracunla còmklao caoyuhua song mi pai ma kap somdet phra mahasamanacao krommphraya wachirayan warorot* (Bangkok, 1929), pp. 211-24.

The two elder *somdet caophraya* died within months of each other in 1855, but their legacy was passed intact to their sons; and the head of the family, *Caophraya* Si Suriyawong (Chuang), dominated the administration from his position as in much the same manner as his father had under King Rama III. He was the elder statesman of the reign, and the natural choice for the post of Regent when King Chulalongkorn ascended the throne at the age of fifteen years in 1868. The period of the Regency (1868-1873) marked the high-point in the fortunes of the Bunnag family. With *Caophraya* Si Suriyawong (Chuang) (since raised to the rank of *somdet caophraya*) as Regent, his son *Caophraya* Surawong Waiyawat (Wòn) as Kalahom, his brother *Caophraya* Phanuwong Mahakosathibòdi (Thuam) as Phrakhlang, affinal relatives as *mahatthai* and Minister of Lands, and numerous relatives in important positions in the Royal Pages' Department and at Court, the family as a political grouping was able effectively to challenge the power of the throne, until they began to pass from the scene in the mid-'eighties. King Chulalongkorn at least once came to consider abdication in his frustration at the checks they put upon his powers.[32]

The Crown and the Nobles

The challenge which the Bunnags posed against the power of the throne in the Fourth and Fifth Reigns was but an extreme variation on a longer-term political problem which concerned the division of power between the Crown and the nobles. In the Bangkok period, the monarchy was on the defensive as early as the reign of Rama II (1809-24). After a campaign against the Burmese in 1810, Rama II found it necessary to appoint several of his brothers to superintend the affairs of the most important of the ministries. For example, Prince Chetsadabòdin (who became King Rama III in 1824) was appointed to superintend the affairs of the Phrakhlang, and thereby entered into a close working relationship with that department, its foreign trade, and members

---

[32] See David K. Wyatt, *The Politics of Reform in Thailand* , Ch. II.

of the Bunnag family which he was to extend and elaborate when he came to the throne. These "superintendents" one encounters throughout Burney's account of his stay in Bangkok in 1825-26, and the impression he gives is that real executive authority remained with the noble ministers. It appears that, despite such attempts to win for members of the royal family a share in administrative power, the monarchy essentially was isolated from the day-to-day workings of government. Lesser members of the royal family found official office closed to them unless they married into the noble families;[33] and, even when they did so, more often than not they found real power beyond their grasp.[34] Having been brought to the throne with considerable Bunnag support, King Mongkut was in a difficult position to attempt to challenge them, and to do so would have been to alienate the single most powerful and effective proponents of modernization and accommodation with the West. Herein lay the real difficulty of Thai politics in the Fourth and Fifth Reigns: that power which was most effective in neutralizing the threat of Western colonialism was also the force which most seriously challenged the position of the throne The political alternatives for Mongkut and Chulalongkorn were not easy. The strongest opposition to the Bunnags was mainly among the old conservatives (and reactionaries); and to strengthen this group would have defeated the main objectives of Mongkut's progressive domestic and foreign policy. On the other hand, few of the other major noble families had responded readily or positively to the problems of relations with the West. They were slower than the Bunnags in sending their children abroad to be educated. The motives of some in espousing modernization were insincere. Others, enamored of the West, became unrealistically radical, while few had sufficiently

---

[33] "Prakat hai but kharatchakan khao rap ratchakan tam opfit tangtang [Decree Urging the Sons of Government Officials to Enter Government Service]," *Ratchakitcanubeksa* [Government Gazette] 7 (1890), 195ff.

[34] As with those princes appointed to superintend the affairs of various government departments from the Second Reign. See, e.g., *The Burney Papers*, I, pp. 55, 61; and Prince Damrong Rajanubhab, *Phraratchaphongsawadan krung rattanakosin ratchakan thi 2* (combined ed.; Bangkok, 1962), pp. 432-36.

strong political positions to be able to render the young King Chulalongkorn the support he needed.

When the time came, between 1882 and 1888, and the Bunnags and the old conservatives began to fade from public life, they had to be replaced with modern men with modern educational backgrounds and forward-looking ideas. Chulalongkorn found that he had no alternative but to rely on his brothers, on whose loyalty he could count, and whose training and early experience fitted them to lead his reforming crusade By 1892, almost all the ministries were headed by the King's young brothers, who as a group provided the kingdom with extraordinarily effective, dynamic, and intelligent leadership through the most dangerous times in Thailand's history. Chulalongkorn permanently reduced the preponderance of the old nobility, but he necessarily crippled the polity by doing so. He created a class of princes fully enjoying executive authority—in heightened modern forms—for the first time in Thai history, as well as a new group of common-born, modern-educated civil servants who served the princes in subordinate positions. The first three decades of the twentieth century were to reveal that the princes wished to retain power, while their subordinates increasingly were determined to seize it. The reign of King Vajiravudh (1910-25) was the era of the new men; and the following reign of King Prajadhipok brought a return to the princes. This succession of political trends came about for reasons essentially accidental; but the two counter-tendencies were no less potent for this fact. Their struggle finally issued in the *coup d'état* of 1932, and a resolution in favor of the new men, the sons of men of moderate backgrounds who, in the middle of Chulalongkorn's reign, had flocked to the new schools, the military academies, and the law school while the old nobility hesitated in their judgments as to what the future was to bring.[35]

Indirectly, by driving its features to extremes, the Bunnags brought about the end of the old nobility as a cohesive and effective political and social force, although it is entirely to their

---

[35] See Wyatt, *Politics of Reform*, chs. 2, 4.

credit that, through diplomatic strategies formulated and executed by Caophraya Phrakhlang (Dit) and Caophraya Si Suriyawong (Chuang), the basic conditions of Thailand's national existence were assured. The continuous participation in public life of a limited number of cohesive families with strong traditions of public service, close links with the royal family, and strong ties to the provinces and established economic interests could contribute substantially to the order and stability of the life of the society. The ultimate fault of the Bunnags is not that they abused political power, for on the whole they did not. They served successive kings with great loyalty in the best traditions of Thai public life. In the end, however, they were simply too outstanding, too capable, too rich, and too powerful. Their participation in public life was excessively continuous and excessively concentrated; their links with the Royal Family were suffocatingly close; they were only too well entrenched in the provinces; and they tended to monopolize indigenous economic life. They could not have failed to come into conflict with a strong king who had his own ideas about the position of the throne and the requirements of modernization. Oral tradition has it that one of the granddaughters of the last great Bunnag statesmen, Caophraya Si Suriyawong (Chuang), once asked him, "Grandfather, why don't you become king?" He is said to have replied, "Why should I bother? I have everything a man could desire." He was only too right.

APPENDIX

MINISTERS OF STATE
IN THE EARLY BANGKOK PERIOD, 1782-1892

° Affinal relative of the Bunnag family
● In the direct male line of the Bunnag family
pat. = paternal; mat. = maternal

A. Krom Mahatthai (Ministry of the North)

1. 1782-1805	Caophraya Rattanaphiphit (Son Sonthirat)	
2. 1809-	Caophraya Rattanathibet (Kun Rattanakun)	
3. -1827	Caophraya Aphaiphuthòn (Nòi Bunyaratthaphan) son of D.1; married dtr. of F.4	
°4. 1827-1849	Caophraya Bòdindecha (Sing Singhaseni) son of B.3; pat. 1st cousin married B.8; niece married A.3	
5. 1849-1863	Caophraya Nikònbòdin (To Kanlayannamit)	
6. 1863-1878	Caophraya Phuttharaphai (Nut Bunyaratthaphan) son of A.3	
7. 1878-1886	Prince Caofa Maha Mala	
8. 1886-1892	Caophraya Rattanabòdin (Bunròt Kanlayannamit) son of A.5	
9. 1892- 1915	Prince Damrong Rajanubhab	

B. Krom Kalahom (Ministry of the South)

°1. 1782-1787	Caophraya Mahasena (Pli) mat. 1st cousin to B.2 and B.4	
●2. 1787-1805	Caophraya Mahasena (Bunnag)	
°3. 1805-1809	Caophraya Mahasena (Pin Singaseni) brother's daughter married to B.8	
●4. 1809-(1811?)	Caophraya Mahasena (Bunma) half-brother of B.2	
°5. (1811)-1822	Caophraya Wongsasurasak (Sæng Wongsarot na Bang Chang) *rachinikun* Bang Chang; granddtr. married son of B.8	
°6. 1822-1824	Caophraya Mahasena (Bunsang na Bang Chang) *rachinikun* Bang Chang; maternal 1st cousin to B.8	
°7. 1824-1830	Caophraya Mahasena (Nòi Si Suriyaphaha) cousin of father of B.2	
●8. 1830-1851	Caophraya Phrakhlang (Dit Bunnag) son of B.2; married dtr. of F.2	

●9. 1851-1869   Caophraya Si Suriyawong (Chuang Bunnag) son of B.8

●10. 1869-1888   Caophraya Surawong Waiyawat (Wòn Bunnag) son of B.9

11. 1888-1894   Caophraya Rattanathibet (Phum Sichaiyan)

C. Krom Müang (Ministry of the Capital)

1. 1782-1785   Caophraya Yommarat (Thòng-in)
●2. 1785-1787   Caophraya Yommarat (Bunnag) = B.2
●3. 1787-1809   Caophraya Yommarat (Bunma) = B.4
4. 1809-   Caophraya Yommarat (Nòi Bunyaratthaphan) = A.3 son of D.1
°5   Caophraya Yommarat (Nòi Si Suriyaphaha) = B.7
6.   -1825   Caophraya Yommarat (Chim) ?son of E.2
7. 1825-   Caophraya Yommarat (Thòngphun)
8.   Caophraya Yommarat (Sæng)
9.   -(1838)-   Caophraya Yommarat (Bunnak Takhethap)
10.   -(1851)   Phraya Phichaichanit (Khunnen)
11. (1851)-   Caophraya Yommarat (Thòngsuk Sinsuk)
12.   -1863   Caophraya Yommarat (Nut Bunyaratthaphan) = A.6
13. 1863-1865   Caophraya Yommarat (Khrut)
14. 1865-1871   Caophraya Yommarat (Kæo Singhaseni) son of A.4
15. 1871-1876   Caophraya Yommarat (Chœi Yamaphai)
16. 1876-1886   Prince Phuttraret Thamrongsak
17. 1886-1889   Committee composed of Prince Naret, Prince Svasti, Phraya Thepprachun (Phum Sichaiyan, B. 11), and Phraya Thammasannitti (Tat Amatyakul)
18. 1889-   Prince Naret Wòrarit

D. Krom Wang (Ministry of the Palace)

1. 1782-1785   Caophraya Thammathikòn (Bunròt Bunyaratthaphan)
2. 1785-   Caophraya Thammathikòn (Thòngdi)
3.   -1809   Caophraya Thammathikòn (Sot)
°4. 1809-1824   Caophraya Thammathikòn (Thet na Bang Chang)
5. (1824-1851)   Caophraya Thammathikòn (Sombun Bantük)
6. 1851-1861   Caophrnya Thammathikòn (Süa Sonthirat) son of A.1
7. 1861-1869   Caophraya Thammathikòn (Bunsi Bunsiri) distant cousin of A.4
8. 1869-1882   Caophraya Thammathikòn (Lamang Sonthirat) son of A.1; granddtrs. married C.14
9. 1882-1887   Prince Pracak Sinlapakhom

10. 1887-1896   Prince Mahit Ratchaharithai

E. Krom Phrakhlang (Ministry of the Treasury and Foreign Affairs)
1. 1782-178x   Caophraya Phrakhlang (Son)
°2.   -1805   Caophraya Phrakhlang (Hon) ?son married a
                    Bunnag
3. 1805-1809   Caophraya Phrakhlang (Kun Rattanakun) = A.2
4. 1809-   Caophraya Phrakhlang (Kòn)
°5. - 1822   Caophraya Phrakhlang (Bunsang na Bang Chang
                    = B.6
●6. 1822-1851   Caophraya Phrakhlang (Dit Bunnag) = B.8
●7. 1851-1865   Caophraya Thiphakòrawong (Kham Bunnag) son
                    of B.8
8. 1865-1869   Prince Wòracaktharanuphap
●9. 1869-1885   Caophraya Phanuwong Mahakosathibòdi (Thuam
                    Bunnag) son of B.8
10. 1885-1923   Prince Devawongse Varoprakar

F. Krom Na (Ministry of Lands)
°1. 1782-1805   Caophraya Phonlathep (Pin Singhaseni) = B.3
°2. 1805-1810   Caophraya Phonlathep (Bunnak Banmæla) dtr.
                    married B.8
3. 1810-   Caophraya Phonlathep (Sakhon)
°4. 181x-182x   Caophraya Phonlathep (Thòng-in) brother of B.3;
                    dtr. married B.8
5. 182x-c1850   Caophraya Phonlathep (Chim) married 1st cousin
                    of B.3
6. c1850-1851   Phraya Sihathep (Thòngpheng)
°7. 1851   Caophraya Phonlathep (Iam Xuto na Bang
                    Chang)
°8. 1851-1869   Caophraya Phonlathep (Long Bun-long) married
                    a Bunnag woman
°9. 1869-1874   Phraya Ahanbòrirak (Nut Bun-long) son of F.8 by
                    a Bunnag mother
10. 1874-1886   Caophraya Phonlathep (Bunròt Kanlayannamit) = A.8
11. 1886-1888   Caophraya Phonlathep (Phum Sichaiyan) = B.ll
●12. 1888-1892   Phraya Phatsakòrawong (Phòn Bunnag) son of B.8

G. Caophraya of the Uparaja
1. First Reign: Somdet Caophraya Wang Na (personal name
                    unknown)
°2. Second Reign: Caophraya Aphairacha (Pin Singhaseni) = B.3
3. Fourth Reign: Caophraya Mukkhamontri (Ket Singhaseni) son of
                    A.4, brother of C.14

THE "SUBTLE REVOLUTION" OF KING RAMA I OF SIAM*

When the old Kingdom of Siam was enjoying what many then thought was its pinnacle of prosperity and power in the late seventeenth century under King Narai (1657-1688), at least one contemporary poet set Ayudhya's splendor in the cyclical perspective of Buddhist conceptions of time. In the belief that human history must move within a narrowly-confined helical track of growth and decay, generation and degeneration, for his people he prophesied an awful fate:

> *As for His Majesty, the King of Kings,*
> *By rule he brings to all their happiness.*
> *Through his decrees, his care and his success,*
> *He strives to bless us all—with joy we shine.*
> ...
> *Beneath his majesty and mighty power*
> *All nations cower; conquered his every foe.*
> *From every quarter, every border, flow*
> *The gifts to show, by tribute, homage true.*
>
> *Ayutthaya is perfect and complete,*
> *Replete, this seat, with honor—with what kings do.*
> *And so with gladness great it will imbue*
> *Its people through its first two thousand years.*

* Originally printed in *Moral Order and the Question of Change*, ed. David K. Wyatt and Alexander Woodside (New Haven: Yale University Southeast Asian Studies, 1982), pp. 9-52. Reprinted by permission of the Council on Southeast Asia Studies, Yale University. For their advice, suggestions, and assistance in the writing of this essay, I am deeply indebted to Craig J. Reynolds, Charnvit Kasetsiri, Lorraine Gesick, Nancy Florida, Jennifer Lindsay, and, especially, Nidhi Aeusrivongse.

Then it shall pass that perils will arise
To compromise all creatures with new fears.
When virtues ten fall deaf on kingly ears,
So smash the spheres; sixteen disasters smite.

The moon, the stars, the earth and, yea, the sky
Are knocked awry—in every realm the blight.
While accidents and portents stun the sight,
The clouds flame bright with world-devouring blaze.[1]

For the poet (who is commonly thought to have been King Narai himself) and the men of his day, the social order was founded essentially upon the principle of replicating among men the cosmic moral order that bound together all creatures in a single hierarchy of moral worth. Its maintenance depended upon the individual's conscientious observance of the Buddhist precepts in order to sustain and promote his merit, so that in his next existence he might ascend in, and ultimately transcend, the moral order. Birth into an aristocratic Ayudhya family, or into the royal family, attested to one's possession of moral merit and legitimized one's power.[2] Uniquely upon the ruler fell the responsibility of promoting conditions under which the members of his society might attend to their moral duties and salvation. According to the Buddhist ideal, the monarch was a King of Righteousness, the "Great Elect" (*Mahasammata*) whose moral contract with his subjects depended in part on his observance of the Buddhist precepts and the ten kingly virtues (*dasabidharajadharma*, the "virtues ten" of the poem).[3] By his legislation ("his decrees"), his actions ("what kings do"), and his

---

[1] "Phleng phayakòn krung Si Ayutthaya [The Long Song Prophecy for Ayudhya]," *Prachum phongsawadan* [Collected Chronicles], pt. 63 (4th ed.; Bangkok, 1968), pp. 117-118; Khurusapha edition, vol. 37 (Bangkok, 1969), pp. 135-136; translated by Richard D. Cushman.

[2] Cf. Lucien M. Hanks, "Merit and Power in the Thai Social Order," *American Anthropologist* 64:6 (Dec. 1962), 1247-1261.

[3] Prince Dhani Nivat, "The Old Siamese Conception of the Monarchy," *Journal of the Siam Society* (hereafter JSS), XXXV, pt. 2 (1947), 91-106. Cf. the Siamese version of the Dharmasastra, "Phra Thammasat," *Kotmai tra sam duang*

"virtues ten," the monarch was seen actively to maintain not only proper, orderly relationships between men but also harmony between men and the cosmos. In this latter task the king was aided by a corps of brahmans, who possessed special knowledge of the workings of the cosmic order which they brought to bear in framing laws, fixing the calendar and the dates for auspicious undertakings, and performing state ceremonies. Failing the proper performance of his duties, "When virtues ten fall deaf on kingly ears," chorused nature becomes man's enemy, thieves triumph over pious men, "none obey the great," and "the learned lose men's trust."

> Once Ayutthaya deserted be,
> The rays of all Three Gems at last go out—
> Yet one more stage of universal rout—
> Until about five thousand years have tolled.

> Though now Ayutthaya in bliss can claim
> To shame all heaven's joys a myriad-fold,
> Yet here—behold!—are whores and sin foretold.
> Alas! Alas! Count the days 'til it shall pass.[4]

Ayudhya's fall came not a thousand years later, but less than a hundred years after the death of King Narai. On April 8, 1767, after a two-year siege, the capital fell to Burmese armies that had been waging war against the kingdom since 1760. In this final campaign, Ayudhya was devastated. Its public buildings were destroyed, the entire countryside was laid waste and looted, and large numbers of the members of the leading families were led away to captivity, and lives of slavery, in Burma.[5] In the warfare,

---

[The Laws of the Three Seals] (hereafter KTSD), vol. I (Bangkok, 1962), p. 16. On the *dasabidharājadharma*, see Prince-Patriarch Wachirayanwong, *Thotsaphit ratchatham lae lak Phraphutthasatsana* [The Ten Kingly Virtues and the Principles of Buddhism] (Bangkok, 1973), pp. 15-31.

[4] "Phleng phayakòn," p. 119 (Khurusapha ed., p. 138).

[5] Many of the captives taken are listed in the Burmese chronicles, *Koun-hpoung-hset mahayazawin taw kyi* (Rangoon, 1967), I, 412-416.

perhaps hundreds of thousands of people died, and their numbers were swelled by deaths from famine and disease. Ayudhya's institutions—political, administrative, social, economic, religious, and cultural—could not readily survive the loss of virtually an entire generation of leaders and the destruction of a large portion of the written records throughout the Central Plain region of Siam.

The result was chaos. To one Buddhist monk who lived through this period, the catastrophe of 1767 quite literally fulfilled the prophecies of a century earlier.[6] He wrote with particularly vivid emotion of the tribulations of the Siamese in the aftermath of the Burmese invasion:

> When Ayudhya fell ... the king fled from the city into the forest. Starving when the enemy captured him, his strength failed and he died a natural death. The populace was afflicted with a variety of ills by the enemy. Some wandered about, starving, searching for food. They were bereft of their families, their children and wives, and stripped of their possessions and tools .... They had no rice, no fish, no clothing. They were thin, their bodies wasting away. They found only the leaves of trees and grass to eat .... In desperation many turned to dacoity .... They gathered in bands, and plundered for rice and paddy and salt. Some found food, and others could not.

---

[6] Somdet Phra Phonnarat of Wat Phrachetuphon, *Sangitiyavamsa: phongsawadan rüang sangkhayana Phra Tham Winai* [A Chronicle of Buddhist Councils] (Bangkok, 1923). This work was composed in Pali in 1789. Pages 401-421 deal with the last days of the Kingdom of Ayudhya. Phra Phonnarat dates the beginnings of Ayudhya's fall from the accession of King Uthumphon in 1758, and he describes a long series of omens in the early 1760s portending disaster in exactly the same language as that of the seventeenth-century prophecy. Compare p. 403 with the middle stanzas of the prophecy cited above (fn. 1). The apocalyptic imagery of both passages must derive from scriptural sources.

They grew thinner, and their flesh and blood wasted
away. Afflicted with a thousand evils, some died and
some lived on.[7]

We know not how accurate is this "description" of the
conditions of 1767, particularly as its author was writing partly
to glorify the king who "repaired the damage;" but all the
evidence we have suggests that the kingdom was laid low,
perhaps to its very foundations.

The man of the hour in 1767, the man on horseback, was a
minor provincial official, a certain Sin who was of mixed Sino-
Siamese parentage and had recently been named governor of the
province of Tak, hence *phraya* Tak (Sin). Slipping through the
Burmese cordon around Ayudhya, Taksin first established a base
of manpower and supplies in the southeastern provinces of the
Kingdom, then moved to the Central Plains, making his
headquarters at Thonburi, and militarily defeated first the
remaining Burmese garrisons in the region and then various
royal pretenders and contenders for the throne. His main
contributions to the revival of Siam were military and
administrative, for he very quickly brought under control not
only all the old Ayudhyan provinces but also extensive regions
never before incorporated within the kingdom. These included
the Lan Na Kingdom centered on Chiang Mai, which had been
a Burmese client state for most of the preceding two hundred
years, the principalities of Vientiane and Champassak in Laos,
and the western half of Cambodia. It might also be argued that
Taksin established new economic foundations for the Kingdom
in the relationship into which he apparently entered with the
immigrant Chinese community of Thonburi (and of Chanthaburi
and southern Vietnam);[8] but too little is known of this to allow any

---

[7] Ibid., pp. 409-410.

[8] Chingho A. Chen, "Mac Thien Tu and Phraya Taksin: A Survey on Their
Political Stand, Conflicts and Background," Paper presented to the Seventh
Conference of the International Association of Historians of Asia, Bangkok,
1977.

firm conclusions to be drawn. All we now know is that, perhaps (or perhaps not) replicating institutional arrangements dating back to Ayudhya times, the Chinese mercantile community of Thonburi and Bangkok came to be closely linked, fiscally, economically, and even socially, to the upper echelons of the Siamese ruling elite by the beginning of the Bangkok period.[9] This was a relationship of profound importance, but the evidence is lacking that would enable us to draw firm conclusions as to its origins and significance to the history of Siam in the late eighteenth century.

For the present, the primary importance of Taksin's actions and policies during this period must be assessed instead in terms of their effect on Siam's administrative cohesion, its military posture, and its international relations. Two of these require little further comment. The internal administrative structure of the Thonburi kingdom was passed on, more or less intact, to the Bangkok monarchy. Though subsequently greatly expanded by the creation of many more provinces in the nineteenth century, and though occasionally challenged by rebellions, the provincial administrative organization was to change little until the modernizing reforms of King Chulalongkorn's and Prince Damrong's era at the end of the nineteenth century.[10] Similarly, on the basis of old Ayudhya patterns, Taksin brought into being and sharpened by almost constant use a formidable military establishment, which, again, was not to change substantially until Chulalongkorn's reign.[11] Neither of these two substantial accomplishments appear to have involved any considerable institutional innovation. The organization of both was founded upon laws dating back to the fifteenth century: both required primarily effective and efficient leadership to function in the service of the state.

Something more innovative, however, may have been at work in the expansion of Taksin's empire to encompass regions never previously ruled by Ayudhya. As Taksin himself left little by way

---

[9] See Sarasin Viraphol, *Tribute and Profit: Sino-Siamese Trade, 1652-1853* (Cambridge, Mass., 1977), esp. pp. 171-173.

[10] See Tej Bunnag, *The Provincial Administration of Siam 1892-1915* (Kuala Lumpur, 1977), esp. pp. 17-39.

of explanation of his policies, the historian can only infer his motivation from his situation and his actions. Taksin, to begin, was a usurper, claiming no blood ties with his Ayudhyan predecessors or with neighboring Tai dynasties. Similarly, he need not necessarily have felt himself bound by any historic accommodations which his predecessors may have reached with neighboring kingdoms. More immediately, throughout his reign Taksin faced the necessity of waging warfare against a Burmese monarchy much more aggressive than any antagonist the Siamese had ever met. The Burmese campaigns against Siam in the 1760s and 1770s were based in part upon Burmese political and military presence virtually encircling Ayudhya on all sides, including a large section of the Malay Peninsula, Lan Na and the Shan states, and Lan Sang in Laos. To break this encirclement, Taksin had to work to expel the Burmese and their allies from these regions, and narrow the zone in which subsequent campaigns would be fought. At the same time, Taksin stood to gain the additional resources and manpower that these conquests could bring him. It is noteworthy, however, that Taksin consistently went further along these lines than King Naresuan (r. 1590-1605) had done under similar circumstances two centuries earlier.[12] In Lan Na, Vientiane, and Champassak, Taksin placed clearly-subordinate vassal rulers upon the throne, whose powers in all three cases were subsequently to be steadily absorbed by the Siamese capital. Much the same was true of western Cambodia, now incorporated as provinces into the Thonburi kingdom, and, to a lesser extent, Cambodia itself.[13] The provinces of the Malay

---

[11] See Noel A. Battye, "The Military, Government and Society in Siam, 1868-1910: Politics and Military Reform during the Reign of King Chulalongkorn," Ph.D. diss., Cornell Univ., 1974.

[12] I will not consider whether these policies were the king's, or those of his chief generals, *caophraya* Cakri and his brother, *caophraya* Surasi, who were to succeed Taksin on the throne in 1782.

[13] On Lan Na, see Nigel Brailey, "The Origins of the Siamese Forward Movement in Western Laos, 1850-92," unpubl. Ph.D. diss., Univ. of London, 1968, esp. pp. 10-23; on Laos, see David K. Wyatt, "Siam and Laos, 1767-1827," *Journal of Southeast Asian History* 4:2 (Sept. 1963), 13-32; and on

Peninsula, and the tributary Malay sultanates further south, also came to be tied more closely to the Siamese court.[14]

The train of these actions and events suggests movement away from what might be termed the multi- or polyvalent world order of classical Indian political theory, exemplified in such treatises as the *Arthasastra*,[15] and towards a more concentrated and hierarchical political order built around the Buddhist ideal of the *cakkavatti*, the "world conqueror," the "wheel-turning monarch" whose moral virtue and power subordinates all neighboring rulers.[16] As Taksin expressed in a letter to the ruler of Vientiane in 1775,

> The power of His Majesty is compounded of Knowledge, Wisdom, and Equanimity. He has the Jewelled Disk and the Jewelled Sword of the Great King of Jambudvipa. He is intent upon becoming greater than the King of Ava and this is not beyond his reach.[17]

The story of Taksin's subsequent elaboration upon this idea, and his quest for recognition as a *sotâpanna*, "stream-winner," an advanced being who had embarked upon the first of the four stages towards Enlightenment, is well-known and need

---

Cambodia, see David P. Chandler, "Cambodia Before the French: Politics in a Tributsry Kingdom, 1794-1848," Ph.D. diss., Univ. of Michigan, 1973, pp. 76-80. The Cambodian episode took place in the midst of Taksin's overthrow and the accession of Rama I.

[14] See Lorraine Gesick, "Kingship and Political Integration in Traditional Siam, 1767-1824," Ph.D. diss., Cornell Univ., 1976, pp. 85-88.

[15] *Kautilya's Arthasastra*, tr. and ed. R. Shamasastry (8th ed.; Mysore, 1967).

[16] There is a good discussion of this concept in Gesick, "Kingship," pp. 49-57.

[17] Letter, Taksin to King Siribunyasan of Vientiane, January 1775, in King Chulalongkorn, *Phraratchawican nai cotmai khwamsongcam khong Phracao paiyikathœ krommaluang Narinthewi* [Commentary on the Memoirs of Princess Narinthewi] (Bangkok, 1908), Appendix, p. 16; translation in Gesick, "Kingship," p. 98.

not be recounted in detail here.[18] The central theme is simply Taksin's donning the cloak of Buddhist moral power in order to legitimize his political expansionism.

The same cloak, of course, could be worn for internal political reasons, and indeed it is these latter that probably encouraged him to put it on in the first place. Within his own society, after all, Taksin was an upstart, a newcomer, a usurper. If he could not, or chose not to pretend to, legitimize his possession of the throne by virtue of royal descent, then he had to justify his actions in moral terms, all the more so because he and his contemporaries believed that Ayudhya had fallen because the merit, the moral power, of its kings had been exhausted. As Gesick has argued, he was attempting to prove the unprovable. He could act the role of the virtuous king, but none could be certain that, as Westerners would put it, his "luck" would hold. In undertaking to gain public recognition as a Buddhist well-advanced, even beyond monks, on the path to Enlightenment, Taksin committed the error, even the sin, of making *personal* that which his society was unwilling to recognize in any save the *institution*. By requiring that monks pay him personal obeisance and veneration, he outraged élite opinion, destroyed his political support, and brought about his own deposition from the throne.[19]

By 1782, then, Taksin's most important effort at fundamental institutional change, the redefinition of the monarchy in exclusively Buddhist terms so as to legitimize the tenure of the incumbent, had failed on the over-identification of monarch and monarchy. While the monarchy might be imbued with an aura of sanctity, Taksin's deposition suggests that popular opinion still demanded that the monarch remain a secular and moral, rather than a religious, leader. King Rama I,[20] who succeeded him in

---

[18] The best recent accounts of this are to be found in Craig J. Reynolds, "The Buddhist Monkhood in Nineteenth Century Thailand," Ph.D. diss., Cornell Univ., 1972, pp. 30-35; and in Gesick, "Kingship," esp. pp. 101-109.

[19] See Gesick, "Kingship," pp. 101-109.

[20] "Rama I" is a twentieth-century name for the first king of the Chakri Dynasty, whose proper title was Phraphutthayotfa Culalok. I use it here simply for convenience.

1782, was left with the task of satisfying this demand in a manner that would provide legitimacy for his dynasty, and thus stability and continuity for his kingdom. He had to do so amidst painful memories of the recent past, a continuing state of warfare with Burma, and a future more clouded by international insecurity than any of his contemporaries could have imagined. The central theme of this essay is that Rama I resolved these dangerous difficulties by legitimizing the Siamese monarchy in a radically, fundamentally new way. He established a completely new relationship between the monarchy and Siamese society that was founded upon rational communication. The Buddhist universe was newly delineated by the exercise of human reason, and this new perception of universal order was employed to inform secular thought and action. Most important, the monarchy became the continuing moderator of dialogue between eternal truths, as uncovered by the exercise of the human mind, and the exigencies of a changing world, and thereby set the stage for the internal dynamics of Siamese intellectual change that were so successfully to withstand the severe challenges of the nineteenth century.

The main features of the reign of King Rama I are well known.[21] Quite apart from the day-to-day business of administering a large and far-flung kingdom, and conducting the warfare that by the end of his reign in 1809 would produce security from further Burman depredations, the king conventionally is credited with having undertaken on a large scale a series of legislative, religious, and cultural activities that had the cumulative effect of restoring the best of the Ayudhyan tradition as it had been in the golden age of King Borommakot (r. 1733-1758). The usual argument has been to the effect that Rama I ably and energetically fulfilled the expectations that Siamese society traditionally had had of its monarchs. A king, as part of the definition of his duties, was expected to issue legislation, ensure the correct performance

---

[21] See Prince Dhani Nivat, "The Reconstruction of Rama I of the Chakri Dynasty," JSS, XLIII, pt. 1 (Aug. 1955), 21-47, and Klaus Wenk, *The Restoration of Thailand Under Rama I 1782-1809* (Tucson, 1968); but see my review in *Journal of Asian Studies* (hereafter JAS), 28:2 (Feb. 1969), 434-435.

of state ceremonies, act as the patron of Buddhism, and generously promote the arts at his court. It is presumed that all the kings of Ayudhya had done so, and, for all his excesses, even King Taksin had made efforts in each of these areas. Viewed from this perspective, Rama I's activities are remarkable chiefly for their scope, their thoroughness, and the king's own undoubted talent, even genius, displayed in numerous activities undertaken in fulfillment of these duties. Rama I, it is pointed out, did not just issue laws but undertook a complete codification of all Siamese law in 1805; he did not just have the Tipitaka copied anew but convoked a full Council of the Buddhist hierarchy for a completely new recension of the Scriptures in 1783; he did not just compose in verse one episode from the epic Ramayana but wrote anew the entire saga. All this work, however, is generally attributed to the king's intention to "restore" or "reconstruct" the glories of Ayudhya.[22] The magnitude of Rama I's accomplishment usually is accounted for by the fact that he had to overcome both the virtual destruction of these legal, religious, and cultural institutions in 1767, and the mischief wrought by Taksin mainly on religious institutions Thai historians thus have not been hard-pressed to find cause for praising the founder of the Chakri Dynasty: he in effect revived and revivified classical Siamese tradition, restored a continuity with the glories of Ayudhya, and reconstructed a healthy, lively state.

Whence comes the impulse to challenge this conventional view of the First Reign? If Rama I and some of his contemporaries explicitly stated that the king deliberately emulated Ayudhyan institutions, why should an historian two centuries later now propose that he really intended something fundamentally new? This historian's urge to suggest precisely that has been slow in the making. It began with the realization that fundamental intellectual changes, having primarily to do with how nineteenth-century Siamese viewed the relationship of man to the cosmos, were already in motion by the beginning of the Third Reign (Rama III, r. 1824-1851). This led first to a careful reading of the documents of the First Reign, and then to their comparison with

---

[22] Note these words in the titles of the works cited above (n. 21).

late Ayudhya materials. Finally, my ideas were stimulated enormously by the recent work of Craig J. Reynolds, Lorraine Gesick, and Nidhi Aeusrivongse more directly concerned with the subject at hand,[23] though in their cases the central issues raised here have not yet been addressed.

The argument I wish now to develop is that, even though Rama I and his contemporaries spoke of what amounted to "reconstruction" or "restoration," the First Reign was not, nor could it have been, simply a "return to Ayudhya." For their part, neither the leaders of Siamese society nor the general public could have been satisfied simply with a king and government content to rule as previous kings had ruled. They held kings responsible for the calamities and chaos of the preceding quarter-century, and they now expected a "better" king, at least in moral terms. On the basis of the various written documents that have come down to us from the First Reign, we might also be tempted to at least suspect that, in addition to wanting a monarchy better defined in Buddhist moral terms, people also wanted a monarchy more responsive to their wishes, more willing to communicate with them as fellow human beings sharing a single vale of woe.

For his part, because of the person he was, the experience he had undergone, and the values and perceptions he had developed, Rama I was unable simply to "go back" to Ayudhya. His very view of Siam's past was filtered through the accumulated memories and impressions of a turbulent lifetime and a range of experience exceptional for a Siamese of his generation. His was an age of critical issues on which men were divided, an age of warfare and far-ranging travel and of new foreign contacts; an age of doubt and uncertainty. An unusually intelligent and resourceful man such as Rama I could not come to the throne in 1782 and act or think as though the preceding two decades had not happened. On the contrary, through much

<hr />

[23] Craig J. Reynolds, "Buddhist Cosmography in Thai History, With Special Reference to Nineteenth-Century Culture Change," JAS 35:2 (Feb. 1976), 203-220; Nidhi Aeusrivongse, *Prawatsat Rattanakosin nai phraratchaphongsawadan Ayutthaya* [Bangkok History in Ayudhya Chronicles] (Bangkok, 1978) and "A Sketch of Early Bangkok Literature" (unpubl. ms., Sept. 1978); and Lorraine Gesick, "Kingship"

of Rama I's work it is quite clear that the past was very much in his thoughts, for the motivation that impelled that work was the determination that the troubles of the past should not be repeated.

The phenomenon of Rama I, then, is the product of interaction between an individual and his society, between past and present. Rama I's generation fundamentally differed from its predecessors for having lived through the 1760s and 1770s; and however much they may have thought they could return to the best of the past, the "past" they imagined was filtered through hard lenses ground in their own experience. As José Ortega y Gasset has put it, "it does not matter whether one generation applauds the previous generation or hisses it—in either event, it carries the previous generation within itself."[24] Rama I's generation deliberately connected itself with their predecessors by affirming the traditions they had upheld; but, at the same time, they redefined those traditions in fundamentally different ways.

In considering the period, the reader will find it useful to bear in mind a few salient facts about the life of Rama I. He was born on March 21, 1737, to a family with a long tradition of service to the Siamese court going back to the reign of King Naresuan.[25] At the time of his birth, Rama I's father was serving in Ayudhya as "the preparer of royal letters and communications for northern directions … and protector of the great royal seal for that purpose,"[26] that is, as secretary to one division within the Mahatthai, the ministry of the northern provinces. His mother was "a beautiful daughter of a Chinese richest family."[27] His only elder brother took up government service in the court of the heir-apparent, but died prior to 1767.

---

[24] *Man and Crisis* (New York, 1962), p. 53.

[25] Birth date from *Ratchasakunwong* [Royal Genealogy] (8th rev. ed.; Bangkok, 1969), p. 1. King Mongkut's Siamese account of the origins of the Chakri Dynasty (ūPathomwong [Forefathers]," *Prachum phongsawadan*, pt. 8; Khurusapha ed. vol. 8, Bangkok, 1964, pp. 229-253) should be read in conjunction with his English version, contained in a letter to Sir John Bowring in Bowring, *The Kingdom and People of Siam* (London, 1857), I, 63-69.

[26] Bowring, *Kingdom and People*, I, 66.

[27] Ibid.

Of his two elder sisters, one was married to the head of one of the palace police units, and the other to the fourth son of a wealthy Chinese family said to be descended from a ministerial family of Ming China and related by marriage to a late Ayudhya minister of finance (*Phrakhlang*).[28] Rama I's younger brother, who was his close lieutenant and later was to serve as his heir-apparent (*uparaja*) was born in 1743. He also had a brother and sister by other mothers. On coming of age, Rama I married a woman of a prosperous family in Ratburi province, and moved there, where he entered the provincial government and by 1762 was the provincial *yokkrabat* (sort of an inspector-general). Little is known of his doings or whereabouts at the time of the great Burmese invasion. We know only that his younger brother was an early adherent to Taksin's cause, apparently as a ranking military officer, and brought Rama I to the king's attention. By 1772, then still only thirty-five years of age, he had attained the ministerial rank of *caophraya* Cakri as head of the Mahatthai; and his younger brother soon thereafter attained similar rank with a specially-created title, *caophraya* Surasi. The two brothers reached such lofty status and responsibilities at such young ages[29] primarily, it would seem, because of demonstrated military and organizational skills and loyalty to the king. Almost constantly in the field together, the two brothers carried on a long series of successful military campaigns in all regions of the kingdom, from Pattani in the south to the far north, and northeast to Vientiane and Champassak, and they were engaged in a campaign against the Cambodian capital when word reached them early in 1782 that Taksin had been deposed.

The conclusions to be drawn from the pre-royal phase of Rama I's career are simple, but deserve emphasis. First, he was still a young man, only forty-five, when he became king, and by then he already had held the highest official rank and responsibilities for a full decade. One would expect him to be confident and self-assured, and

---

[28] Mongkut, "Pathomwong," pp. 232-34.

[29] A late Ayudhya decree (1740) suggested that even minor provincial officials should be at least 31 years of age: KTSD, V (Bangkok, 1963), p. 149 (Phraratchakamnot kao, 50).

not overly deferential to age and inherited status: he had dealt with enough kings and would-be kings to recognize their human qualities or lack of such. His family background had provided him with an early understanding of government, both in the capital and in the provinces, and his family connections, especially by marriage, gave him a wide circle of acquaintances in both public and private life. By reason of his constant campaigns away from the capital, ever since about 1775, he was comfortable with the necessity for making quick, independent judgments and decisions, and he had been thoroughly exposed to the life and culture of ordinary rural people. However, as we shall see, Rama I was more than a man of action. He was unusually well-educated in his own culture and capable of both thoughtful reflection and studied analysis, the product perhaps of an interest in people and a talent for listening and learning. By the time he came to the throne, he had formed clear perceptions of the state of his kingdom, and was prepared to take immediate steps to improve it. Most importantly, Rama I moved through an extraordinarily fluid situation; one in which the nature of the state, and even of human society itself, had been thrown open to question by the chaos of the times, and in which virtually a whole generation of his elders was absent, having dropped from sight in 1767.

A great deal of research needs to be done before a comprehensive assessment of Rama I's work and reign can be accomplished.[30] This present more modest effort will examine only briefly four major undertakings of the First Reign in the fields of religion, state ceremony, legislation, and literature, with a view primarily to delineating their intellectual orientation. After doing so, we will conclude by asking whether the First Reign should continue to be viewed as a period of "restoration" or "reconstruction."

Religion

Rama I's chief works in the area of religion were the new Ecclesiastical Laws ("Kotmai phra song") issued between 1782

---

[30] In particular, we need a full and careful publication of all documents and manuscripts surviving from the First Reign.

and 1801, the commissioning of a new edition of the "Three Worlds" cosmology in 1783, and the convening of the Grand Council to revise the Tipitaka in 1788. The balance of these efforts falls at the very beginning of his reign, and they might be taken to represent the new king's judgment as to where he must place his highest priority.

That Rama I should have begun with Buddhism is hardly surprising, all the more because of the havoc wrought by King Taksin on the Buddhist establishment and on public opinion informed by Buddhism. As Reynolds has pointed out, Taksin was not so completely unorthodox as to ignore the traditional expectations of royal patronage: he had commissioned a re-copying of the Tipitaka in 1769 and of the *Traiphum* ("Three Worlds") cosmology in 1776.[31] However, the unorthodoxy of his pretensions to supernatural power in the last years of his reign were seriously divisive, and provoked the reaction that soon brought his reign (and his life) to an end.

To Rama I, the question was not just a matter of differences of opinion within the monkhood, or even of popular or élite dissatisfaction with Taksin's aberrant behavior: much more was at stake. Rama I considered that the state was in a moral crisis, that it had been in such a state since before the fall of Ayudhya, and that moral crisis had led to the fall of Ayudhya.[32] The individual decrees of The Ecclesiastical Laws are replete with references to the low state of religion and the Buddhist monkhood, expressed in the most stringent language. To cite but a few examples:

> *Monks nowadays have completely abandoned the*
> *Vinayapaññati [rules of conduct] and are heedless*
> *of advice, instruction, and control.[33]*

---

[31] Reynolds, "Buddhist Cosmography," p. 209.
[32] The historical dimension of Rama I's argument will be taken up again below.
[33] KTSD, IV 177 (Law 3, May 8, 1783).

Nowadays, monks, having been ordained, fail to obey
the Vinaya, and their behavior evidences their
immoral lives .... Monks commit cardinal sins
fearing more the perils of the present than they fear hell.[34]

Having explained that customarily the Buddhist realm
(*phutthacak*) and the secular realm *(Phraratcha-anacak)* had
cooperated in upholding Buddhism, he goes on to say that

> Nowadays, it can be seen that the Buddhist realm
> became complacent, considering that Buddhism
> was secure, and so the cooperation lapsed to the
> point where the Burmese (? lit., the Great Dacoits)
> could destroy the religion.[35]

Monks, he continued, had failed to maintain their discipline
and their studies, and wandered about in the shops and markets,
visited musical and dramatic performances, played chess and
gambled and, in short, behaved like laypeople.[36]
There are several remarkable things about these laws. First, the
king's language is unexpectedly harsh and scathing, considering
that he is writing about monks who by definition, as well as by
custom, have always been accorded special deference in Siamese
society. Second, his critique of monastic behavior and the state of
ecclesiastical discipline is based consistently upon a thorough
acquaintance with, and understanding of, canonical Buddhism,
specifically the Vinaya, and of Buddhist history.[37] His critique,
then, is not a matter of measuring a present situation against an
Ayudhyan situation, but rather of assessing the present in terms of
eternal truths. He does not do so, however, without first indicating
his active acceptance of the philosophical logic that lay behind

---

[34] KTSD, IV, 193-194 (Law 6, July 13, 1783).
[35] KTSD, IV, 209-210 (Law 8, Feb. 10, 1790).
[36] There are many more examples: see, for instance, pp. 171 (Law 2, May
5, 1783), 181 (Law 3), and 190 (Law 6).
[37] Cf. esp. KTSD, IV, 190-193 (Law 6).

the prescriptions of the canon. His critique, then, is a return to first principles, not only because they exist in the Siamese tradition, but also because he rationally and deliberately chooses to affirm them. Next to their bluntness, the rationalism of the Ecclesiastical Laws is their most striking feature.[38] Unlike the laws of all his predecessors (and more of this below), the Ecclesiastical Laws present reasoned cases for the prescriptive decisions they announce. The decrees describe existing situations, give case examples that illustrate it, outline fully the various grounds—canonical, historical, moral—upon which the situation should be condemned, and then enunciate laws which, consonant with canonical precedent and administrative capacity, should work to correct it. These laws are tightly constructed and well thought through. They bespeak an authority very different from that of the Ayudhya kings, "whose very word was law."

The Ecclesiastical Laws also represent the king's assumption of religious authority in a manner unique to the First Reign. So far as we know, in all the surviving corpus of pre-Bangkok law only two decrees encroach into the religious sphere and are addressed specifically to the Buddhist monkhood. The first is a decree of 1738 dealing with a specific case of monastic interference in the administration of justice.[39] King Borommakot says, in effect, that monks should mind their own business and leave government affairs to officials, because secular and religious affairs must be kept distinct. The second is a curious re-statement of the 227 rules of conduct for monks, addressed to them in homely language by King Taksin in 1774.[40] This decree certainly marks a break with

---

[38] I am particularly struck by this quality because I recently read through the entire five volumes of KTSD at a single sitting (over four days). Coming to the Ecclesiastical Laws in the middle of the fourth volume after days with the Ayudhyan laws was an extraordinary experience, to be highly recommended to those who persist in considering Rama I a latter-day Ayudhyan king.

[39] KTSD, IV, 306-311 (Phraratchakamnot kao, 8, Jan. 12, 1783).

[40] *Buddhajayamangala 8 læ phraratchakamnot khong phracao krung Thonburi wa duei sin sikkha* [The Eight Glories of Buddhism, and Royal Decree of the King of Thonburi Concerning the Precepts of the Monastic Life] (Bangkok, 1967), pp. 28-59, dated Feb. 13, 1774.

previous practice, but hardly a sharp one: he does not specifically invoke royal authority, but simply reminds monks of the rules they are bound to obey. By contrast, Rama I goes very deeply into religious affairs, and in one decree goes even further than he realizes is proper, by deciding a question of interpretation of the canon.[41] The king clearly was uncomfortable in doing so, and closed the decree by strictly forbidding any future resort to him of monastic quarrels over questions of the interpretation of the Vinaya. The remainder of his Ecclesiastical Laws, however, display no such reticence or defensiveness about royal involvement in ecclesiastical affairs. As the patron and protector of Buddhism in his kingdom, the king considered it his responsibility to provide a framework, legal and institutional, in which monks could fulfill their responsibilities in order that the moral decay of the age might be arrested and Buddhism might again flourish.

Already, in the Ecclesiastical Laws of the first few months of his reign, King Rama I repeatedly had indicated the significance of scriptural scholarship and textual study to proper monastic life.[42] One customary act of royal patronage of Buddhism practiced was to commission the copying of a set of the Tipitaka. Taksin had done so at least twice, first in 1769 copying from an original set in Nakhòn Sithammarat, and then in 1776 presenting another copy to a Thonburi monastery during obsequies for his mother;[43] and he is said also to have sought additional manuscripts of the sacred texts in Cambodia.[44] In some ways just as important was royal patronage for copying the *Traiphum* cosmology, which to pre-modern Siamese was rather like a textbook of basic science,

---

[41] KTSD, IV, 195-206 (Law 7, Oct. 27, 1783). This unusual situation is discussed in Reynolds, "Buddhist Monkhood," pp. 44-50.

[42] KTSD, IV, 167-168 (Law 1, Sept. 16, 1782), 175 (Law 2), 180-181 (Law 3), 184-185 (Law 4, July 13, 1783), etc.

[43] "Phraratchaphongsawadan krung Thonburi chabap phan Chanthanumat [Royal Chronicles of Thonburi, phan Chanthanumat edition]," *Prachum phongsawadan*, pt. 65 (2nd ed.; Bangkok, 1960), pp. 32, 81; Khurusapha ed., vol. 40 (Bangkok, 1969), pp. 45, 114-115.

[44] G. Cœdès, *The Vajirañana National Library of Siam* (Bangkok, 1924), p. 21.

outlining the principles in terms of which all existence was structured.[45] King Taksin commissioned a magnificently-illustrated copy of the *Traiphum* in 1776, and the manuscript copy, generally regarded as the modern standard edition, was copied at a provincial monastery in 1778.[46] The manuscript probably was fairly widely copied in the late eighteenth and early nineteenth centuries, and was even more widely known by mural representations of its contents.

This textual continuity, which goes back to the fourteenth century, was broken sharply by King Rama I. In August of 1783, he convened an assembly of officials and high-ranking monks at which time various texts were chanted and the king posed questions to the monks. The discussions must have had some bearing on questions of cosmology and on the constitution of human society, for being dissatisfied with the learned monks' statements or answers, he "ordered the leading monks *(phraratchakhana)* and royal pundits to research the Tipitaka in the Royal Library and from the relevant passages to compile an edition of the *Traiphumikatha* in order to promote both faith and knowledge.[47] The task apparently was accomplished, though perhaps not quickly. The next we hear of the text is in 1802, when the king voiced his dissatisfaction with the unevenness, inconsistency, and deficiencies of the *Traiphumikatha,* and ordered

---

[45] See Reynolds, "Buddhist Cosmography," p. 409.

[46] Klaus Wenk, *Thailandischen Miniaturmalereien nach einer Handschrift der Indischen Kunstabteilung der Staatlichen museen Berlin* (Wiesbaden, 1965), pp. 14-15. Reynolds, "Buddhist Cosmography," p. 409, refers to the 1776 and 1778 copies as "revisions," but it is difficult to term them so without comparison with earlier texts, which has not been done. The 1778 copy was not commissioned by Taksin: it was copied by a monk in Samut Prakan who makes no mention of royal patronage in his colophon. The 1778 copy is the basis of all the modern printed editions, including the French translation by G. Cœdès and C. Archaimbault, *Les trois mondes* (Traibhumi Brah R'van) (Paris, 1973). A new critical edition, *Traiphumikatha rü Traiphum Phra Ruang,* ed. Phaithun Maliwan (Bangkok, 1974), is based on the 1778 copy, with comparisons to a 1787 copy and to a fragmentary version from late Ayudhya times.

[47] *Traiphum lok winitchai, camlòng cak chabap luang* [Exegesis of the Three Worlds, Copied from the Royal Edition] (Bangkok, 1913), p. 3.

that it be rewritten as a comprehensive work, consistent with the Pali canon and its commentaries. He requested that *phraya* Thammapricha (Kæo), head of the Royal Pundits, take charge of this work; and three leading monks were co-opted to join him: Phra Phutthakhosachan as his assistant, Phra Thamma-udom as researcher, and the Supreme Patriarch as advisor. This committee completed its work in only two months, on December 17, 1802, when their work was presented to the king.[48]

Working certainly on the basis of the 1783 draft, what the committee produced was anything but another re-casting of the fourteenth-century *Traiphum.* While the old *Traiphum* began at the bottom of the moral scale of existence with the creatures of hell and worked upwards through the human world and the worlds of the gods to *nibbâna*, the 1802 text dealt with man first, then lower orders, higher orders, and the way to *nibbâna.*[49]

This difference is important as an indication of the perspective from which Rama I's Siam saw the world. What it suggests is that man, in the middle of the scale of existence, is in the vulnerable position of standing to gain or lose most by his actions. It is far easier for man to rise or fall than it is for lower and higher creatures. This fact makes the governance of human society all the more important, and it would appear that the chief theme of this work is the justification of the kingship which provides the framework within which men can work out their moral fates. The summary given at the end of the fragmentary published version states this so succinctly that it demands quotation in full:

> The gist of this book is as follows: When mankind arose in the world, and began to gather in groups, those groups raised up a person of truth, justice, ability, force, and power to preside over them in order that they might be governed so as to live in

---

[48] Ibid., pp. 4-5. Cf. Reynolds, "Buddhist Monkhood," pp. 56-57.
[49] Ibid., p. [6]. Unfortunately, the only published text of the "Exegesis" is fragmentary, consisting only of the first of four sections.

peace and prosperity, safe from all dangers. When mankind had further progressed and polities *(ban müang)* had been formed, a Bodhisatva appeared in the world of men, a man of merit, bravery, and ability surpassing all other people, so the assembled people invited him to become their leader, and he was named the King, the Great Elect (*phrachao maha sommutti khatiyarat*). In that first era, he was the first King. His Majesty was steadfast in practicing the ten kingly virtues (*dasabidharajadharma*). All his ministers and courtiers and all the populace trusted and were faithful to him, and all classes and lineages of people were in concord with one another. All the monks, brahmans, and people lived in peace and prosperity. The country *(prathet ban müang)* fully shone with glory, and abounded in all kinds of goods, force, and power. Thus it can be seen that any people *(chat)* and country *(ban müang)* is good that is presided over by a King (*phramahakasat*): that country will develop in full glory, steadfast and independent through the ages, just as it was in the earliest times.

Matapitukataññukatavedita = Appreciation of parental virtue.

Sasanadalhasaddha = Firm faith in the religion.

Annamaññasamaggi = Mutual concord.

Issaramukhâdisaccam = Loyalty towards he who presides as King.

If these four principles are inculcated in and habitually practiced by the individual, by the family, in the villages, and in the country, the individual, the family, the villages, and the country will be replete with the peace, prosperity, and virtue that are the highest blessings in this world and the next.[50]

---

[50] Ibid., pp. 117-118.

None of this may be particularly novel. The fourteenth-century *Traiphum* so argues, as do the canonical texts on which the *Traiphum* and the 1802 "Exegesis" were based. What is new in the First Reign is the form in which the old arguments are restated and the prominence given to the world of men and kings. Men now are moving to the center of the stage, and kings play the leading roles without which the play cannot go on. Particularly striking are the parallels drawn between the Bodhisatta—the First King, the Great Elect—and King Rama I. Both arose out of troubled times in order to create moral order. To his contemporaries, Rama I could be seen "as" the Mahasammata, and at least one saw him as a Bodhisatta.[51]

Having begun in 1783 the process of scholarship and writing that ultimately was to lead to the "Exegesis" of the "Three Worlds" cosmology, Rama I then undertook, in 1788, a much more ambitious task. Like other kings before him, early in his reign he had begun commissioning copies of the Tipitaka for use in monastic scholarship, and even had sought to obtain copies of the Pali texts in other Southeast Asian scripts. In 1788, however, from a combination of motives, he determined to convene a Sangha council for the full revision of the entire Pali canon and ancillary works.[52] In addition to being an occasion for demonstrating royal patronage of Buddhism on a grand scale, and for engaging contending factions of monks in a common harmonious endeavor, this Grand Council (*sankhayana*) was considered to be a momentous event in universal Buddhist history. Phra Phonnarat, the Siamese historian of the occasion, reckoned that there had been only eight previous councils since the first was convened not long after the Buddha's demise to assemble the Tipitaka for the first time; and the most recent had been held at Chiang Mai in 1475.[53] The task of the 250 monks and royal pundits was formidable: to review the entire Pali canon, comparing various

---

[51] Phra Phonnarat, *Sangitiyawong*, p. 424.

[52] Revnolds discusses this fully in "Buddhist Monkhood," pp. 50-55.

[53] Phra Phonnarat, *Sangitiyavamsa*, pp. 340-345. There have been only two since, at Mandalay, Burma, in 1860 and 1956.

manuscripts, and by research and deliberation to establish a definitive text for fresh copying on palm leaves. They completed their work in five months, in April, 1789, and the results of their labors were embodied in 288 manuscripts, a total of 3,568 bundles of palm leaves.[54] This set, frequently copied since, has comprised the standard texts for Thai Buddhism to the present day.[55]

By his direct sponsorship, and his daily attendance at the convocation to make food-offerings to the monks, Rama I fully associated himself with this undertaking and played the role of royal patron of Siamese Buddhism in a highly-visible manner. Rama I was acting in a very traditional fashion, in a tradition that was not only Siamese but also embraced all of the Buddhist world. However, not just any king could carry out such a portentous task. After all, the purity and textual integrity of the scriptures was of enormous importance to the health and prosperity of Buddhism. Few but the most powerful kings had ever dared to attempt their revision. If the task were poorly done, the sponsoring king stood to lose merit and thereby endanger not only his throne but also his kingdom. In sponsoring the Grand Council, Rama I displayed a characteristic confidence in the ability of human minds to meet the delicate challenge of ascertaining and interpreting holy writ. The Tipitaka revision was not something that tradition required he do: the recopying of the texts had fulfilled his formal duties in this area. His actions in 1788 imply that he was saying that tradition alone was not enough, an attitude very much in keeping with his other activities.

---

[54] Cœdès, *National Library,* p. 22, notes that another copy was produced a few months later, including extracanonical works not incorporated in the first version, numbering 354 manuscripts in 3,686 bundles.

[55] The next comparable act of royal patronage was King Chulalongkorn's commissioning of the first printed edition of the full Tipitaka, now in Siamese rather than *khòm* (Khmer/Pali script), in 1893.

State Ceremony

For all the weight Rama I placed on Buddhism as the legitimizing ideology of kingship, he was by no means exclusively a Buddhist king. Much of the ritual of the court calendar was brahmanical in origin, and continued to be carried on by a corps of brahmanical specialists kept at court for that purpose.[56] The regular performance of the state ceremonies of the Ayudhya court had been disrupted by warfare, the loss of critical ritual texts, and the death or disappearance of ritual specialists. Taksin had begun the task of reconstructing the ritual life of the court, by seeking out former court officials and such ritual texts and specialists as could be located, for example, in Nakhòn Sithammarat.[57] There was some feeling at the beginning of the First Reign that the unfortunate end of Taksin's reign might have been due, at least in part, to the fact that Taksin had never undergone a full, proper coronation. Still pressed by the threat of war with the Burmese, and engaged in moving his capital across the river from Thonburi to Bangkok, Rama I underwent only a provisional coronation, "taking possession of the throne," in June, 1782. On January 1, 1783, however, he convened a group of knowledgeable officials and Buddhist monks to consult the old treatises and remembered forms in order to draw up a coronation manual;[58] and at the same time he ordered the royal regalia and

[56] Cf. Prince Dhani, "Old Siamese Conceptions," and H. G. Quaritch Wales, *Siamese State Ceremonies: Their History and Function* (London, 1931).

[57] See the forewords written by Prince Damrong Rajanubhab for "Rüang tamra krabuan sadet lae krabuan hæ tæ boran [An Ancient Treatise on Royal Processions]," *Latthithamniam tangtang* [Various Customs] (hereafter LTT), pt. 10, Khlang Witthaya ed. vol. I (Bangkok, 1961), 451-456; and *Tamnan phram müang Nakhòn Si Thammarat* [Chronicle of the Brahmans of Nakhon Si Thammarat] (Bangkok, 1930). Note that one lengthy treatise on royal processions dating from Taksin's reign was expressly commissioned by Rama I, who was then *caophraya* Chakri: "Tamra krabuan sadet," p. 457.

[58] Prince Damrong Rajanubhab, *Phraratchaphongsawadan krung Rattanakosin ratchakan thi 2* [Royal Chronicle of the Second Reign], Khlang Witthaya combined First and Second Reign edition (Bangkok, 1962), pp. 340-348. One of Prince Damrong's chief sources for this account, once extremely rare, has been reprinted: *Ruang rachaphisek lae cotmaihet borommarachaphisek ratchakan thi 5* [On Coronation, and Documents Concerning the Coronations in the Fifth Reign] (Bangkok, 1966), pp. 8-15.

utensils to be fashioned.[59] A minor decree on ceremonial matters from 1782 indicates how the king wished things to be done: "His Majesty wishes that things be carried out as in [the time of] King Borommakot, and not like *Phraya* Taksin."[60] It was on this basis that Rama I's grand coronation took place in 1785.

In the first few years of his reign, Rama I had issued a number of orders dealing with ceremonies. On occasion there are specific references to practices in the reign of King Borommakot, as if by way of justification.[61] One of the most significant things about the documents that have survived, however, is the public quality of the proclamations read out at the re-instituted regular ceremonies of the year, which characteristically explained the origins and purpose of the ceremony in didactic fashion.[62]

It should also be noted that Rama I seems to have been responsible for beginning that process of "Buddhaization" which Kirsch has described, by which the Buddhist elements of Siamese religious observance began to gain ground at the expense of the

---

[59] "Tamra krabuan sadet," pp. 495-496.

[60] Ibid., p. 495, dated April 9, 1782, only three days after his accession to the throne.

[61] E.g., ibid., pp. 510, 515. Other documents concerning state ceremonies in the First Reign may be found in the following parts of LTT (citations for the Khlang Witthaya ed., Bangkok, 1963): "Phraratchaphithi cakkraphat rachathirat læ phraratchaphithi aphatphinat [Royal Ceremonies for the Health of the King and the Relief of an Epidemic]" (pt. 8), I, 385-404; "Laksana kan Phraratchaphithi sokan nai ratchakan thi 1 [On the Royal Sokan Ceremony in the First Reign]" (pt. 12), I, 581-652; "Tamra bæp thamniam nai ratchasamnak [Treatise on the Customs of the Royal Household]" (pt. 15), II, 1-142; "Rüang mairapsang bang rüang nai ratchakan thi 1 læ thi 2 [Various Royal Orders from the First and Second Reigns]" (pt. 17), II, 265-352; and "Tamra bæp thamniam nai ratchasamnak khrang krung Si Ayutthaya [Treatise on the Customs of the Royal Household in the Ayudhya Period]" (pt. 19), II, 475-560. There is a great deal of repetition amongst these various publications. Prince Damrong's foreword to part 15 is particularly helpful.

[62] Prince Dhani, "Reconstruction of Rama I," p. 40, referring to such decrees as the following, collected in Prince Sommot Amòraphan, *Prakat kan phraratchaphithi* [Proclamations for Royal Ceremonies] (2 v.; Bangkok, 1916), I, 53-55 (?); II, 1, 10, 19.

brahmanical and animistic elements.[63] He seems to have been most concerned to limit the role of the supernatural (into which Taksin and some rebels had delved)[64] and emphasize the primacy of a more philosophical Buddhism. It was in this vein that in 1782 he ordered that his subjects revere none higher than Buddhism. He admitted there was a place for the propitiation of various spirits, and even urged officials to promote proper respect for them, but he warned them not to place them above Buddhism. Turning his attention to phallic worship he stated that he found no sanction for it in the Tipitaka, and that he was concerned that foreign visitors found it offensive. He forbade the keeping of lingas, and ordered officials to gather and destroy them, on penalty of death.[65] In much the same spirit, three years later he required that officials participating in the annual oath-of-allegiance ceremony in the Temple of the Emerald Buddha should complete their obeisances to the Triple Gems of Buddhism, the Emerald Buddha, and Buddhist relics before paying their respects to the guardian and tutelary deities or to the statues of previous rulers.[66] In both cases his argument was founded on a clear view of the primacy of Buddhism in Siamese religion, and conveyed in the clear, straightforward style of his decrees on state ceremonies. He was by no means undertaking any radical attempt to transform Siamese religion. Indeed, it is worth noting that he had a learned Buddhist monk compose a lengthy scholarly invocation to the guardian spirits and gods of the universe (*thewada*) to inaugurate the Buddhist Grand Council in 1788.[67] Rama I was in advance perhaps only of the popular Buddhism of his day. The views he expressed have to be regarded as representative of the better- informed, more devout of the populace. It is significant that in his patronage of Buddhist practice and teaching, and in his establishment of state ceremonial, he seems to

---

[63] A. Thomas Kirsch, "Complexity in the Thai Religious System: An Interpretation," JAS 36:2 (Feb. 1977), 241-266.

[64] See Reynolds, "Buddhist Monkhood," pp. 41-42.

[65] KTSD, V, 320-325 (Phraratchakamnot mai, 35, Aug. 21, 1782).

[66] KTSD, V, 353-357 (Phraratchakamnot mai, 40, Apr. 22, 1785).

[67] "Kham prakat thewada khrang sangkhayana," *Prakat kan phraratchaphithi*, II, 10-19.

have taken the lead in attempting actively to improve the position of Buddhist values and practice in everyday life. He was not content simply to preside over an on-going system of order or to return to the recent "glories" of Ayudhya: he was seeking deliberately to "purify" and refine a traditional order so as to be "better" than his precedessors.

Legislation

Nowhere are the qualities of the First Reign displayed more fully and clearly than in the famous "Laws of the Three Seals," the product of the grand recodification of Siamese law in 1805. Here the tension between tradition and innovation is particularly evident both in the substance and in the style of the code.

At the beginning of his reign, Rama I's actions in the field of legislation were, at least in part, conventional. For the most part, he could simply reaffirm the accumulated legal corpus he inherited from his predecessors, and in confirming the judgments of the courts act in accordance with the received wisdom of tradition. There were problems in doing so: as late as 1795 it was estimated that only one-ninth or one-tenth of the Ayudhyan legal literature had survived the holocaust of 1767, and a retired judge from old Ayudhya had to be brought in to act as a consultant.[68] In addition, the unusual disorder of the Buddhist monkhood in the wake of warfare and Taksin's eccentricities required special legislation unprecedented in the legal tradition of Ayudhya.

It was not unheard of for kings, in the course of reviewing court judgments or considering appeals, to find on examination and reflection that the existing laws were not adequate to cover a new situation, or to find that older laws no longer were in accord with present-day sensibilities. King Borommakot, for example, found several old laws too lenient on offenders, and revised them by decree in the 1750s.[69] Rama I did much of the same

---

[68] KTSD, V, 295-299 (Phraratchakamnot mai, 28, March 7, 1795).

[69] KTSD, V, 188 (Phraratchakamnot kao, 64, May 12, 1754); and 188-192 (Phraratchakamnot kao, 65, June 12, 1755).

through out his reign,[70] though the overwhelming bulk of his judicial decisions probably simply confirmed the existing law.[71] Nonetheless, the number of separate, new pieces of legislation from the First Reign prior to 1805—some eighty separate decrees, royal ordinances, laws, proclamations, etc.—seems slowly to have brought the king to consider a more ambitious approach to his legislative duties.

Finally, at the beginning of 1805 a divorce case was brought to the king by disquieted judges who felt that a decision in accordance with the law would violate their sense of justice. In brief, the case involved a certain woman Pom, who had successfully sued in the provincial courts for a divorce from her husband Bunsi, with restoration of her premarital property. Bunsi appealed, alleging his wife's pre-litigation adultery with one of the judges in the case, and arguing that if he had sued for divorce, his wife, being the guilty party, would not have regained her property.[72] The judges in the case agreed with Bunsi, but could find no justification in the existing legal codes for denying Pom's petition. The King agreed that this decision offended his sense of equity. He had the various legal libraries searched for laws that might clarify the issues, but found none. In a royal decree of January 31, 1805, he reviewed the case and the issues. He pointed to what he had accomplished by the Tipitaka revision of 1788-89, and the procedures that had been followed then, and saw the present situation to be analogous: the laws of previous kings had disappeared, the remaining texts were in a state of confusion, and justice itself was threatened. He therefore appointed a commission of eleven judges and royal pundits to revise or edit (*chamra*) all the legal texts from beginning to end. They were to make the laws accord with the Pali (presumably of the Tipitaka), eradicate errors and duplication, and arrange the various sections

---

[70] E.g., KTSD, IV, 262 (Phraratchabanyat, 3, 1786).

[71] For example, a decree of 1788 stating that the Chief Justice's judgment was in accordance with "ancient tradition" and should be affirmed (KTSD, IV, 263-264, Phraratchabanyat, 5).

[72] The case is given at the beginning of the "Laws of the Three Seals," KTSD, I, 1-3, dated January 31, 1805.

logically; "and then His Majesty would himself strive to revise those laws that were irregular or defective so that they would be in accordance with justice, as His Majesty graciously wishes that [the laws] would be of use to kings who would reign in the future."[73]

It was hardly unusual for law cases reaching the King on appeal to provoke a re-examination of the law, and on occasion a revision of, or addition to, the existing codes.[74] The corpus of Ayudhya law surviving in the 1805 recension has preserved our knowledge of dozens of individual cases, dating back in some instances as far as the fourteenth and fifteenth centuries (if the dates can be trusted).[75] In all such examples, however, individual cases had raised only their own peculiar issues. For example, when in 1643 Chinese seafarers quarrelled over liability for the loss of a chartered ship, the king found it necessary only to add a new section to the law on hiring, lending, buying, and selling.[76] It is difficult to believe that anyone in 1805 would have expected Rama I to do anything more than that when faced with a troublesome divorce case. He could simply have added a clause to the law on husband and wife.[77]

Why did he not do so? Why did he decide instead on a wholesale revision of the laws? A minimal approach to an answer is to argue that the king found his court without the full set of laws any good monarch ought to have. But why, if for twenty-three years he had constantly been reviewing legal cases, presumably making frequent reference to the old codes, and if he had complained ten years earlier about the lack of nine-tenths of the old texts, should it have taken him so long to act? It can be argued that he first tried the traditional approach, legislating only when and where specific legal needs became apparent. I

---

[73] KTSD, I, 3-6.

[74] See above, note 67.

[75] For example, KTSD, I, 197, 316; II, 209, 244; III, 1, 22, 111, 132, 164, 290; IV, 89, 98, 155.

[76] KTSD, III, 132-135. (This is a fascinating case!)

[77] Indeed, he actually did so in the months while his legal commission was at work: KTSD, II, 248-250 (Phra aiyakan laksana phua mia, §75, March 25, 1805), dealing specifically with a matter of divorce.

would like to suggest that it took the king two decades to become sufficiently acquainted with the law (and perhaps to lose a certain layman's awe of the legal tradition) to first realize the need for a thorough revision, and to dare to undertake it.

The most formidable obstacle in the way of assessing Rama I's legislative activities is our lack of knowledge of Ayudhya law. We know almost nothing of Ayudhya law save for what was incorporated into the Three Seals code. The law codes of other Thai kingdoms such as Lan Na and Lan Sang are of almost no assistance to us because they are much less comprehensive, and were constructed on different principles.[78] Our best evidence has to be the 1805 code itself.

The "Three Seals" law is probably not all that Rama I might have hoped it would be. It was put together in eleven months, including copying time, resulting in a text that now amounts to five volumes, with 1,698 printed pages. Some decrees are repeated twice, and there is a good deal of minor duplication and messy organization. It remains, however, a remarkably systematic and relatively well-organized work. It is structured around the legal categories and principles of the ancient Indian legal tradition, best represented by the "Laws of Manu" *dharmasastra* tradition as domesticated in the Southeast Asian world by the Mons.[79]

Judging from internal evidence, the commission of 1805 proceeded by grouping laws under the various legal categories specified by the *Dharmasastra* (*Thammasat*), the eternal truths of law. Within each category, subcategories are ranged, and everywhere earlier laws precede late ones. The framework of logical arrangement everywhere seems to have been made highly visible, partly by repeated quotations (in Pali) from the Thammasat, and partly by inserted comments indicating the end of one section and the beginning of another.[80]The critical

---

[78] There is an extensive published literature in Thai and Lao on the legal traditions of Lan Na and Laos which awaits scholarly treatment.

[79] The Siamese debt to the Mons in this regard is specifically acknowledged: KTSD, I, 8.

[80] A few random examples: KTSD, III, 113-114, 163, 242, 246, etc.

significance of this logical framework, however, is that it functions primarily to relate all law to a single absolute standard of justice. It seems entirely characteristic of Rama I that he should have required that the new law code be so constructed. He had called for doing so in his decree establishing the legal commission; and the standard evident throughout the code is the same as that of his decrees and actions discussed above. It is not a standard simply stretching back in time as the accumulated, timeless fruit of the actions of his royal predecessors and ancient lawgivers. Instead (and this may simply be a matter of emphasis or degree), it is a standard interpreted and stated in and for a specific historic time by specific historic individuals. Perhaps unintentionally, but probably not, the cumulative effect of a reading of the laws is the evidence they give of individual kings, over more than four centuries, legislating on the basis of values that have become increasingly more Buddhist, and increasingly attuned to Siamese conditions, values, and sensibilities.[81]

The 1805 code contains an enormous variety of legislation, most of it general in nature. One of the hallmarks of Rama I's own contributions to it, in the form of specific legislation in response to specific situations, is the style of his decrees. Invariably these begin by describing the facts of a case, and then proceed to a reasoned discussion of the need for legislation in both moral and practical terms. Often the king will refer to religious, historical, or legal precedent before prescribing specific laws.[82] These are quite unlike the legislation of any previous Siamese king. Even when Ayudhya kings cited the cases that provoked specific decrees, they never went any further to justify legislating, whereas Rama I constantly does so, and does so in reasoned fashion. It was not in the nature of traditional Siamese kingship to have to give reasons for doing anything, yet Rama I was always doing so. Something seems to have changed: Was it simply a matter of changing times? Had the relationship between king and subject changed? Or the relationship between man and the world? It was not just Rama I, for all his successors conducted legislation in much the same manner.

---

[81] See, for example, the law on immoral dealings with a child, KTSD, IV, 281-282 (Phraratchabanyat, 17, 1794).

[82] See the "Phraratchakamnot mai [New Decrees]," KTSD, V, 193-372.

Further light on this question might be shed by an examination of some aspects of the literary life of the First Reign

Literature and History

The role of literature in premodern Siamese life has hardly begun to be systematically investigated. There is ample evidence, in folk tales, toponymy, and mural painting, of quite widespread general acquaintance with such literary classics as the *Ramayana*,[83] but very little by way of written evidence before the First Reign. In addition, far too little scholarly work has been done on the great literary works of the early Bangkok period for us now to be able to draw any definite conclusions about the considerable literary accomplishments of the First Reign. For the present, we can only comment briefly on the range of literary activities in the First Reign, and attempt a rough assessment of their significance.

Rama I's most ambitious literary undertaking was his effort to reconstitute (or perhaps to construct for the first time) the full Rama saga, very little of which had survived the sack of Ayudhya. In the early years of his reign the king appears to have ordered the systematic collection of all available material concerning the Ramayana. When this was completed, in 1796 or 1797, he personally directed an enormous cooperative effort to write down the entire saga in verse.[84] This is the only complete version of the Ramayana known in Siam, a work of enormous scope and length.[85] The work clearly was completed by many

---

[83] See Christian Velder, "Notes on the Saga of Rama in Thailand," JSS 56, pt. 1 (Jan. 1968), 33-46.

[84] Velder, "Saga of Rama," p. 36; Prince Dhani, "Reconstruction," pp. 32-33; P. Schweisguth, *Étude sur la litterature siamoise* (Paris, 1951), pp. 186-190; Ki Yupho, "Lao rüang nangsü Ramakian [Concerning the Ramakian]," in King Taksin, *Bot lakhòn Ramakian* (Bangkok, 1963), pp. 132-178. Cf. also Sathian Koset (Phya Anuman Rajadhon), *Upakòn Ramakian* [Ramakian Handbook] (Bangkok, 1972), pp. 233-269; and S. Singaravelu, "A Comparative Study of the Sanskrit, Tamil, Thai and Malay Versions of the Story of Rama, With Special Reference to the Process of Acculturation in the Southeast Asian Versions," JSS 56, pt. 2 (July 1968), 137-185.

[85] King Rama I, *Ramakian* (2 vols.; Bangkok: Sinlapa Bannakhan, 1967). This edition runs to 3,181 pages. The colophon gives the date of completion as Nov. 19, 1797.

hands, and is uneven in style, and repetitious; but the king himself is said to have revised and approved the entire work.[86]

A number of motivations may have impelled the king to sponsor and direct this work. The simple fact of royal patronage of the arts may have been important in establishing a certain cultural leadership role for the court, for no other institution in Siamese society had the resources to fully serve this function. The completion of such a centrally important text as the *Ramayana* could function to provide the capital's artists with ample material and inspiration for decorating the large numbers of new buildings that were constructed in those early years of the new capital. However, Rama I is said to have also intended that literary materials, presented in dramatic form both outdoors and within the palaces and homes of the ruling élite, might be used to inculcate and popularize ideas and values.[87] Not only is there much in the Rama saga of considerable utility for these purposes, models of virtuous conduct, faithful love, bravery, loyalty to king, justice, and the like, but also there is much that was directly applicable to the king's own situation. To begin with, the geographical setting of the story is clearly Siam, and the royal seat of the hero Rama is obviously Bangkok. The saga's Rama ascends his throne because of his virtue and bravery after a long period of dark and dangerous warfare. He triumphs because he is virtuous and brave, and worthy of the loyalty of those who assist him. As depicted by the royal author and his literary assistants, the saga's Rama is no prisoner of fate, compelled to work out a foreordained karma; nor is he a pampered princeling favored by benevolent gods. The hero Rama is in charge of his own destiny, and his success depends upon his own wits, his virtue, and his valor. Just as the world of men had moved to the "head" of the *Traiphum*, so too had man, now unable to depend on divine assistance, taken charge of his own world, led by a ruler whose primary virtues were moral rectitude, decisiveness, and bravery.

The literary efflorescence of the First Reign underlines in many different ways the changes that were taking place in the

---

[86] Schweisguth, *Étude*, p. 184.
[87] Ibid., pp. 184-185.

Siamese world in the last half of the eighteenth century. The catastrophe of 1767 had been profoundly unsettling. Men had not been able to avoid death and destruction through divine intervention, and Rama I and his contemporaries recognized that they could avoid similar calamities in the future only by accepting responsibility for their fate and acting in consonance with the moral order to improve themselves and their society. The world around them, moreover, was becoming more dangerous, and their own kingdom was now much more clearly seen as but one amongst many. They were not unappreciative of what they could learn from others, and a great deal of the literary output of the First Reign reflects a propensity for borrowing widely from throughout the world known to them. Like Javanese rulers of the same period, Rama I encouraged a great deal of translation and adaptation of foreign literature: for example, the *Rachathirat*, the chronicle of the Mon kings of Pegu; the *Dalang* and *Inao* from Java; the *Unarut*, based on a section of the *Mahabharata*; the *Duodecagon* from Persia; the *Mahavamsa* and *Jinakalamali* translated from Pali; and the *Sai Han* and the "Romance of the Three Kingdoms" from Chinese.[88] (And should, perhaps, Rama I's edition of the *Ramayana* be seen in the same light?) It is important that most of the foreign classics translated during the First Reign were recognized as providing more than entertainment. The Mon, Persian, and Chinese works in particular were held up as repositories of admirable political and martial values and of appropriate modes of behavior. Note, however, that such virtues now are confirmed, or even validated, from *outside* the Siamese-Buddhist tradition. This universalization of values again implies something about the ability of man to define his own identity and actively choose his own values, an ability now denoting a cultural self-confidence that had not been nearly as readily apparent in Ayudhya a few decades earlier.

It is difficult to assess the significance of the fact that a good deal of the literary production of the First Reign was prose, rather

---

[88] Prince Dhani, "Reconstruction," pp. 33-36; and Saeng Manavidura, "Some Observations on the Jinakalamalipakarana," in N. A. Jayawickrama, tr., *The Sheaf of Garlands of the Epochs of the Conqueror* (London, 1968), pp. xxxiv-xxxv.

than the poetry customarily composed at court, for we know too little of the prose of the Ayudhya period. We may safely assume that the prose translations from foreign languages were intended to be read, rather than performed, and that they functioned mainly as entertainment. Already by the Second Reign (1809-1824) such works as the *Sam kok* (the "Romance of the Three Kingdoms") were well-known to literati and government officials in the capital,[89] in a way that secular prose works never before had circulated.

But when one speaks of premodern Siamese literature, it is still verse to which one refers; and however novel the First Reign prose may have been, the poetry certainly was no less so. In a short, unpublished essay, Nidhi Aeusrivongse delineates strong differences between the verse of late Ayudhya and that of the early Bangkok period.[90] In Ayudhya verse, there was a marked dichotomy between court and folk traditions. The metrical patterns of court poetry (*khlong* and *chan*) were elaborate, flowery, stilted, and far removed from the everyday language and the sort of word-play common in Thai villages. Folk metres (in *phleng*, "songs"), on the other hand, were much simpler and closer to ordinary language. Court literature was written down in order to be performed and fulfilled didactic and ritual functions; while folk poetry was never written, but was simply performed for entertainment. In the closing decades of the Ayudhya period these two traditions began to converge, but it is only in the early Bangkok period that a truly new literature begins to emerge. The most important characteristics of the early Bangkok literature, evident already in the verse of the First Reign, demonstrate what amounts to the ascendency of the folk tradition over the literary heritage of the Ayudhya period. The metrical forms of early Bangkok court poetry (with the exception of that of a few persistent classicists) were based on the simpler *klòn* metre, ultimately derived from vernacular folk sources.

---

[89] *Sam kok* [Romance of the Three Kingdoms]. (12th ed.; Bangkok, 1968), I, Preface.

[90] Nidhi, "A Sketch of Early Bangkok Literature," Sept. 20, 1978. I am deeply indebted to Dr. Nidhi for writing this lengthy essay for me. My debt to him should be obvious in the paragraphs that follow.

The didactic and ritual functions of Ayudhya court poetry atrophied, to be replaced by a much greater willingness simply to entertain. With the writing down of massive, complete literary works carrying through a long involved line of action, these works no longer could be performed in full, but could be read for enjoyment. Where virtually all the court poetry of the Ayudhya period had begun with a ritualistic invocation to Hindu gods and/ or the Buddhist Triple Gems, that of the early Bangkok period either lacks such formulae entirely, or begins with a secular introduction. The best example here is Rama I's *Ramayana*, the *Ramakian*: The invocation at its beginning ".. is in fact a eulogy of Rama I, but it is different from ... [similar invocations in the poetry of King Narai's reign] because while Narai's eulogy consists of poetical allusions to Hindu gods, Rama I's eulogy is a matter-of-fact description of what the king had done for the state and Buddhism."[91] Similarly, the poetry of the early Bangkok period depicts the real, empirical world; not an unattainable, ethereal never-never land inhabited by much "better" people than mere mortals, but a recognizable world peopled by others not unlike those around us. In short, in style, form, and content the literature of the First Reign much more closely approached life than the poetry of the late Ayudhya period. Both for this reason, and because it was increasingly widely circulated in written form, it was accessible to a much broader public (though, without printing, by no means yet a mass audience) than Ayudhya court poetry had been.

Finally, in a manner parallel to his literary endeavors, Rama I undertook to rewrite Siamese history in order to create a more relevant past for the service of his own age.[92] Working on the basis of earlier such efforts made in the reign of King Taksin, Rama I's chroniclers were preoccupied by several critical themes. In their treatment of the last kings of Ayudhya, they naturally

[91] Ibid.

[92] These comments are based closely upon the important new work of Nidhi Aeusrivongse, *Prawatsat Rattanakosin*. On the same subject, see also Craig J. Reynolds, "Religious Historical Writing and the Legitimation of the First Bangkok Reign," in *Perceptions of the Past in Southeast Asia*, ed. Anthony Reid and David Marr (Singapore, 1979), pp. 90-107.

were concerned to explain the reasons for the fall of Ayudhya, and this primarily in terms of moral decay. They argued that the Ban Phlu Luang dynasty (1688-1767) had unjustly seized power from a good king; they measured each king's moral worth in heavily Buddhist terms, irrespective of administrative accomplishments or martial success, and they viewed the dynasty as lacking in "royal majesty," particularly of the sort confirmed by such things as omens. Because the last kings of Ayudhya were not good Buddhist monarchs, Ayudhya fell. At the same time, of course, they implicitly were making a case why Rama I deserved to be king, justifying his seizure of power from Taksin, and providing the society with a set of criteria in terms of which Rama I could be judged.

The chroniclers' extensive elaboration of a standard by which kings should be judged exclusively in Buddhist moral terms is of immense significance. It was developed at the expense of simple "divine right" or legitimation by descent. Given the fact that both Taksin and Rama I may possibly be the two kings of lowliest origins in Siamese history, they could hardly do otherwise than create a firm new basis for royal legitimacy in abstract philosophical and moral terms.[93] However, with this development a good deal of the mystery and magic began to drain away from the monarchy.

We need not conclude that Rama I and his advisers invented a new theory of royal legitimacy when they came around to rewriting the chronicles. Rather, the views that came to be expressed in the chronicles, like those in the *Traiphum* and in the "Thammasat" section of the "Three Seals" code, first expressed in their most general form many centuries earlier, were recognized by the leaders of Rama I's generation as "empirical" truth, consistent with their own experience. They took from their own past, then, not an intact order, but rather the fundamental principles upon which they conceived that order to have been built. In their own struggle to understand what was happening to them and to their society, they discarded the accretions of custom and habit that encrusted the traditional order, and they reinterpreted eternal

---

[93] Nidhi, *Prawatsat Rattanakosin*, p. 36.

truths in the light of their own experience and understanding. Unsystematic ideas about animistic spirits or brahmanical deities were not very useful in this effort, while Buddhist thought came increasingly to be seen as pertinent and utilitarian. Theirs was ultimately a more critical, rationalistic, and pragmatic way of looking at the world than the vision of their Ayudhyan forefathers, and yet it was a way that still provided them with positive prescriptions for improving their lives.

Rama I ran a series of risks from the beginning of his reign. He was a usurper, even though there is no evidence that he actively participated in the overthrow of Taksin, or even that he was ever anything but loyal to Taksin. However, as a usurper he was vulnerable. He did little to lessen that vulnerability in the ways that others might have done. He did not marry any of the female descendents of the Ayudhya or Thonburi lines though he could have done so. Taksin had never taken the definitive steps that would sever the connection with the Ayudhyan monarchy: He never underwent a full coronation, and he never formally proclaimed the transfer of the capital from Ayudhya to Thonburi. Rama I, on the contrary, did both, and both these steps were fraught with risk. The chronicle of Ayudhya sponsored by Rama I and edited by Sondet Phra Phonnarat towards the end of the First Reign is the first version of the royal chronicles that treats Ayudhya as a concluded era, of thirty-four kings and 417 years. The name of Ayudhya was continued in the formal name for Bangkok, but there had been a clear and definitive break with the past, and for that break Rama I actively took the responsibility.

"A Subtle Revolution"

None of the arguments presented above have been based on thorough examination of the relevant sources. All the most critical texts—the *Traiphum* and *Traiphum lok winitchai*, the ceremonial texts, the "Three Seals" code, and the *Ramakian* and associated literature—still are in need of exhaustive study by specialists. At the same time, none of those thus far responsible for the English studies of Rama I's "reconstruction" or "restoration" have either covered all this material or have asked of it the questions with which we have been concerned here. If conclusions now are to be drawn from this study, let them for the present be regarded as hypotheses to be tested in further research as the study of Siam's intellectual history gets under way.

The primary thrust of the argument stated above is that, although Rama I formally reaffirmed Ayudhyan traditions, accomplished no formal structural or institutional changes, and lived up to all the traditional expectations that Siamese of that age had of kingly behavior, he sharply broke with Ayudhyan tradition. Far from "restoring" or "reconstructing" Ayudhya, he fundamentally changed it. He did so, however, in a subtle way, so successfully that the changes he introduced hardly seemed significant at the time.

All of Rama I's innovations went in essentially the same direction. All of them involved a change in focus that brought rational man clearly to the center of the stage of history, mentally in control of his own world through the exercise of his critical faculties. Though it was more a shift in degree than an absolute change, man began increasingly to self-consciously and critically examine the rules by which he lived and constantly gauge them against his improving understanding of the eternal truths of Buddhism. One critical aspect of this shift in focus was in the redefinition of Siamese kingship, and in the prescribed activities and ceremonial that had surrounded it. These might be expected to be the elements of Siamese civilization most resistant to change, simply because of the extent to which the structure of the entire society was refracted through the prism of kingship. Perhaps it was easier for Rama I and his contemporaries to address this challenge because of the extent to which traditional kingship had been discredited, or at least de-mystified, by the collapse of 1767 and the excesses of Taksin's reign. It is difficult to believe that Rama I could have accomplished much along these lines if a substantial segment of the élite of his generation had not shared at least some of his perceptions of the proper role of the monarchy and of religion. It fell to the king himself, however, to take the initiative in all the major undertakings we have examined above. At every critical juncture, in issuing the first new Ecclesiastical

Laws in 1782, in calling for a new *Traiphum* in 1783, in initiating the revision of the Tipitaka in 1788, in organizing the writing of a complete *Ramayana* in 1797, in establishing a commission to codify the law in 1805, and in commissioning a new history towards the end of his reign, Rama I chose the difficult and even the dangerous course of innovation instead of the easier course of copying from the manuscripts of the past. He repeatedly chose creativity in preference to repetition or replication.

The king, however, did not exist in a vacuum, and the history of the First Reign, even its intellectual history, is hardly the history of a single individual, however creative he may have been. It is not just that countless other individuals—monks and laypeople, jurists and poets, and high and low officials—were intimately involved in the major projects we have outlined here. It is also that every one of those projects involved some sort of "audience" to whom texts were addressed; texts accessible to them both collectively and individually, orally or through reading. The very act of "text-making" implies the necessity for communicating that both parties to the relationship seem to have felt. In order to build some sense of social and, especially, moral community, the bases of that community had to be shared and mutually understood.

What Nidhi says about the literature of the early Bangkok period is susceptible to broader application: He conceives of a greatly expanded role for a bourgeois-official class in the public life of the early Bangkok period.[94] Without now discussing the social history of the period, we can note that the official class of early Bangkok, though genealogically connected with the official families of late Ayudhya, differed from them in several important respects. Many of them had close relationships with the immigrant Chinese mercantile community (as Taksin and Rama I both had), some wealth based on commerce in goods and money rather than simply based on official control of manpower, and some cosmopolitan sense of belonging in a world

---

[94] Nidhi, "A Sketch," p. 6.

that extended far beyond Siam. They were sensitive to foreign opinion and at times were intrigued with foreign ideas, and yet they were proud of themselves and of their accomplishments in the harshly real world of their own age. Certainly they had shared in the construction of their Siam, and they must have felt that they deserved to share fully in the life of the state. Perhaps the translations of foreign literature into Siamese symbolically represents the integration of some of their interests and values into Siamese tradition and, in a sense, validates their position.

Siam could never be the same again because of the choices that Rama I had made. Many members of the Siamese élite in the two generations succeeding him would go on to do much, as he had done, to build on the education, the foundations of which he had laid, to use their trained, well-informed minds to continue to distill the eternal truths of human experience out from the broth of Siamese tradition, and to use their perception and understanding of those truths to attempt reform and improve the world in which they lived. It was such habits of mind, instilled in Rama II, Rama III, Dit and That Bunnag, Prince Wongsathiratsanit, Prince Paramanuchitchinorot, King Mongkut, and their peers, that would stand Siam in such good stead when they confronted the dangers and opportunities posed by the West to their society in the decades that followed Rama I's death in 1809.

What are we to call this intellectual shift of the First Reign? To associate it with such terms as "the Enlightenment" or "rationalism" is to attribute to it qualities and associations it did not necessarily have. In some ways it amounted to the beginnings of a sort of Buddhist "Reformation," to the extent that it involved a return to first principles and the clearing away of the accretions of centuries of custom and long-standing habit. It was clearly a change totally or mainly within an existing cultural tradition, drawing upon the intellectual strengths of that tradition. It is perhaps worth saying that Rama I's "subtle intellectual revolution" may serve to remind us that "Siamese tradition" was by no means unchanging, and that Europe and America were not the only lively centers of new ideas in the last quarter of the eighteenth century.

If the hypotheses outlined above withstand the critical examination of another generation of historians, we may soon reach the point where we wish to consider how it was that so much of the world, including many areas of Southeast Asia, came to be so exciting in the last half of the eighteenth century. We will certainly wish at least to look more closely at Rama I and his court in the hope of identifying more clearly the individual and environmental impulses of creativity. We will wish to discover the social and economic forces that underlay the power of this new Siam. At the very least, we still need to know a great deal more about Rama I himself. If this essay succeeds only in arousing new interest in his reign, it will have done the study of Siamese history some service.

Genealogy of the Ruling Family of Nan

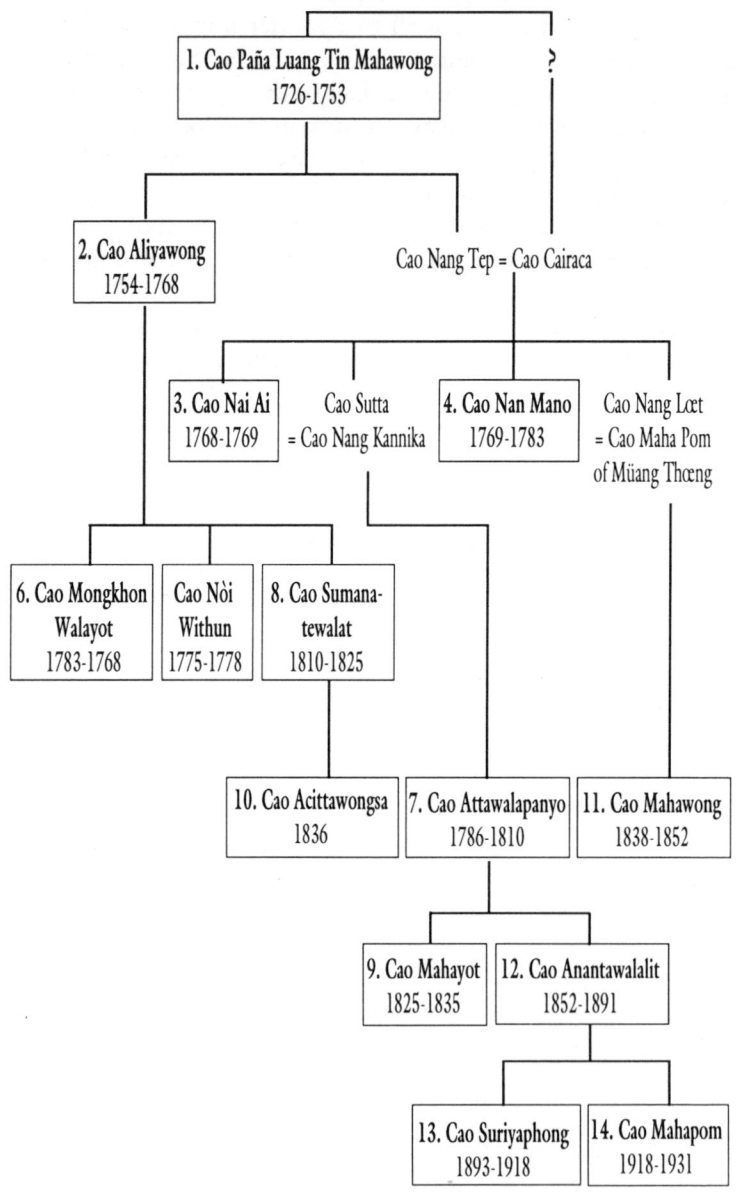

ASSAULT BY GHOSTS:
POLITICS AND RELIGION IN NAN
IN THE EIGHTEENTH CENTURY*

In the chronicles of the old principality of Nan, in northern Thailand, there appears the following episode centering on Wat Phrathat Chæ Hæng, the great Buddhist reliquary monument and associated monastery that since the fourteenth century has stood at the heart of Thai life in Nan.

On reaching the ninth month in that year 1157 [May/June 1795] there was a strange occurrence at Müang Ngua. It was a warning to the people from the *devas*. It took the form of ghosts going around the city assaulting monks and people. After these beatings they dropped written messages, saying that they had come from the *deva* guardians of the cetiya of the Chæ Hæng Reliquary, and that the cetiya containing the holy relics was now in a very bad state of disrepair and that no attempt had been made to restore it to its original condition. The holy shrine had to be restored to its beauty as when it was first built, and the *devas* would continue annoying and assaulting until it was rebuilt and made as beautiful as when it was first built. "When the shrine has been repaired and made beautiful we will cease annoying and tormenting you," the messages said. Cao Mongkhonwalayot then went to Cao Atthawalapañño,

---

* *Crossroads* 4:2 (1989), 63-70. Reprinted with the permission of the Center for Southeast Asian Studies, Northern Illinois University.

the governor, and told him about the occurrences in Müang Ngua and the warning of the *deva* guardians of Wat Chæ Hæng. Cao Atthawala appointed his uncle Cao Mongkhonwalayot, Nai Aliya, and several monks to supervise the work of reconstruction. Thereupon, in the second month [October], Cao Phraya Mongkhonwalayot, the uncle, accompanied by the princes and their men, and by the leading monks of Müang Ngua, began the construction and restoration of the Holy Reliquary of Phu Phiang Chæ Hæng. The work took five months to complete. On Tuesday, the eighth day of the sixth month [February 15, 1796], Cao Atthawalapañño performed the ceremony of placing the finial atop the cetiya. When the restoration was completed there was a celebration. The ghosts that had been tormenting the monks and the public disappeared.[1]

---

[1] *The Nan Chronicle,* tr. Prascet Churatana, ed. David K. Wyatt (Ithaca, 1966; Cornell University Southeast Asia Program, Data Paper 59), p. 56, slightly revised. I have a new version of this translation forthcoming. There are three manuscript versions of this tale so far known to me: (1) "Phün wongsa mahakasat thang lai tangtæ Phraya Samantarat phon ma læ phün wongsa caonai ton sawœi ratchasombat nai müang Pua læ müang Nan," palm-leaf ms., Wat Phranet, tambon Wiang Nüa, amphœ Müang, cangwat Nan, from microfilm in the Social Research Institute, Chiang Mai University, SRI 82.107.05.043, ff° 157-158, a version virtually identical to that published in *Prachum phongsawadan,* pt. 10 and translated as *The Nan Chronicle;* (2) "Prawat tang müang Nan," palm-leaf ms., Wat Phra Kœt, amphœ Wiang Nüa, cangwat Nan, from microfilm in the Social Research Institute, Chiang Mai University, SRI 82.107.05.045 f° 171/1 ff.; and (3) "Phün wongsa caonai ton sawœi ratchasombat nai Müang Pua læ Müang Nan," Wat Dòn Kæo, t. Nai Müang, a. Müang, c. Nan, from microfilm in the Social Research Institute, Chiang Mai University, SRI 82.107.05.044, f° 126 line 4 ff. There are few significant differences between these texts, the earliest of which appears to date from (perhaps) the 1830s. The well-known chronicle of the Chæ Hæng reliquary covers only the period down to the eighteenth century. A modern version of the reliquary chronicle first printed in Northern Tai script in 1923 takes this "ghost story" from version (1) above (or its sources).

It is obviously difficult to take this story at face value; but it is also unwise to dismiss it as simple foolishness or superstition. A careful examination of the story might serve to tell us something about the relations between religion and politics in the eighteenth-century northern Tai world, and perhaps something also about the way in which these people thought about their own history and how it should be written and transmitted to subsequent generations.[2]

Though to do so might seem to betray modern prejudices against "superstition" and ghosts and guardian spirits, it would not be unreasonable to dismiss the supernatural elements and begin with the assumption that it was men, and not "spirits" who wandered the roads and pathways of Müang Ngua[3] "assaulting monks and people." But who were these people? and what motivated them so seriously to disturb the public order as to provoke a response from the ruler? The answers may lie in the earlier history of Nan, up to the year 1795.

Nan's history had long been troubled. The principality's independence lasted only until 1448, when Nan became a dependency of Chiang Mai. When the Burmese took Chiang Mai in 1558, they also took Nan, though the men sent to rule Nan thereafter usually were Chiang Mai Tai rather than Burmese. Warfare, both before the Burmese hegemony and during it, regularly devastated and depopulated the area of the upper Nan valley; and such troubles were to continue down to 1795.

---

[2] There surely are other such stories in the Northern chronicles. One that has come to my notice is that in "The Padaeng Chronicle," *The Padæng Chronicle and the Jengtung State Chronicle Translated*, tr. Sao Saimöng Mangrai (Ann Arbor: Center for South and Southeast Asian Studies, Univ. of Mich., 1981; Michigan Paper on South and Southeast Asia, 19), pp. 113 ff. This story does not, however, seem susceptible to the sort of explanation offered here for the Nan "ghost story."

[3] Müang Ngua cannot be located on the maps publicly available. Because Müang Ngua and the Phrathat Chæ Hæng temple are so closely associated in the text, I assume Ngua probably should be taken as the area located in the two kilometer stretch between the temple and the Nan River, on land sloping gently to the west.

A key juncture occurred early in the eighteenth century, when a commoner (that is, one not born in a family of ruling *cao*) in charge of Nan "realized that Nan had no ruling prince"[4] and persuaded the Burmese to allow the appointment of a prince of the Chiang Mai ruling house as ruler of Nan in 1726; a man known as Cao Phraya Luang Tin Mahawong. The man who urged this appointment later realized that he had made a mistake, the chronicle tells us without explanation, and shot himself in the mouth.

Cao Aliyawong Wanthòk, the eldest son of Cao Luang Tin, was ruling when all the north country exploded in chaos during the Siam-Burma wars of the 1760s. Even a cursory examination of the four reigns beginning with Aliyawong reveals grave divisions and problems within the Nan polity.

Cao Aliyawong in 1765 sent his nephew, Cao Nai Ai, with troops to assist in the Burmese capture of Ayudhya; but Aliyawong himself defeated Burmese troops in 1766 and fled to Laos when the Burmese counterattacked in 1767.

The Burmese rewarded Cao Nai Ai by appointing him governor in 1768, but within a few months he made a trip to Laos and died there, perhaps by poison. The Burmese then appointed Cao Nai Ai's brother, Cao Nan Mano, as ruler in 1769, and he remained so only to 1775.

At this point, Cao Noi Witun, one of the sons of Cao Aliyawong, was serving under the Burmese in Chiang Mai, but joined the Lan Na rebellion against the Burmese. When the Siamese forces called in from the south finished helping the rebels expel the Burmese, they took Witun to Lampang, and then sent him to Nan as governor. There his cousin, Nan Mano, yielded and fled, ultimately into Laos. Witun's success was short-lived: the Burmese counterattacked, and Witun and his father, the former ruler Aliyawong, held them off only in the extreme south of Nan, at what is now Tha Pla in Uttaradit province. For a year or two, neither Witun nor Nan Mano lived in Nan, and governing authority there seems to have been tenuous indeed. Finally, in

---

[4] *The Nan Chronicle*, p. 30.

1778 Cao Kavila (the ruler of Lampang who was soon to become the first ruler in the new house of Chiang Mai) brought an army to the region, charged Witun with disloyalty to Siam, and sent him to Thonburi, where he soon died. Cao Mano now had a clear field to rule alone, and he returned from Laos to govern from Müang Ngua—apparently in the vicinity of the great Buddhist reliquary at Wat Phrathat Chæ Hæng, across the Nan River from the present-day site of the city of Nan.

There followed a period of extraordinary confusion, even when compared with the decades that had gone before. One army after another—from Siam in the south, from Chiang Mai, and from Burmese Chiang Sæn—raided the Nan valley for population, and at one point Mano was taken to Chiang Sæn and then to Thœng, where he died in 1784. On his death, the Burmese named his nephew, Cao Atthawalapañño, as governor of Nan. This prince accepted the post, but remained in Müang Thœng, some 110 km. over the mountains to the northwest of Nan.

Meanwhile, late in 1783 the new King of Siam in Bangkok, Rama I, named Noi Witun's brother, Cao Cantapachot, as ruler of Nan with the title of Cao Phraya Mongkhonwalayot; and this prince stationed himself at Tha Pla, in present-day Uttaradit province. Mongkhonwalayot failed to withstand another Burmese invasion of his state in 1785, and surrendered his province without a fight. Lan Na armies restored order, even to the point of contributing some captured families to the repopulation of Nan; and the stage was set for a confrontation when Cao Atthawalapañño returned to Nan. The tale given by the chronicles is complex and somewhat opaque, but there appears to have been something like what we used to call a "Mexican stand-off" between Atthawalapañño on the one hand and, on the other hand, Mongkhonwalayot and his brother Sumanatewarat.[5] In its wake, Atthawalapañño went to live in Ban Tit Bun Hüang, which I think is just to the south of the present city of Nan, and thus across the river from Müang Ngua. In the following year, 1786, Mongkhonwalayot resigned the rulership in favor of

---

[5] *Ibid.*, pp. 48-49.

Atthawalapañño. Two years later, in 1788, Atthawalapañño went to Bangkok and obtained formal appointment as ruler, while his uncle (and Mongkhonwalayot's brother), Sumanatewarat, was named heir presumptive (*cao phraya hò na*).

At this point our list of named characters in the "ghost story" is nearly complete, and we can pause to consider who they are and what they stand for. First, note that, in the "ghost story," it is the former ruler Mongkhonwalayot who reported the "ghost" incident to his nephew the ruler, Atthawalapañño. By 1795, these two men had for some time represented two opposing tendencies in the immediate politics of the period. Mongkhonwalayot, by now an elderly man, like his brother Noi Witun had sided with the new Lan Na house of Cao Kavila and with Siam in the trials of the preceding two decades. Cao Atthawalapañño, on the other hand, like his two uncles who had preceded him as prince, had more often taken the Burmese side in those conflicts. As can be seen on the accompanying genealogical chart, these political alignments followed the blood lines of two of the children of Cao Luang Tin Mahawong: the descendents of Cao Nang Tep, his daughter, sided with the Burmese, while those of Cao Aliyawong, one of his sons, sided with Siam.

Or is something else going on? It is curious to note that the rulership seems to have alternated between the two sides of the family after the death of the founder of the line, with Cao Aliyawong's line taking reigns numbered 2, 5, 6, 8, and 10, and Cao Nang Tep's line taking reigns numbered 3, 4, 7, 9, and 11 (up to 1851). Is this, like the alternation between rival ruling lines in Kedah in the same period, a balancing of otherwise irresolvable claims? It is difficult to see it as a balancing of rival resource bases, as the chronicles give us little hint of such power; but it is surely noteworthy that the king in Bangkok appointed Atthawala's uncle as his designated heir. On balance, it is probably preferable to consider the split between the two sides of the ruling family as both genealogical and generational, since Mongkhonwalayot was a generation older than Atthawalapañño— uncle and nephew, respectively.

Now it is curious that Atthawalapañño should have been chosen by Bangkok to rule Nan in 1786, given his long association with the Burmese. Indeed, his counterpart and contemporary in Phræ, Cao Mangcai, similarly had served the Burmese and only late rebelled against them. King Rama I in 1787 was still suspicious of Phraya Phræ, for he had lived with the Burmese for a long time, and the king was not certain whether or not his return was a stratagem designed to deceive him. He did not quite trust Phraya Phræ enough to send him back to be governor of Phræ, the position he formerly held. Therefore Phraya Phræ was given a house to live in and was to serve in an official capacity in the capital city [Bangkok].[6]

At the same time, the ruler of Yòng was trusted only sufficiently to be allowed to serve Cao Kavila in Lampang and Chiang Mai. The Burmese, after all, still controlled the Chiang Sæn region, a base from which Phræ, Nan, and Yòng could relatively easily be attacked. And if the king in Bangkok distrusted the ruler of Phræ, some in Nan might have felt justified in mistrusting Cao Atthawalapañño.

In the late 1780s and early 1790s, Nan was extremely weak after decades of almost constant warfare. The chronicle states that "As Müang Nan had been sacked and devastated by war, by now it was an empty city."[7] Under the circumstances, the most important task for a ruler was to increase and hold manpower, without which even defense would be impossible. Cao Atthawala's actions during the first years of his rule can be seen as efforts in this direction, but they may also have caused uneasiness in some.

Cao Atthawala was a curiously peripatetic ruler. On returning from Bangkok in 1788, the chronicle states that "He did not go directly to Nan, but stopped at Müang Ngua. Later,

---

[6] Caophraya Thiphakòrawong, *The Dynastic Chronicles, Bangkok Era, The First Reign*, tr. Thadeus and Chadin Flood (Tokyo, 1978), I, 133-34; Thiphakòrawong, *Phraratchaphongsawadan Krung Rattanakosin chabap Ho Samut hæng Chat, ratchakan thi 1 ... ratchakan thi 2* (Bangkok: Khlang Witthaya, 1962), pp. 141-42.

[7] *The Nan Chronicle*, p. 52.

the people of Nan welcomed him to the city by meeting him at with a stately procession."[8] After entering the city he took up residence in Ban Tit Bun Hüang. A month later he moved to Müang Ngua, after turning over Ban Tit Bun Hüang to a group of "elders." The next year he returned to live in Ban Tit Bun Hüang. In 1792, the chronicle records, he again moved to Ban Tit Bun Hüang, but there is no mention of where he might have been in the interim. And then, in 1793-94, he began moving the capital of Nan 30 kilometers to the south, to Sa. After major construction, including a new dam across the Sa River before its confluence with the Nan River and a major religious foundation, "he then [late in 1794] settled in Müang Sa, leaving Müang Ngua in charge of Cao Mongkhonwalayot and Nai Aliya."[9]

It surely is significant that our "ghost story" immediately follows this reference to the move of the capital, both textually and chronologically. The logic of our texts at this point creates the strong presumption that the "ghosts" of Chæ Hæng were protesting not just the neglect of the ancient monument, but also the geographical reordering of hierarchy within the principality.

What would the removal of the capital from the Chæ Hæng/ Ngua/Nan City region to the Sa region have meant? On a material level it reduced the demand for goods and services generated by a prince's household of two hundred or more persons.[10] Among other things, the loss of this wealthier and high-status group would have diminished both daily alms to and princely patronage for the monks of Wat Phu Phiang Chæ Hæng, undermining their prestige and their ability to sustain religious education and other services. For more than four hundred years, Wat Phu Phiang Chæ Hæng had been the focal

---

[8] *Ibid.*
[9] *The Nan Chronicle*, p. 55.
[10] *The Nan Chronicle* (pp. 54-55) gives this figure in reporting that in 1792 "Cao Atthawalapañño, with Cao Mongkhonwalayot, the vice-governor, his family and servants, two hundred in all, moved back to the old city, Ban Tit Bun Hüang."

point of Buddhism in Nan. Though that shrine clearly had fallen on hard times in the period of warfare and depopulation in the late eighteenth century, it had not lost its place in the symbolic hierarchy in the minds of the local population. Chæ Hæ ng was at the center of the traditional world of Nan, and many might have been at least offended, and some perhaps outraged, at losing their place in that world, all the more so because of the psychological shocks of thirty years of warfare and instability.

What, then, happened around Chæ Hæng in August of 1795? It is curious that the "ghosts" working on behalf of the *deva* guardians of Wat Chæ Hæng, though taking the form of *pret* and *yak*, did not necessarily behave as *pret* and *yak*. If I understand such things correctly, such supernatural beings normally work rather more subtly than resorting to simple physical violence: one does not normally think of *pret* and *yak* as beating people up. Nor, one would think, would *pret* and *yak* drop written messages to underline their purpose. Contemporaries wishing to give the *deva* the benefit of the doubt might explain away these actions by concluding that the *deva* were working through ordinary human beings whom they had possessed for the purpose. There is no particular reason to doubt that, indeed, people were being assaulted, and that messages calling for the restoration of the Reliquary were being found.

The monkish chroniclers reporting such episodes, however, were put in a bind. They could not directly write that public protest had brought about the restoration of the Reliquary and the move of the capital back to Nan, for to admit the existence of such protest would work to diminish the authority of the ruler. By expressing the tale in religious and supernatural terms, however, they could both preserve what they considered to be an important episode in their history and make a subtle point for the edification of future princes; that is, "we" care about what happens to "us."

The point was not lost on Cao Atthawalapañño, thanks no doubt to the urgings of his uncle, the former ruler Cao Mongkhonwalayot. The Reliquary cetiya was refurbished. Five years later, in 1800, the ruler had the old city cleaned up; and the next year he "visited the King in Bangkok to ask his permission to move the seat of the government back to the old city of Nan."[11] The remainder of his reign was most successful, literally crowned in 1805 when King Rama I conferred kingly status on Cao Atthawalapanyo, after the Cao had played a major role in expelling the Burmese from the Chiang Sæn region.

What, then, does this episode in the Nan chronicles contribute to our understanding of religion and politics in early northern Thailand? It might lead us to read rather more closely the chronicle evidence concerning religious foundations and renovations. While those interested in political and royal events might be tempted quickly to pass over these, it is readily apparent from the Nan chronicles' treatment of religious affairs that it is preëminently in Buddhist restorations and renovations that rulers—particularly those who come to rule from outside the polity—can be seen as doing what they conceive to be "the people's will." And where popular political protest is virtually unheard of in most of the Northern chronicles, at least this single episode might lead us to undertake a much closer scrutiny of the sources than they previously have been afforded.

SIAM AND LAOS 1767-1827*

In January of 1827 Cao Anu, the ruler of the Lao state of Vientiane, led his armies in a rapid and unopposed march across the Khorat Plateau of Northeast Siam in a sudden attack on his suzerain, the third king of Thailand's Cakri Dynasty. Reacting to Anu's presence only in late February when the Lao vanguard reached Saraburi, three days' march from Bangkok, the Thai soon mounted a counterattack which scattered and expelled the Lao forces. The sack and complete destruction of Vientiane followed, together with a massive resettlement of Lao people on what is now the Thai side of the Mekong, and in the next few years the Thai brought all the former Vientiane territories under direct administration.[1]

The drama of the 1827 rebellion has in many historical accounts overshadowed the important sixty-year period which preceded it and provided the conditions under which it occurred. The object of this paper is to consider this period and distinguish within it a number of elements and events which contributed to the eventual outbreak of rebellion, as well as to attempt to throw some light on a neglected period in the histories of Siam and Laos. This study is based primarily on printed Thai sources, particularly the chronicles of the three major Lao states of this period (Luang Prabang, Vientiane, and Champasak) and the first three reigns of the Chakri Dynasty, and several collections of Thai documents. With these relatively limited sources, only tentative conclusions may be urged, particularly as so few Lao documents

---

*Journal of Southeast Asian History, IV:2 (September 1963), 13-32. Reprinted with the permission of the Department of History, National University of Singapore.

[1] A good account of the Vientiane Rebellion may be found in Walter Vella, Siam Under Rama III (Locust Valley, N.Y., 1957), 80 ff.

for this period are available. Their main import, however, is nonetheless clear: the Vientiane rebellion had its roots in a long period of increasingly active Thai involvement in Lao affairs.

I. The First Thai Invasion of Vientiane, 1778-1779.

The most important ingredient in the events of the 1770s in Laos was the continuing struggle between Siam and Burma, which did not diminish in intensity in the decade following the Burmese sack of Ayudhya in 1767. In order both to strengthen their own forces and to deny strength to their enemy, each side became involved in Lao affairs. The opportunities for both sides were heightened by the deep-seated hostility which existed in the relations between the Lao states themselves, a product of the dynastic schism of the first decade of the century which had resulted in the division of the Kingdom of Lan Chang, and had been aggravated further by Burmese interference, in particular, in Lao affairs.[2] There were thus two major kingdoms with which alliances could be sought, and an alliance made with one of the two would tend to throw the other into an alliance with the opposing side.

Two other elements important in the history of this period should also be mentioned. First, continued Burmese involvement in Laos depended upon their easy access to Laos, which was possible only so long as the Burmese retained a foothold in the Chiang Mai area. When the Burmese finally lost Chiang Mai for the last time in 1798, their influence in Laos came to an end; and, in practice, their activities in Laos were limited from the mid-1770s.[3] Secondly, one should note in the following paragraphs the political effects of Laos' geographical position, which in the end made its continued existence dependent on the will of its neighbors.

In preparation for the final massive attack on Ayudhya, the Burmese commander at Chiang Mai attacked Luang Prabang in

[2] Paul le Boulanger, *Histoire du Laos français* (Paris, 1931) mentions no Thai involvement in Laos in the 18th century until after 1767.

[3] Prince Damrong Rajanubhab, *Thai rop Phama* [Thai Wars With Burma] (Bangkok, 1962), 639, 784.

1764, aided by an army from Vientiane. In addition to many horses, elephants, and supplies for war, the Burmese also carried off one of the king's younger brothers as security for the treaty they obtained, and at the same time concluded an alliance with Vientiane. The prince later escaped, and returned to Luang Prabang to be crowned as King Vongsa. This king set about, early in the 'seventies, to settle his score with Vientiane.[4]

Impressed with renascent Siam, fearful of a vengeful Luang Prabang, and aware that the Burmese, occupied with both Siam and China, could be of no assistance, King Siribunyasan of Vientiane bid for an alliance with Siam in a letter written on 6 April 1770. King Taksin of Thonburi responded favorably and in April of 1771 wrote to confirm the pact and told Siribunyasan to remember that "your enemies will be considered as our own." Explaining that he was moving troops up to Chiang Mai, he suggested that a present of 300 horses would be greatly appreciated.[5]

In his commentary on a major document of this period, King Chulalongkorn expressed some doubt as to Taksin's motives in this correspondence. Taksin, he thought, was not averse to opening friendly relations with Vientiane on a basis of equality only because he intended to bring Vientiane under Thai control in due course. He had no real hopes of obtaining horses from Vientiane, and was not truly interested in adding Siribunyasan's daughter to his household, although he suggested he would accept her. His was but a single goal: to strengthen Siam.[6] In the course of events which followed, such a policy is well in evidence.

---

[4] Phraya Pramuan Wichaphun, *Phongsawadan muang Lan Chang* [Chronicles of Lan Chang] (2nd ed., Bangkok, 1941), 56-7, gives a clear account of this expedition, but dates it in 1756; while Prince Narathip Praphanphong, *Phraratchaphongsawadan Phama* [Royal Chronicles of Burma] (Bangkok, 1962), II, 117-8, gives 1766. I follow here Prince Damrong's *Thai rop Phama,* 336, which shows evidence of having sifted all the relevant sources—Lao, Burmese, and Thai.

[5] Texts of these and succeeding letters are translated in Maha Sila Viravong, *History of Laos* (New York, 1958), 87 ff.

[6] Chulalongkorn, *Cotmaihet khwamsongcam khong krommaluang Narinthewi...la phraratchawican nai phrabat somdet phra Cunlacòmklao caoyuhua* [Memoirs of Princess Narinthewi, With Commentary by King Chulalongkorn] (Bangkok, 1958), 131-2.

This correspondence was interrupted by new warfare. The
Burmese, by the Kaungton Treaty of 1770, put an end to their
war with China and again turned their interests to the East.[7]
Shortly thereafter, early in 1771, Luang Prabang launched its
attack of revenge against Vientiane, and laid siege to the city for
two months.[8] Beleaguered in his capital, King Siribunyasan
appealed, not to the Siamese, who were again on the defensive,
but to the Burmese, who quickly sent 5000 troops from Chiang
Mai under the command of the famous general Posuphala to
attack Luang Prabang from the rear.[9] Apparently the Luang
Prabang army was warned of the approach of the Burmese, for
they hastily retreated home and held off the enemy for fifteen
days. The outcome of the battle is not clear. While some sources
state or imply that the city was taken and sacked,[10] others
indicate that concern for their position at Chiang Mai in the face
of a Siamese attack forced the Burmese to retreat, leaving Luang
Prabang under a negotiated peace as a vassal of Burma.[11]

When King Siribunyasan ascended the throne of Vientiane,[12]
his claim was supported by two officials of the Kingdom, named

[7] D. G. E. Hall, *Burma,* (3rd ed., London, 1960), 91.
[8] "Phongsawadan müang Luang Phrabang [Chronicle of Luang
Prabang]," in *Prachum Phongsawadan* [Collected Chronicles], vol. 11
(Bangkok, 1919), 41. Cited hereafter as *PMLP.*
[9] Maha Sila, 89. The Luang Prabang chronicles state that Vientiane
solicited aid directly from Ava; but Posuphala was commander of Burmese
forces at Chiang Mai, the only Burmese troops, in all probability, which could
have come to Vientiane's rescue in time. This is borne out in the annals of
Chiang Mai, as presented by Phraya Prachakit Kòracak, *Phongsawadan Yonok*
[Chronicles of Yonok] (Bangkok, 1961), 472.
[10] Le Boulanger, 155, 196.
[11] *PMLP,* 14; and Prince Damrong Rajanubhab, ed., "Phongsawadan
müang Luang Phrabang [Chronicles of Luang Prabang]," in *Collected
Chronicles,* vol. 5 (Bangkok, 1915), 254. Cited hereafter as Damrong-PMLP.
Phraya Prachakit 473, states that a Siamese attack in the Chiang Mai area caused
the sudden Burmese withdrawal from Luang Prabang.
[12] For the date of the accession of Siribunyasan, Le Boulanger gives 1760,
as does *History of Laos,* 58, 64. On the other hand, Phraya Pramuan, 36; Yim
Panthayangkura, "Lamdap ratchawong kasat hæng Prathet Lao [Genealogical
Table of the Kings of Laos]," *Sinlapakòn* 6:3 (Sept. 1962), suppl.; and Berval,
41, give 1767. Charles Archaimbault, in an admirable study of "Histoire de

Wò and Ta. These two personages came in the succeeding years to figure in the history not only of Vientiane, but also of Champasak, several present-day provincial capitals in the Thai Northeast, and Siam as well. Out of a mass of legends in nearly twenty versions of their story, the following sequence of events emerges, albeit none too clearly.

Wò and Ta, in return for their efforts on behalf of Siribunyasan's claim to the throne, asked for the honor of being appointed to high state position, but as they were not of royal blood, Siribunyasan refused them. They then left Vientiane and went across the Mekong to Nòng Bua Lamphu, near Udon in Northeast Thailand, where they founded their own independent principality. One version of the tale states that they were further offended when Siribunyasan asked for the hand of Ta's daughter as a common concubine.[13] In any event, out of their own frustrated political ambitions and Siribunyasan's desire to eliminate his rivals, matters soon came to a head. After three years of intermittent warfare between Vientiane and Nòng Bua Lamphu, Wò and Ta finally appealed to the Burmese for aid. A Burmese force was sent from Chiang Mai to help them, but was intercepted en route and persuaded by Siribunyasan's envoys to attack Nòng Bua Lamphu. In a brief encounter with joint Burmese-Vientiane forces, Ta was killed and the town taken, while Wò managed to escape to Champasak with some of his followers. The Burmese forces returned to Chiang Mai, carrying with them some of Siribunyasan's children and court officials as hostages against Vientiane's good behavior during a projected invasion of Siam. It appears that at this time the Burmese asked Vientiane to attack Nakhòn Ratchasima (Khorat) in conjunction with this invasion.[14]

Campasak," *Journal Asiatique* CCXLIX, fasc. 4 (1961), 558, indicates that the Wò-Ta tale related below could have taken place following the accession of Siribunyasan's predecessor in 1741. I am most grateful to M. Archaimbault for his kindness in discussing this article with me, although for the judgments expressed here I alone am, of course, responsible.

[13] Tœm Singhathit, *Fang khwa Mænam Khong* [Right Bank of the Mekong River] (Bangkok, 1956), I, 141.

[14] As Chulalongkorn, 135, indicates. The sequence of events presented here follows Chulalongkorn. The main weakness of this version of the tale is

When Taksin attacked Chiang Mai in 1774, he discovered some Lao officials among the Burmese forces and sent off a blistering protest message to Vientiane.[15] Carried to Vientiane by six envoys, the letter complained that Vientiane had not lived up to the treaty with Siam, and threatened that Taksin would be compelled to attack Vientiane unless Siribunyasan sent food supplies for the current campaign against Burma, together with a Lao contingent to fight on the Thai side.

In his reply, written on 23 March 1775,[16] Siribunyasan protested that he had done his best to live up to the treaty, but that he had been compelled to aid the Burmese because they held some of his children and officials as hostages. He promised to observe the treaty as fully as possible, but explained that he could do so only covertly until the hostages were returned, and asked that Siam give assistance to any of them that might escape through Siam. Siribunyasan's reply to Taksin's protest was accompanied by corroborating messages written by high court officials and the Supreme Patriarch of the Lao Buddhist order.

that events move too rapidly for the geographical and human elements involved. Thus, following Chulalongkorn's version, it is but four years from the time of Wo's flight to Champasak in 1773 to his death in 1777 following the complex series of events related below. Archaimbault's 1741 date (p. 558), on the other hand, moves too slowly, over a space of almost forty years, and must meet the additional objection that the Burmese were in no position in 1741 to be active in Laos as they were established only in Chiang Sæn by 1741, and not in Chiang Mai until early in the 1760s (see Damrong, *Thai rop Phama*, 297-338, esp. pp. 331-4; and Phraya Prachakit 454-6). The alternative to these two versions is that given by Mòm Amòrawongwichit, "Tamnan müang nakhon campasak [History of Champasak]," in *Collected Chronicles*, vol. 70 (Bangkok, 1941), 30-33 (hereafter cited as *TMNC*), which dates Wo's flight from Nong Bua Lamphu in 1770 or 1771. If this date is correct, the Burmese would have arrived in Vientiane owing, not to the appeals of Wo and Ta for aid, but rather to the Luang Prabang invasion of Vientiane. Since, however, the Burmese are said to have rushed back to Chiang Mai following their siege of Luang Prabang (see note 11 above), even this answer to the problem is not free from doubt. All that can be stated with any certainty is that Wò was expelled from Nòng Bua Lamphu by a Vientiane-Burmese force, and at this time the Burmese forces returned to Chiang Mai with hostages from Vientiane.

[15] Text in Maha Sila, 91-2.
[16] Text in Maha Sila, 92.

Taksin's reply, written on 31 May 1775, was more conciliatory. The threat to invade Vientiane was withdrawn, since a captured Burmese officer had corroborated Siribunyasan's excuses; and Taksin expressed his desire—in the spirit of the treaty of 1771—to take revenge on Burma for its poor treatment of Vientiane. For such an expedition, however, Taksin stated that he needed money, elephants, horses, and soldiers. If Vientiane could supply these items, Taksin promised to rescue the Vientiane hostages in Ava. This message was sent with a large quantity of gifts, mostly textiles but including two rifles as well.[17]

Siribunyasan's reply to this last letter displayed a mixed reaction.[18] He offered his daughter to Taksin, but stipulated that she must be sent for and escorted back to Thonburi. He also offered the Thai 500 oxcart loads of rice, but stated that Siam must fetch this as well. On the other hand, in order that he might have suitably-equipped troops for aiding the Siamese, he requested that he be sent 2000 rifles. Evidently the King of Vientiane had accepted the fact of Siamese power, but his response to Taksin's request indicates that he wished to keep their relations on an equal basis. While he must have felt constrained to accept some of Siam's demands in view of the disparity in their military power, he attempted to gain some status in his own right by marrying his daughter to Taksin, and he also required that Siam make some efforts on his behalf.

Taksin's response to this letter, written in September of 1775, was quite friendly.[19] He stated that his envoys would come to Vientiane to fetch the princess and the 500 cartloads of rice, and that in addition to sending the rifles, instructors would also be sent to teach the Lao soldiers their use. He added that the Siamese army would soon be striking directly at Ava. This is, however, the last letter in this highly interesting correspondence which has been preserved. Relations were soon broken off, either due to a report from Luang Prabang that Vientiane was cooperating with the Burmese again and because the Lao did not subsequently aid

---

[17] Maha Sila, 95-7.
[18] Maha Sila, 99.
[19] Maha Sila, 99-100.

in attacking the Burmese,[20] or due to subsequent events which touched off the Siamese invasion of Vientiane in 1778. Both reasons are equally likely, and either is sufficient.

Before turning to the invasion of Vientiane, it is necessary to look first at the other Lao kingdoms. The annals of Luang Prabang are virtually blank for this period, save for passing mention of the inauguration of friendly relations with Siam. Le Boulanger[21] states that in 1774 the King of Luang Prabang solicited Taksin's protection and proposed a defensive alliance against the Burmese. The two published Luang Prabang chronicles, however, state that Taksin wrote to the King in 1774 asking that friendly relations be established, and that a mission from Luang Prabang signed a treaty of alliance in Bangkok in 1776.[22] In assessing this new direction in Taksin's foreign policy, several factors may be pertinent. First, it may be that in resuming his correspondence with Vientiane in 1774, Taksin also took the opportunity to establish contact with Luang Prabang as part of his offensive against the Burmese strongholds in the north. On the other hand, it is also possible that King Cao Vongsa heard of the correspondence between Taksin and Vientiane and wished to avoid complete isolation. Finally, by 1776 Taksin may have been anticipating the invasion of Vientiane that came in 1778. Unfortunately, none of these possibilities can be confirmed with the evidence at hand.

The principality of Champasak appears to have had consistent history of domestic political turmoil. Its ruler, Saiyakuman, was in constant conflict with the Uparaja (or Viceroy). In 1758 the latter, Thammathewo, brought an army of supporters to attack the city, forcing Saiyakuman to flee to the village of Dòn Mot Dæng, near the present city of Ubon. The Uparaja was prevented from pursuing the ruler only by the efforts of their mother, who managed to settle their quarrel and obtain the restoration of Saiyakuman to his duties in the city.[23]

---

[20] Maha Sila, 100.
[21] Pages 155, 196-7.
[22] PMLP, 44-5; Damrong-PMLP, 254.
[23] TMNC, 29-30.

The major cause of the 1778 Thai invasion of the Lao lands—according to the Thai annals—lay with the troublesome Wò, who had earlier fled to Champasak.[24]Saiyakuman established Wò and his entourage at the village of Ban Du Ban Kæ. Informed of Saiyakuman's protection of the refugees, Siribunyasan prepared an army to attack the village. Concerned, no doubt, for the effects a Vientiane army might have on his own authority, Saiyakuman quickly dispatched a mission to Vientiane which secured the recall of the army and the opening of friendly relations between the Lao states.[25] Finally, in 1777, Wò and Saiyakuman quarreled, and the former withdrew his followers and their families to the village of Dòn Mot Dæng (apparently a convenient refuge) and, submitting tribute through the governor of Nakhòn Ratchasima, put himself under the suzerainty of the Siamese.

King Siribunyasan of Vientiane, hearing of Wo's quarrel with Saiyakuman, sent an army against Dòn Mot Dæng. Wo's appeals for help from Champasak and Nakhòn Ratchasima were not answered in time, and he was captured and executed by the Vientiane force. His son, Thao Kham, and several other officials escaped, and sent a message to Nakhòn Ratchasima asking that the Thai take revenge on Vientiane.[26]

Tœm rightly points out[27] that Taksin would hardly have gone to war over such a minor personage as Wò. His invasion of Vientiane was rather another step to be taken towards the strengthening of Siam; a move indirectly against the Burmese, but also, as the addition of new vassals along the eastern frontier would appear to indicate, a precaution against any eventual troubles with Annam or Cambodia. Taksin had previously had pretexts for attacking Vientiane, but they had arisen at times when he was preoccupied with Burma. At this point, however,

---

[24] Chulalongkorn, 135. Tœm, I, 143-4, gives 1771, following TMNC, 32.
[25] TMNC, 32.
[26] TMNC, 33. Maha Sila, 101-2, also states that Thao Kham suggested to Taksin that Vientiane was cooperating with the Burmese. Cf. also Chulalongkorn, 128.
[27] Vol. I, 145-6.

there was a temporary lull in the west,[28] and several pretexts upon which to base an invasion of Vientiane, including perhaps the accusation of Thai Kham that the Lao were in league with the Burmese, as well as the murder of a vassal, Wò.

In November and December of 1778 the Thai armies moved out towards Vientiane. General Cakri took a force of 20,000 men overland, while his brother, General Surasi, went to Cambodia, where he raised a vassal naval force of 10,000 men and headed up the Mekong, capturing Champasak, Nakhòn Phanom, and Nongkhai en route, as well as several smaller towns which were then vassals of Vientiane.[29] The two forces joined in subduing the small towns surrounding Vientiane and laid siege to the capital for four months. They finally stormed the city, aided by a small force dispatched by Luang Prabang, and captured many members of the ruling family, the city's prized Buddha images, the Phrabang and the Emerald Buddha,[30] and a very large number of Lao families which were later settled in the region of Saraburi, northeast of Ayudhya.[31] King Siribunyasan, however, managed to escape to the town of Khamkœt, on the Vietnam border. Vientiane was left in charge of a prominent Vientiane general, Phraya Supho, and the Thai army returned home in April of 1779.[32]

---

[28] During the relatively quiet reign of King Singu in Burma, 1776-1782. Cf. Hall, *Burma*, 92.

[29] For this invasion, a standard source is the Royal Autograph Edition of the Thai annals: Prince Damrong Rajanubhab, ed., *Phraratchaphongsawadan chabap phraratchahatlekha (Bangkok,* 1962), II, 418-23. For an incomplete account of the procuring of the naval force in Cambodia, see J. Moura, *Le royaume du Cambodge* (Paris, 1883), II, 91. Other accounts of the expedition may be found in Maha Sila, 101-2; Le Boulanger, 155-6; Tœm, I, 145-9; and *TMNC*, 33-4.

[30] Which were, as the Thai sources put it, "invited" to Thonburi.

[31] Maha Sila, 103.

[32] The Thai annals state that there were two military expeditions in the Champasak area during this period, but give Wò as the cause of neither. In addition to the major attack on Vientiane in 1778-9, in the course of which Champasak was taken, the *Royal Autograph Edition*, II, 414-5, and the *Phraratchaphongsawadan krung Thonburi* [Royal Chronicles of the Thonburi

As a result of this invasion, both Vientiane and Champasak lost their independence and their ruling families and temporarily were governed by military commanders, although, at least in the case of Vientiane, the ruler was indigenous to the city. As for Luang Prabang, which had aided in the capture of Vientiane. it too became more closely aligned with the Siamese. Both the Luang Prabang chronicles state that Luang Prabang entered the battle at the request of General Cakri,[33] and that subsequently Luang Prabang either "asked to be allowed to become" a vassal of Siam, or "was forced to accept Siamese suzerainty."[34] All three Lao kingdoms thus came under the spreading umbrella of Thai power.

Period] (Collected Chronicles, vol. 65, Bangkok, 1960), 83, mention a military expedition, in the Champasak area in 1777. This expedition was undertaken, they state, to put down a revolt of *müang,* Nang Ròng, tributary to Khorat, whose ruler allegedly was conspiring with the Uparat of Champasak and the governor and Uparat of Attapü (tributary to Champasak). According to these accounts, the Thai sent an army to the area, led by General Cakri, which executed the governor of Nang Ròng and then captured Champasak, Khong, and Attapü and executed the plotters. The Thai army returned home in April of 1777. This story is corroborated by the memoirs of a contemporary, Princess Narinthewi (Chulalongkorn, 6-7, 124 ff.), who remembered the army returning from Champasak in September and setting out again in December for Vientiane.

The Uparat of Champasak and the rulers of Attapü, mentioned in the Thai account as having been executed in 1777, were the reported grounds for another Thai expedition against Champasak early in the following decade, mentioned in *TMNC,* 34-5. The same people and events are thus reported by both sides, but the three Champasak annals Archaimbault used place the event after the 1778 invasion, while the Thai annals place it before the invasion. I have chosen to follow the Champasak chronology, primarily because of an editorial footnote to the Thonburi Annals, p. 83, which notes that as late as 1780 General Cakri was referred to, in a document still extant, as "Caophraya Cakri," and not "Caophraya Mahakasatsuk," the title which the Thai annals state was conferred on him following the 1777 invasion of Champasak, thus indicating that the expedition involving the Uparat of Champasak may not have taken place until the following decade.

33 MLP, 45-6; Damrong-PMLP, 254-5.
34 Maha Sila, 102-3.

II. Laos to the Accession of Cao Anu, 1780-1804

The sources which deal with the 1778 Thai invasion of Vientiane offer interesting material relating to the differing relationships holding between Bangkok and the Lao states on the one hand (Vientiane, Luang Prabang, and Champasak) and between Bangkok and the northeast provinces of old Siam on the other. While these relationships are by no means clearly defined, and in practice varied greatly, certain general characteristics are readily apparent.

During the period with which this paper is concerned, the area in present-day Northeast Thailand under direct Thai administrative control, greatly expanded to cover virtually all of the Thai Northeast, except for a narrow band along the Mekong. By the end of the First Reign (1782-1809) this area included such *müang* (town/ province) as Sisaket, Ubon, Yasothòn, Roi-et, Kalasin, and Khònkæn, as well as many more towns clustered more closely around Khorat. The governors *(caomüang)* of these towns were quite independent within their own jurisdictions. They did not, however, have the power to execute evildoers, to appoint higher officials within the *müang,* or to make war. Such decisions were referred to Khorat or Bangkok.[35] Provinces in the Northeast were attached to various ministries and officials in Bangkok as a part of the financial support of the latter, and to them the *müang* had to render revenue and labor service. For such purposes, periodic censuses were made of every *müang* by officials from the capital. Their boundaries were set and, in this period, often shifted by Bangkok in order to create new *müang* in the area. A policy of the First Reign, continued by its successors, was to reward *caomüang;* for increases of population and territory by awarding them titles which reached as high as *phraya.*[36] In general, in the sphere of administrative control. these Northeast provinces did not differ greatly from the rest of the Kingdom.[37]

---

[35] Tœm, I, 496-7.

[36] M. C. Sipphanphansanœ Sonakun, *Prawatsat Thai samai krung Rattanakosin yuk ræk ... chabap rang* [Thai History in the First Part of the Bangkok Period... Draft Edition] (Bangkok, 1958), 61.

[37] For this section, see Mòm Amòrawongwichit, "Phongsawadan huamüang monthon Isan [Chronicles of the Provinces of Monthon Isan]," in *Collected Chronicles,* vol. 4 (Bangkok, 1915), 29-222, *passim.*

The areas of Laos that came under the suzerainty of Bangkok in the First Reign enjoyed quite a different relationship with Siam. The powers of their rulers were very much greater. They had the powers of capital punishment, of making war with Thai consent, and of independently appointing all but the four highest officials of the realm, and, as documented in the cases of Champasak and Luang Prabang, these appointments were generally made locally by a council of nobility and then submitted to Bangkok for approval. Their obligations to provide revenue and corvée labor were very much curtailed, and amounted to little more than an annual tribute of the "silver and gold trees" and providing armies in time of war. Each of the three Lao states had its own vassals and, to some extent, carried on limited independent foreign relations. In short, the Lao areas were more properly "vassals," comparable to the Malay vassals of Bangkok, although because of the cultural affinities between Thai and Lao the relationship was more open to the close ties of royal marriages, the education of Lao princes in Bangkok, and cultural and religious exchanges.

Within this framework of relations there was, during the 1780s and '90s, considerable scope for Thai diplomatic and military initiative. Rama I came to the throne of Siam fresh from the invasion of Vientiane,[38] and throughout his reign had occasion to deal with Lao affairs. The main features of his activity were the appointments of higher officials and rulers in several of the Lao states, and several cases of military intervention.

In Champasak, Cao Saiyakuman, in the period following the Siamese invasion, was faced with a continuation of his old feud with the Uparaja. The latter had died in 1767, but his influence in state affairs continued. Thao Kham Phong, a son of Phra Ta who had come to the area with Wò in 1773, had married the daughter of the late Uparaja and proceeded to gather a strong following. Saiyakuman was then forced to award Thao Kham Phong an important military position in charge of a large area around present-day Ubon. Then, in 1780, the governor of Attapü,

---

[38] He was the former General Cakri.

Cao O, a son of the late Uparaja, together with his brother, was accused of oppressing the population under his control and was captured and executed by a force from Champasak. Hearing of this incident, Bangkok sent a royal commissioner to Champasak in 1782 who was to bring Saiyakuman and his court back to Bangkok for examination, but as Saiyakuman fell ill along the way, he was permitted to return home.[39]

In 1791 a man popularly believed to possess magical powers gathered together a following and attacked Champasak, spurred by news of the ruler's illness. While the city was surrounded, Saiyakuman died at the age of 81 after a reign of 54 years. Informed of the incident, Siam sent a force from Khorat to subdue the rebels; but Thao Kham Phong and Thao Fai Na, the son of Wò. were able to put down the rebellion and executed the rebel leader. When the Thai forces arrived they reconstituted the local government, moved the capital north to the present Muang Kao Khan Kœng, and appointed Thao Fai Na ruler of Champasak, under the name of Cao Phra Wisaiyarat Khattiyawongsa.[40]

Vientiane, however, was quite another matter. After the invasion of Vientiane in 1778, all the members of the royal family of the state—with the important exception of Cao Siribunyasan—were brought to Bangkok, and it was from this group of prisoners that the next three rulers of Vientiane were chosen.

Siribunyasan returned to Vientiane in 1781, and appears to have regained control over the state, although the sources do not present any clear account of how this came about. At his death

---

[39] There is no mention of this episode in the Thai annals (see note 32 above). For this paragraph, see *TMNC* 34-5.

[40] *TMNC* 35-6. Chao Phrommathewanukhrò, *Tamnan müang nakhòn Champasak* [History of Champasak]," *Collected Chronicles* vol. 70, 57-8 (cited as Phrommathewanukhrò-TMNC), states that Saiyakuman died upon his return to Champasak in 1782 (see para. above), and that the Siamese were unable to choose a new ruler from among the three members of the ruling family they had removed to Bangkok The leadership vacuum was filled, the account relates, first by the man with magical powers, and then by the sons of Wo and Ta, out of whom Thao Fai Na, after a visit to Bangkok was appointed *caomüang*.

in 1781, the Siamese enthroned Cao Nanthasen, son of Siribunyasan, as ruler of Vientiane, and returned the Phrabang image.[41]

Luang Prabang, after having entered into more direct relations with Siam at the time of the invasion of Vientiane in 1778, had broken off relations with Burma. It annually sent the "silver and gold trees" to Siam, and maintained tributary relations with China.[42] After a short interregnum following the death of King Cao Vongsa, the nobles of the kingdom finally agreed in 1791 on the choice of his son, Anuruttha, to succeed him, but before enthroning him sent a mission to Bangkok to secure Siam's approval and recognition for their nominee.[43]

Less than a year later,[44] Cao Nanthasen reported to Bangkok that Anuruttha was conspiring with Burma against Vientiane, and shortly thereafter received authorization to attack Luang Prabang.[45] The Vientiane army laid siege to the city for two weeks and

---

[41] Both Hall, A *History of Southeast Asia* (London, 1955), 381, and Le Boulanger, 157, state that Siribunyasan voluntarily returned to Vientiane and submitted to Siam on learning that his children were being well-treated in Bangkok. The "Short Chronicle of Vientiane" ("Phongsawadan yò müang Wiangchan," *Collected Chronicles, vol.* 70, 183) states only that Siribunyasan returned to the city in December of 1780. The chronicles of the First Reign of the Cakri Dynasty of Siam state that Siribunyasan returned to Vientiane and killed Phraya Supho, whom the Thai had left in control, and took over the city. Officials opposed to him then reported the event to Bangkok, whereupon the Thai king appointed Nanthasen ruler of Vientiane. "Not long afterwards," the source reports, Siribunyasan died. Caophraya Thiphakòrawong, *Phraratchaphongsawadan krung Rattanakosin ratchakan thi 1* (Bangkok, 1962), 45-6. Hereafter cited as *First Reign Chronicle*.

[42] Damrong-PMLP, 255, states that tribute was sent to China every five years until 1782, when the interval was changed to ten years, at an increased rate of tribute. The dates given in the Chinese sources, however, indicate that this change took place before 1760. Cf. J. K. Fairbank and S. Y. Teng, "On the Ch'ing Tributary System," *HJAS* 6 (1941), 166-8.

[43] Maha Sila, 136; Damrong-PMLP, 256; and René de Berval, *Kingdom of Laos* (Saigon, 1959), 42.

[44] Or perhaps still in 1791.

[45] Both Le Boulanger, 157, 198-200; and Hall, *History*, 381, state that the attack was made on the initiative of Nanthasen because of "dynastic troubles" in Luang Prabang. The Thai sources, on the other hand, state that the attack was made for the purpose stated and that it was authorized. *First Reign Chronicle*, 182-3. Cf. also Sipphanphansanoe, 61; and Maha Sila, 110.

was unable to penetrate the city walls. The commander of the invading forces then sent a letter to Queen Thæn Kham, widow of King Suryavong, promising to make her ruler of Luang Prabang if she would open the gates of the city. With the aid of a friend in the city's garrison this was done, and the city fell to Vientiane. As in other cases of suspected treason,[46] Cao Anuruttha and his family were sent to Bangkok.[47] Evidently out of respect for Siam, however, Vientiane did not attempt to unite the two kingdoms, and only annexed the Hua Phan cantons at this time.[48]

In 1794, a member of the Luang Prabang royal family, sent to rule over the city by Vientiane, sought the release of Cao Anuruttha from prison in Siam, doing so through the good offices of China. The Chinese sent envoys to Bangkok via Hsen Wi and down the Nan River. They were granted an audience with Rama I and obtained Anuruttha's release. Orders then were sent to Vientiane that all families who had been deported from Luang Prabang in the 1792 invasion be returned to their homes, and Anuruttha and his family were sent home laden with gifts.[49]

At about this time,[50] Siribunyasan returned to Vientiane in 1781, and appears to have regained control over the state, although the sources do not present any clear account of how this came about. At his death Cao Nanthasen of Vientiane was recalled to Bangkok. Some sources state that he lost his throne simply because he did not rule well;[51] but most mention that he was accused of conspiring with the ruler of Nakhòn Phanom to revolt

---

[46] E.g. the Uparat of Champasak at an earlier date.

[47] Maha Sila, 110; Sipphanphansanoe, 61; *First Reign Chronicle,* 183.

[48] Berval, 42.

[49] PMLP, 49-50; and Damrong-PMLP, 257 8 give this story in full, with some variations. The Chinese embassy seems unlikely, especially by the route mentioned. The *First Reign Chronicle* states only that Anuruttha was later restored to his throne, without mentioning the circumstances.

[50] The First Reign Chronicle mentions this event after discussing the restoration of Anuruttha, while the actual dates mentioned for the events would put them in reverse order. Le Boulanger states that Chao Nanthasen was recalled because of the attack on Luang Prabang, and at that time Anuruttha was restored to his throne.

[51] E.g. Sipphanphansanoe, 61.

against Siamese domination. Both were summoned to Bangkok for an investigation, and while in Bangkok, Cao Nanthasen died.[52]

His brother, Cao Inthavong, was sent from Bangkok to succeed him. He was assisted by his younger brother, Cao Anuvong (or Anu), who was made Uparaja. He immediately began to render his obligations to his suzerain in full. Anu was sent to command Lao contingents fighting at the side of the Thai army in 1795, 1798, 1799, and 1803. Anu distinguished himself in these campaigns, most of which were against the Burmese, and was twice commended by King Rama I. The reign of Cao Inthavong marked a high point in Thai-Vientiane relations on this account, at any rate: the last two times Lao soldiers had participated in the Thai-Burmese wars were in 1765 and 1774, both times on the Burmese side. Relations appeared to be perfectly harmonious, although Le Boulanger expresses some doubt as to this conclusion:

> Politically clever, [Anu] hid his true sentiments and maintained the attitude of deference to his suzerain which circumstances had imposed on him. He acquired the confidence of the Thai court, and the annals of the Thai recognized his courage and the incontestable services which he rendered to Siam for about five years. When Cao In died, he was immediately appointed as his successor.[53]

Vientiane, however, also continued to carry on relations with Vietnam. .Some of her vassal towns had been paying equal tribute to Annam and Vientiane as long ago as 1780[54] and in 1790 Vientiane was attacked by a joint Vietnamese-Xieng Khouang

---

[52] *First Reign Chronicle,* 211-12: Maha Sila, 110; and Phraya Chanthangonkham, "Phongsawadan müang Nakhòn Phanom sangkhep [Condensed Chronicles of Nakhòn Phanom]," in *Collected Chronicles, vol. 70,* 239.

[53] Le Boulanger, 159. On the content of this paragraph, see also Maha Sila, 111.

[54] And probably before. Cf. Pierre Grossin, *Notes sur l'histoire de la province de Cammon (Laos)* (Hanoi 1933), 17.

force, which appears to have resulted in Cao Inthavong sending tribute to Annam as well.[55] Vientiane forces cooperated with Gia-long against the Tay-son rebellion, and in 1798 Vietnamese officers came to Vientiane to aid the Lao army, later accompanying it on missions against rebel remnants. Vientiane sent tribute missions to Gia-long in 1801 and 1802; and upon his accession, in 1804, Cao Anu immediately notified the court at Hué.[56] It appears possible, then, that Vientiane's relations with Vietnam were nearly as close as its relations with Siam, although the Siamese sources give little such information.

Finally, in 1804, Cao Inthavong died. The King of Siam sent presents by an embassy to his cremation, and named the Uparaja, Cao Anu, to succeed him.[57]

In summary, then, during this period Siam's position in Laos was maintained by both diplomatic and military means. Bangkok named the rulers of Champasak (1791) and Vientiane (1781, 1794/5, and 1804), and approved the choice of a ruler for Luang Prabang (1791). Siam repeatedly took measures to suppress suspected revolts in Laos and, whether as a conscious policy or not, maintained the political fragmentation of Laos. During the reign of Cao Anu of Vientiane, this was to be seriously threatened.

III. The Reign of Cao Anu, 1804–1827

Although his reign was to bring about the destruction of his state, Cao Anu came to the throne under most favorable auspices.[58] He was highly respected and honored by the Siamese

---

[55] *First Reign Chronicle.*, 177. This attack may have been provoked by a prior attack by Vientiane on Xieng Khouang in 1787, occasioned by the latter's submission to Vietnam, although none of the other sources mention this. Maha Sila, 109-10. Cf. also Eugene Picanon, *Le Laos français* (Paris, 1901), 174-5.

[56] Charles B. Maybon. *Histoire moderne du pays d'Annam (1592-1820)*(Paris, 1919), 385; Le Thanh Khoi, *Le Viet-Nam, Histoire et Civilisation* (Paris, 1955), 336; and, for the date of the accession of Chao Anu, Bui Quang Tung, "Chao Anou, roi de Vientiane; a travers les documents vietnamiens," *BSEI* 33 (1958), 401.

[57] *First Reign Chronicle*, 274.

[58] To paraphrase Le Boulanger, 159.

for his loyal services in the Thai wars with Burma, and he received his investiture at the hands of Siam. Much of the early part of his reign was spent in expanding and beautifying his capital. He constructed a new royal palace, bridges, and religious monuments.[59] In this aspect of his rule, Anu appears to have been acting in the best traditions of Buddhist monarchy.

In the political realm, however, Anu's actions and policies admit of less certain interpretation. Some writers, notably Le Boulanger, have construed virtually every action of Anu from 1794 as preparation for the rebellion of 1827. It is possible that from his youth Anu harbored a grand design for restoring the Kingdom of Lan Chang, but lacking any reliable indications of Anu's intentions, at least for the early part of his reign, his actions and policies must be taken at their face value.

Early in his reign, Anu reaffirmed the old tribute relationship between Vientiane and Vietnam. Tribute was regularized by three missions sent in 1804 to notify Gia-long of Anu's accession.[60] It was to be sent every three years, and to consist of male elephants, rhinoceros horns, ivory, and cinnamon. When the tribute for 1808 did not arrive punctually, Gia-long sent a mission demanding it, which quickly provoked the desired response. There were only three more tribute missions, in 1811-12, 1814, and 1817, and none after that.[61]

The Luang Prabang Annals record very little for this interim period. They mention that King Anuruttha died in 1815, and that King Rama II supported the Uparaja as his successor. The latter was enthroned in 1816 as Cao Mangthaturat, and was, in the following years, to show himself a devoted friend of the Thai monarchs.[62] Champasak, on the other hand, figures prominently in the annals of the period. In 1811,[63] the ruler of Champasak died, and a son of the former ruler, Saiyakuman, was named to replace him, but the latter died within three days. King

[59] Maha Sila, 111; *Short Chronicle of Vientiane*, 181-204.
[60] Bui Quang Tung, 401. Cf. also Le Boulanger, 160-1 fn.
[61] Maybon, 385; Le Thanh Khoi, 336.
[62] PMLP, 51.
[63] TMNC, 37; Phrommathewanukhrò-TMNC, 59, says 1810.

Rama I sent a high ranking official to his cremation. This envoy was given a precious crystal image of the Lord Buddha as a present for King Rama I, but returned to Bangkok without installing a ruler in Champasak. Finally in 1813 Cao Manòi was appointed by Siam to rule the state, with a descendant of the rival Thammathewo's family as Uparaja. Cao Manòi and his Uparaja were later involved in a dispute which was mediated by Bangkok and resulted in the jailing of the latter. Clearly Siam's control over Champasak was stronger than that over either of the other two principalities.[64]

In 1819 a revolt broke out in the territory of Champasak among the Kha peoples, led by a renegade monk named Sa. Sa claimed magical powers, which he demonstrated by using a mirror to create fire. Gathering a large number of followers, he marched on Champasak. Cao Manòi put up very little resistance, and the city was quickly taken, the ruling families escaping to the region of Ubon. Troops from Ubon and Khorat quickly retook the city, but were unable to capture the monk Sa, and returned home, sending Cao Manòi to Bangkok, where he later died. Sa was finally captured by a force from Vientiane, led by Anu's son, Yò.

The Siamese were confronted with the problem of reinstating strong rule in Champasak. Cao Manòi and his predecessors had proved themselves too weak to withstand even internal revolt. During a lengthy discussion in Bangkok over the naming of a ruler, Cao Anu urged the naming of his son to the post. Prince Chetsadabòdin (later Rama III) was in favor of such an appointment, and prevailed over Prince Phithakmontri, who argued that such an appointment would dangerously strengthen Vientiane. The Thai were forced to make the decision on the basis of political and military requirements, and so chose Yò, who, it was felt, would be strong enough—with his father's help, if necessary—to prevent Vietnamese encroachment in the Mekong valley.[65]

---

[64] Maha Sila, 144; TM-NC, 37-8.

[65] Prince Damrong Rajanubhab, ed., *Phraratchaphongsawadan krung Rattanakosin ratchakan thi 2* [Royal Chronicle of the Second Reign of the Bangkok Period] (Bangkok, 1916), 270-4; *TMNC*, 38ff.; Le Boulanger, 160; Maha Sila, 144-5.

Following the Champasak episode, Anu began to prepare for revolt. He instructed his son, Cao Yò, to fortify his territory[66] and began a campaign to obtain at least the neutrality of Luang Prabang in the event of conflict with Siam. In 1820 he sent envoys to Cao Mangthaturat of Luang Prabang to propose the restoration of friendly relations between the two states and "the union of their forces against the suzerainty of the West [Siam] whose power was growing in a menacing fashion."[67] Cao Mangthaturat refused, but in the following year Anu again sent a mission in an attempt to bribe him. This mission seems at least to have won Mangthaturat's neutrality, for he did not report the incidents to Bangkok, and over the following years maintained envoys in both Bangkok and Vientiane to keep him informed of developments.[68]

The rulers of both Vientiane and Luang Prabang came to Bangkok for the cremation of Rama II in 1825. Mangthaturat of Luang Prabang handed over the administration of his state to senior officials and came to Bangkok bearing tribute. In a rather curious gesture, he asked the permission of King Rama III to enter a monastery to make merit in recognition of the favors which Rama I and Rama II had shown Luang Prabang. He stayed in the monastery for a year and wished to stay longer, but an epidemic broke out in Luang Prabang in 1826, and he asked to be allowed to return home. Upon his departure, King. Rama III bestowed upon Mangthaturat "the five insignia of kingship" in recognition of his great loyalty to Siam. Leaving behind two of his younger sons, whom he had enrolled in the Royal Pages Corps, Mangthaturat returned to Luang Prabang.[69]

---

[66] *TMNC, 39;* Le Boulanger, 161.

[67] Le Boulanger, 201.

[68] Le Boulanger, 201-2.

[69] Damrong,-PMLP, 261-2. The five royal insignia are the golden slippers, the royal staff or baton, the scepter or sword, the state crown, and the fly whisk. Cf. also Tœm, 154. It is possible that Chao Mangthaturat stayed in Bangkok at this time to avoid any involvement in Anu's forthcoming revolt, and returned home only when the danger of revolt appeared past—perhaps when the rumor of a British invasion had died out.

Cao Anu also came to Bangkok for the royal cremation. His actions there show some of the seeds of the rebellion which followed his return home. First, following the cremation, some of the Lao in Anu's entourage were called up for the Thai corvée, and put to work cutting palm trees at Suphanburi.[70] Secondly, Anu made a number of demands on Rama III, acting on the assumption that he was an important vassal of Siam and a necessary ally, particularly at a time when it appeared that Siam was threatened by British actions in Burma and Malaya and by Vietnamese pressure on Cambodia.[71] Anu asked that the Lao dancers and artisans in the royal service be returned, but he was given only one singer.[72] He also requested that the Lao families who had been deported from Vientiane in 1778-9 and settled in Saraburi— amounting to some ten thousand persons—be returned, but as this would leave a large depopulated area near the capital, the request was refused.[73] The denial of his requests and the treatment or members of his entourage must have convinced Anu that his value to Siam was not as high as he had supposed. In addition, he may have taken offense at the favors shown to Cao Mangthaturat of Luang Prabang in response to the latter's submissive behavior.

Anu returned to Vientiane and began to plan his revolt. He mended his fences with Vietnam and appears to have relied upon Vietnamese support in the event that he should require it.[74] He called together the nobles of the state and outlined his plans. He pointed out that a new and inexperienced ruler was on the throne in Siam and that the Thai armies were weak. The governor of Nakhòn Ratchasima was absent, and this was the only town along the route to Bangkok that could make any show of resistance. His most convincing argument, however, consisted of a fresh rumor

[70] Maha Sila, 113; and Caophraya Thiphakòrawong, *Phraratchaphongsawadan krung Rattanakosin ratchakan* thi 3 [Royal Chronicle of the Third Reign of the Bangkok Period] (Bangkok, 1938), 24.

[71] Le Boulanger, 166; Thailand, Krom Sinlapakòn, comp., *Cot)maihet rüang prap khabot wiangcan* [Documents Concerning the .Suppression of the Vientiane Rebellion] (Bangkok, 1926), 6; and Tœm, I, 154-5.

[72] *Third Reign Chronicle*, 24.

[73] Cf. esp. Tœm, I, 154-5.

[74] Sipphanphansanœ, 63; Tœm, I, 155; and Vella, 80.

from Bangkok to the effect that the British were sending a naval force against Bangkok.[75] Vientiane, he explained, could send an army through the Thai Northeast, using the rumor as an excuse, stating that the Lao force was going to the aid of Siam.[76] He envisaged a lightning campaign for loot and captives, with its first objective the repatriation of the Lao settlers in the Saraburi region, and he did not intend to occupy Bangkok for any length of time. In late January 1827, the Lao troops began their attack from Vientiane and Champasak, the latter army under the command of Cao Yò.[77]

In a letter written to Bangkok after the start of the rebellion, Cao Mangthaturat reported having received a diplomatic mission from Vientiane in 1826. The mission had brought word that the British and Burmese were attacking Bangkok, and that Vientiane was going to the aid of the Siamese and needed reinforcements from Luang Prabang.[78] Mangthaturat stated that he had not believed the story, and had sought the counsel of his nobles in working out some stratagem to stall the Vientiane envoys. He told the latter that he would send troops, but that they would be late, and in the interval sent word by his son to Bangkok of Vientiane's intentions. Not long afterwards he received a message from the town of Nan, stating that it had been requested by Bangkok to assist in attacking Vientiane.

---

[75] A letter from John Gillies to John Crawfurd, dated 2 September 1825, notes the currency of the rumor in Bangkok during the former's stay there that year. Gillies states that the rumor was started by the Dutch, and that it caused some alarms in the Thai Government; but by the time he left Bangkok, he wrote, he had managed to discourage such reports. Thailand, Ratchabandit Sapha, trans. and comp., *Khao tòn ton ratchakan thi 3* [News from the Beginning of the Third Reign] (Bangkok, 1932), 5.

[76] Chao Anu's use of this rumor is shown in a curious letter he wrote King Rama III from Nakhòn Ratchasima dated 26 January 1827, in which he stated that he was on his way to Bangkok with a large army to defend the city against a joint British-Burmese attack. He admitted that he was doing so without the King's orders, knowingly risking the death penalty. *Chtmaihet nakhòn Ratchasima* [Documents of Nakhòn Ratchasima] (Bangkok, 1954), 1-3. I am grateful to Kachorn Sukhabanij for calling this letter to my attention.

[77] *Third Reign Chronicle*, 38-9.

[78] *Vientiane Rebellion Documents, 64.*

Mangthaturat joined his small force with the Nan troops and provided supplies for the Thai army in their campaign, but his general participation in putting down the revolt was minimal.[79] The task of pacifying the Lao states, from Champasak in the south to the Hua Phan cantons and Luang Prabang in the north, was carried out on a massive scale by the armies of Siam, which gained at this time an overwhelming predominance in Laos which lasted until the last years of the century.

Conclusion

Viewed within its historical context, the Vientiane rebellion comes into clearer focus as the logical consequence of growing Thai domination in Laos. While earlier Thai interference in Lao affairs had been undertaken largely as a defense against the Burmese, and seems to have been accepted by Vientiane and Luang Prabang as such, the character of Siamese control was gradually broadened and came to be supported by the full military strength of Siam. By the beginning of the nineteenth century, Siam began to focus her attention on her eastern frontiers, and Laos became a major scene of Thai activity.

In his attempt to resist growing Siamese encroachment in Laos, as well as to check its continued political fragmentation, Cao Anu failed, and lost both his struggles. The Kingdom of Vientiane was abolished, its population forcibly removed to Siam, and its former territories fell under the direct control of Thai provincial administration. Likewise, the Thai installed a new line of rulers at Champasak and drew that state more firmly into the administrative system of the Thai Northeast. Luang Prabang remained weak, to carry on alone the shade of old Lan Chang.

[79] For events in Luang Prabang during this period, see PMLP, 52-4; and Damrong-PMLP, 262-4. The latter notes that in 1828 the Uparat of Luang Prabang was accused by the Thai of sheltering some fleeing Vientiane families, and was call to Bangkok where he soon died. Chao Suk Sœm, the son of Mangthaturat who had carried the message to Bangkok concerning Anu's plans, was named to replace him. See also *Vientiane Rebellion Documents*, 64-6; and Le boulanger, 164-70, 201-3.

In its expansion into the Lao country, Siam over extended herself. While Laos prior to 1778 had felt the adverse effects of political disunity, the result of the 1827 rebellion was to accentuate it further. The Thai had perpetuated the existence of a weak and divided Laos as an instrument of their own self-strengthening. But such a Laos was to prove more a liability than an asset in the years that were to follow.

THE BUDDHIST MONKHOOD
AS AN AVENUE OF SOCIAL MOBILITY
IN TRADITIONAL THAI SOCIETY*

From ancient times, education as a social institution has been widespread in Thailand, in every village and town, where the monasteries have provided instruction. According to Buddhist principles, such a form of instruction was, indeed, necessary, in order that the Sangha be provided with a secure knowledge of the Dhamma and Vinaya and a proficiency in Pali. In addition, education served a wider social function in providing the government and administration with literate men for its service and Thai culture and civilization with its men of letters and arts. Most men went to study their ABCs in the *wat* as children, and after ordination as novices or monks, returned to civil life and their farms, orchards, cattle, and commerce as their ancestors before them. Sons of the nobility did the same, entering the government service on leaving the religious life. However, if such was always the case—that is, if each son always followed the vocation of his father—then there would have been only two major groups in old Thai society: farmers and government officials; and there would have been no upward mobility in Thai society. For much of the time this may have been the case; but there is some evidence to indicate that sometimes sons of provincial farmers entered government service in the capital. In many such cases such men often moved into government positions through the system of religious education.

---

* Originally published in *Sinlapakòn*, the bimonthly journal of the Fine Arts Department, *10:1* (May 1966). Translated from the Thai version by the author.

When Europeans visited Thailand in the reign of King Narai, they found that "the most learned become priests, and from these priests the chiefs of the temples are chosen, who are held in high honor by the people."[1] Two centuries previously, the "Law of the Military and Provincial Hierarchy" (AD 1454) shows that educated monks and novices received higher *sakdi na* grades than those who were not educated.[2] Thus we may infer that some sort of religious examinations were in existence from the reign of King Borommatrailokanat; and we know for certain that they were held during the reign of King Narai.[3] The importance of this lies in the fact that if there were such examinations at any time, then undoubtedly some monks and novices came from the provinces to the capital in order to study with learned monks teaching in the Royal Monasteries under Royal Patronage. Among these, some, after passing the examinations, must have entered government service, especially those who while in the monkhood had taken the opportunity to acquire special knowledge and skills, such as astrology, medicine, law, or high proficiency in Pali. Such men could enter the service of the Department of the Royal Astrologers (*krom hon*); the Department of the Royal Physicians (*krom mò*) the Department of the Royal Scribes (*krom phra-alak*), or the departments dealing with religious and legal affairs (*krom thammakan, krom sangkhakari, krom ratchabandit,* etc.).

In the Bangkok Period there are numerous examples of such social mobility from the monkhood into government service, especially at the beginning of the Fourth Reign (1851–1868), when many monks left the monkhood for government service on the accession of King Mongkut. Among this group were many monks who had attained high degrees in the religious

---

[1] "Translation of Jeremias van Vliet's Description of the Kingdom of Siam," *JSS*, Vll, i (1910), 76.

[2] "Phra aiyakan tamnæng na thahan huamuang," *Kotmai tra sam duang (Laws of the Three Seals;* Bangkok, 1962), I, 315 (Section 27).

[3] Simon de la Loubère, *A New Historical Relation of the Kingdom of Siam* (London, 1693), p. 115.

examinations; for example Phraya Sri Sunthòn Wohan (Fak Salak), a Standard IX degreeholder (the highest degree, the Ph.D. of its day), Phraya Sri Sunthòn Wohan (Nòi Achanyangkun), Standard VII; Prince (Krommamün) Noribanmukhamat, Standard VIII; Phraya Itsaraphan Sophon (M.R. Nu Itsarangkun na Ayutthaya), Standard VII;[4] and many others. By 1854 more than sixty monks had left for government service; and H.M. King Mongkut was greatly upset, fearing that religious education would deteriorate with the exodus of so many learned monks to government service, leaving insufficient monks to provide religious instruction in the Royal Monasteries. In a decree issued on 3 May 1854 His Majesty gave a brief history of this educational system since the beginning of the Bangkok Period, stating that he had granted generous monthly stipends to the learned monks, holders of ecclesiastical appointments and graduates of the examinations to the extent of more than 64,320 baht per year. Nevertheless, between 1851 and 1854,

> some ecclesiastical officials, learned monks, and degreeholders, selfishly concerned only with their own dignity and rank, portraying themselves as educated men had sought out royalty and nobles in the Ministry of Interior, the Ministry of War, and the Foreign Office, assuming that these dignitaries could assist them in requesting royal permission to leave the monkhood and become high officials in these and other ministries. Such presumptions on the part of these monks is not in accordance with the Royal Desire, and should be absolutely dismissed from mind. It is the Royal Desire to obtain only men of good family and background, the sons of nobles, for high positions in the Ministries of Interior, War, and Foreign Affairs. It is not His Majesty's wish that monastery-dwellers (chao *wat*) should become *phraya*, *phra*, *luang*, *khun*, or *mün* in these ministries.

---

[4] Bangkok, National Library (comp.), *Parian ratchakan thi 5* (Ecclesiastical Degree Holders of the Fifth Reign; Bangkok, 1920), I, p. (2).

These monastery-dwellers may become officials only in the departments of the Courts of Justice (*krom lukkhun*), Royal Scribes (*krom phra-alak*) Church Administration (*krom thammakan*), Royal Pundits (*krom ratchabandit*) and Ecclesiastical Courts (*krom sangkhakari*), Monastery-dwellers who are not men of good family are absolutely forbidden to seek office in any but these five departments.[5]

Six months later, on 2 November 1854, a further decree had to be issued:

In the reign of His Majesty King Nang Klao (Rama III, 1824–51), not many learned monks left the monkhood; but now, unlike before, more than sixty have left. Henceforth, if any ecclesiastical official (*phraratchakhana*) or degree-holder (*parian*) leave the monkhood, he will become a *phrai luang*, attached for compulsory labor service to the Royal Printing Press, and will continue to be so attached until he obtains a guarantor. Upon obtaining a guarantor, he will remain liable for one month's (annual?) service at the press. If these men persist in presenting themselves before officials, high or low, seeking their patronage in obtaining release, such release will not be granted, and a punishment of fifty strokes of the rattan will be inflicted on them.[6]

From these decrees, it may easily be seen that there was a serious problem in the Sangha at the beginning of the Fourth Reign, with many more high ecclesiastical dignitaries and learned monks leaving the monkhood for government service than ever before. Another difference between this and earlier periods was that, while formerly monks of non-noble origins had tended to enter those departments dealing with education,

---

[5] King Mongkut, *Prachum prakat ratchakan thi 4* (Collected Decrees of the Fourth Reign; Bangkok, 1960-61), Decree No. 33.

[6] Decrees of the Fourth Reign. Decree No. 48.

religion, and other sciences, they were now beginning to show a desire to enter other departments. These two decrees manifested King Mongkut's explicit determination to maintain the old customs.

King Mongkut's policy continued successfully to be followed up to the middle of the Fifth Reign, around 1892. For this periodwe have definite evidence in the lists of names of monks and novices passing the religious examinations between 1870 and 1900, which were published in two volumes in 1920.[7] In collating these lists, the statistics in Table 1 emerge. In each of the examinations, among the monks and novices taking part some had taken them previously while others were entering them for the first time, and some continued on to take them in later years while others left the monkhood, some for government service and others for occupations unknown, as shown in Table 2.

It will immediately be observed that, of those monks awarded religious degrees in this thirty-year period, the proportion of those leaving the monkhood, 45%, was quite high, and is quite regrettable. The Sangha had to lose men who had gained a deep and strict religious and Pali education; men who would in the future have attained high ecclesiastical distinction, perhaps even men who might otherwise have become Supreme Patriarchs. It must be admitted, however, that those who left the Sangha may not have been suited for the monastic life, and if they had remained in the Sangha they might not perfectly have served the advance of Buddhism. Nevertheless, as King Mongkut had observed earlier, their leaving the monkhood was a waste of the funds expended on their education. But finally we must note that those funds were not totally wasted, for among those degree-holders who left the Sangha, at least as many as fifty-seven served the government in high positions, as shown in Table 3. In addition to these fifty-seven men there may have been many others who entered government service but who were not included in this published list. Thus, although the Sangha had to suffer the loss of many monks and novices in this manner, they were not lost to the work of the government, the society, and the nation.

---

[7] Degree-Holders (2 vols.; Bangkok, 1920).

In examining Table 3, one observes that most of the monks who left for government service did so between 1882 and 1890. That period was a time when the government service was growing very rapidly and was greatly in need of large numbers of educated men. At the same time, however, there were yet but few modern schools. Therefore the government had to take its civil servants from wherever it could get them. Monks and novices who had entered the ecclesiastical examinations and emerged with degrees were men who had obtained the highest education available in the country, and so the government had to receive them as civil servants in newly-created positions for the sake of the progress of the nation. After about 1890 there were two circumstances which caused the number of monks entering government service to decrease. First, once the Education Department was established (1887) many modern schools were established and increasing numbers of their graduates entered the government service. Secondly, after the Mahamakut Academy took over the administration of the religious examinations in 1894, the examinations were much more strict than previously[8] and the monks who entered them seemed to be more firmly committed to the monastic life than previously. For these two reasons, there were fewer monks and novices leaving the monkhood for government service than before.

When the standards attained by monks in the examinations are correlated with the positions which they attained in Government service (Table 4), it may be seen that examination degrees were not important in determining government rank: there were Standard VII graduates who became *khun* and a Standard III graduate who become a *caophraya*. It must be admitted, however, that government positions attained depended to some extent on the age of the monk when he left the monkhood and were not determined solely by the monk's proficiency in Pali.

As called for by the decrees of 1854, monks and novices who left to enter government service in the Fifth Reign entered ministries, departments, and offices whose work was concerned

---

[8] Degree-Holders, II, pp, 2–8.

with religion, education, and scholarship, as had been traditional (Table 5). Those thirty men, more than 50% of the total, who entered the service of the Ministry of Public Instruction, must have found their work congenial. Just as when they were still monks, they could still teach, read and write textbooks, and take a hand in the administration of the Sangha. Although they did not attain ranks as high as those who entered the service of other ministries, this did not matter, for they were likely to be performing work which suited their abilities, interests, and educational attainments. There were in addition some five or six men who began their governmental careers in the Education Department during the time when Prince Damrong Rajanubhab was Director and then moved with him to the Ministry of Interior in 1892. These were men whom Prince Damrong considered outstanding, such as Caophraya Yommarat (Pan Sukhum).

In the entire group of fifty-seven men who left the monkhood for government service in this period, Caophraya Yommarat is the best example of social mobility. He was born in a village near Suphanburi. His parents were too poor to raise him, and sent him to a monastery in the town to study. He later went to Bangkok, and entered the ecclesiastical examinations in 1882. He passed Standard III, and then left the monkhood for government service in 1883, going for teacher training at Suankulap School. For ten years he was teacher to four of King Chulalongkorn's sons, both in Bangkok and abroad. He returned to Bangkok to a position in the Ministry of Interior in 1894, his rank rising gradually to *phraya* and *caophraya*, and he served as Minister of Public Works and Minister of Local Government.[9] None of the other fifty-six men became *caophraya*, but twelve attained the

---

[9] Prince Damrong Rajanubhab, "Rüang prawat caophraya yommarat (On the Life of Caophraya Yommarat)," in *Samnao phraratchahatlekha suan phra-ong phrabat somdet phra Cunlacòmklao Caoyuhua thüng Caophraya Yommarat (Pan Sukhum) kap prawat Caophraya Yommarat* (Copies of H.M. King Chulalongkorn's Personal Letters to Caophraya Yommarat [Pan Sukhum], Together with a Biography of Caophraya Yommarat; Bangkok, 1939), pp. (22)-(112).

rank of *phraya.* Such improvement of social status as this is termed "social mobility." The fifty-seven monks and novices who left the monkhood for government and attained rank as *khun, luang, phra, phraya,* and *caophraya* during this thirty-year period indicate that the ecclesiastical examinations were a vehicle of social mobility in Thai society in former times. Further research may show that it was a vehicle by means of which the Thai nation continuously obtained outstanding men. As such, it is an important factor in the social history of Thailand.

TABLE 1
RESULTS OF THE ECCLESIASTICAL EXAMINATIONS,
1870-1900

BE	AD	Standard Attained							Total	Ten-year Total
		3	4	5	6	7	8	9		
2413	1870/71	12	—	—	—	—	—	—	12	59
2419	1876/77	16	24	4	—	1	2	—	47	
2425	1882/83	34	15	9	—	—	1	—	59	261
2429	1886/87	61	22	10	5	1	—	—	99	
2433	1890/91	69	19	9	—	5	—	—	103	
2436	1893/94	1	—	—	—	—	—	1	1	
2437	1894/95	25	26	9	3	3	—	—	66	358
2438	1895/96	7	10	1	—	1	—	—	19	
2439	1896/97	17	16	5	—	2	—	—	40	
2410	1897/98	8	12	10	—	2	—	—	32	
2441	1898/99	75	19	13	1	6	—	—	114	
2442	1899/00	12	3	2	—	1	—	—	18	
2443	1900/01	39	18	5	3	3	—	—	68	
	Total	376	184	77	12	25	3	1	678	

TABLE 2
NUMBER OF SUCCESSFUL CANDIDATES LEAVING THE MONKHOOD

BE	AD	Entered exams	To later exams	Total	Left for Government service number	%	Left for other	Total leaving monkhood number	%
2413	1870/71	12	-9	3	2	66	0	2	66
2419	1876/77	47	-15	32	5	16	5	10	31
2425	1882/83	59	-22	37	9	24	12	21	57
2429	1886/87	99	-24	75	15	20	33	48	64
2433	1890/91	103	-26	77	9	12	49	58	75
2336	1893/94	1	-1	—	—	—	—	—	—
2437	1894/95	66	-26	40	6	15	6	12	29
2438	1895/96	19	-14	5	1	20	—	1	20
2439	1896/97	40	-25	15	1	7	6	7	44
2440	1897/98	32	-15	17	5	29	3	8	40
2441	1898/99	114	-42	72	3	4	14	17	24
2142	1899/00	18	-5	13	1	8	3	4	31
2443	1900/01	68	-34	34	—	—	3	3	9
	Total	678	-258	420	57	13.6%	132	191	45.5%

TABLE 3
RANKS ATTAINED BY SUCCESSFUL CANDIDATES
LEAVING MONKHOOD

BE	AD	Khun	Luang	Phra	Phraya	Cao-phraya	Other	Total
2413	1870/71	2	—	—	—	—	—	2
2419	1876/77	1	—	1	2	—	Caokrom 1	5
2425	1882/83	3	2	1	2	1	—	9
2429	1886/87	4	5	3	2	—	Ph.D. 1	15
2433	1890/91	3	3	1	2	—	—	9
2436	1893/94	—	—	—	—	—	—	—
2437	1894/95	2	4	—	1	—	—	6
2438	1895/96	—	—	—	—	—	—	1
2439	1896/97	—	1	—	—	—	—	1
2440	1897/98	—	—	2	3	—	—	5
2441	1898/99	1	1	1	—	—	—	3
2442	1899/00	—	—	—	—	—	Army capt. 1	1
2443	1900/01	—	—	—	—	—	—	—
Total		16	16	9	12	1	3	57

TABLE 4
CORRELATION BETWEEN ECCLESIASTICAL ATTAINMENT AND GOVERNMENT RANK

Ecclesiastical Attainment	Government Rank Attained						
	Khun	Luang	Phra	Phraya	Cao-phraya	Other	Total
3	7	10	3	—	1	2	23
4	5	2	3	8	—	—	18
5	3	2	3	1	—	1	10
6	—	1	—	—	—	—	1
7	1	1	—	3	—	—	5
Total	16	16	9	12	1	3	57

TABLE 5
GOVERNMENT MINISTRIES ENTERED BY FORMER
MONKS

Ministry and / or Department		Total
Ministry of Public Instruction		
Education Department	17	
Royal Pundits' Dept.	5	
Chulalongkorn University	1	
Ecclesiastical Affairs Dept.	1	
Department unknown	6	
Total, Ministry of Public Instruction		30
Royal Secretariat (and Royal Scribes' Department)		4
Ministry of the Palace		2
Ministry of Interior		10
Ministry of Foreign Affairs		1
Ministry of Justice		7
Ministry of Public Works		1
Ministry of the Capital		2
Ministry of Finance		3
Ministry of Defense		4
Subtotal, all ministries		66
Minus men serving in more than one department		-9
Total, all ministries		57

EDUCATION AND THE MODERNIZATION OF THAI SOCIETY*

Profoundly important to the modernization of Thai society was the introduction of modern education during the reign of King Chulalongkorn (1868-1910). New schools on the Western model and a curriculum greatly different from that of the Buddhist monastery education of a few decades earlier contributed substantially to the definition of new roles and groups in Thai society and to the formation of a new generation of modern men which by the reign of King Vajiravudh (1910-1925) had assumed direction of the public life of a Thai nation becoming modern. The manner in which these changes were promoted and accomplished depended greatly upon the political and economic circumstances of the day, and resistance or indifference to modern education delayed its impact upon the masses of the population of Thailand until late in the reign and beyond. Similarly, the same circumstances, and the general state of Thai society in the latter half of the nineteenth century, were reflected in the responses of different elements of the society to modern education. These responses, expressed in the enrollments of the early schools as well as in isolated public and private statements of opinion concerning education, affected the composition of the Thai elite at a critical state in the nation's history, and their legacy remains apparent in many ways.

---

* In *Change and Persistence in Thai Society: Essays in Honor of Lauriston Sharp*, ed. G. William Skinner and A. Thomas Kirsch (Ithaca: Cornell University Press, 1975), pp. 125-150. Reprinted with the permission of the Cornell University Press.

Both the introduction of modern education in Thailand and the responses of Thai society to it were rooted in the forms and content of traditional monastery education. As Phya Anuman has noted,[1] Thailand's Buddhist monasteries had been centers of instruction and learning since the beginnings of the kingdom in the thirteenth century. Certainly as an ideal, and as often as possible in practice, education was intimately associated with religious attainment in the lives of individuals and in the life of the society as a whole. Although slaves found it difficult to gain release from their obligations so as to spend a period of service in the monkhood or novitiate, a substantial proportion of the male population must have been able to do so, and thereby acquire rudimentary literary and general training in the principles of their religion. Although most monasteries doubtless confined their educational offering to such simple fare there is substantial evidence that some monasteries, particularly those in the capital and in major provincial towns, were able to offer more specialized instruction to serve the demands of both village and court for specialists in the arts and sciences. The informal, unstructured patterns of monastery instruction could allow young men to pursue their interests in acquiring such skills as medicine or astrology for use in their home villages or allow the especially talented young man a channel into the specialized branches of the bureaucracy. Royal patronage extended to selected monasteries enabled such specialized instruction to develop throughout the country and provided a framework of bureaucratic and personal contacts through which a few especially gifted monks might come to the attention of the king.

Although monastery education pre-eminently functioned within a religious context, the essentials of which remained stable over long periods of time, there was considerable religious and cultural development in the Ayutthaya and Early Bangkok periods which both grew out of and was reflected in the monasteries. The domestication of Indic arts and sciences was primarily the work of

---

[1] Phya Anuman Rajadhon, *Chiwit chao Thai samai kòn* [Thai life in times past] (Bangkok: Ratchabandit Sathan, 1967), passim.

monks and their pupils, and their influence on the development of Thai vernacular culture must have been considerable It is not surprising that the first textbook of Thai language and poetics, based on a desire to emulate French missionary education in the seventeenth century, was written on royal command by a former monk;[2] nor was it perhaps unusual that a monk studied foreign languages early in the eighteenth century.[3] The range of interests covered by some monastery schools was considerable, and the best of these schools were by no means concerned only with narrowly defined religious pursuits. Because ambitious and intelligent men would have it so, and because the monasteries, so intimately bound up with the life of the society, could ignore neither the intellectual currents that swept the kingdom and the region nor the requirements of Thai society for specialized instruction, there seems to have existed in Thai monastery education a receptivity to change and a capacity for critical self-examination which the society could tolerate and, at times, encourage.[4]

As Akin Rabibhadana has demonstrated,[5] the extent to which traditional educational patterns served as avenues of social mobility was extremely limited as late as the reign of King Mongkut (1851-1868). The class of nobles, the *khunnang* who served the king, was rigidly defined in law and practice, and few who were not themselves the sons of nobles could gain either entrance into the Royal Pages Corps or appointment to public positions. Accordingly, the education of the sons of nobles was by no means rigorous, and "the elders of families other than the royal family still believed in the old principle that the literate arts were

---

[2] *Phraratchaphongsawadan krung Sayam* [Annals of Siam], British Museum recension (Bangkok: Kaona, 1961), pp. 149- 50

[3] W. A. R. Wood, *A History of Siam* ...(London: Fisher Unwin, 1926), p. 223. n. 3

[4] David K. Wyatt, *The Politics of Reform in Thailand* (New Haven: Yale Univ. Press, 1969), ch. 1.

[5] Akin Rabibhadana, *The Organization of Thai Society in the Early Bangkok Period, 1782-1873* (Ithaca: Cornell University Southeast Asia Program, 1969), ch. 8. ·

subjects for clerks, and it was unnecessary for a person of high status to study them seriously."[6] Although there were some exceptions, and some slight changes in the syllabus of monastery schools between the seventeenth and nineteenth centuries, most boys, whether the sons of nobles or of peasants, still were instructed in the 1850s as their ancestors had been two centuries earlier. The sons of nobles and craftsmen alike gained a basic acquaintance with the rudiments of reading and writing during their period in the monastery, and then learned the vocation of their family by a period of apprenticeship as pages at court or in the establishments of princes and nobles and by working beside their fathers or male relatives and family friends. As long as the traditional arts and sciences were essentially unchallenged, and as long as the court and bureaucratic nobility remained unreceptive to new educational qualifications, there was little inducement to major changes in educational patterns and little demand for such either from the court or from upwardly-mobile young men.

In the second quarter of the nineteenth century a few young men already were unsure of the capacity of traditional ideas and institutions to deal morally and intellectually with a world beginning rapidly to change around them. The prince-monk Mongkut, passed over for the succession to the throne in 1824, sought by a return to first principles a revitalization of the Buddhist monkhood and the religious life of the society so as to counter the increasing materialism and moral uncertainty that grew from important shifts in Asian trade and changes in the organization of Thai society.[7] These same economic and social developments were promoted by and worked to the benefit of a small group of the Thai nobility, of whom the chief was Caophraya Phrakhlang (Dit Bunnag), who served concurrently as minister of the Southern Provinces, Finance, and Foreign Relations

---

6 Prince Damrong Rajanubhab, "Rüang prawat khòng Caophraya Phatsakòrawong" [On the life of Caophraya Phatsakorawong], in *Khamklòn khòng caophraya Phatsakòrawong* [The Verse of Caophraya Phatsakorawong] (Bangkok, cremation, 1922), p. iii.
7 See Akin, ch. 7.

throughout the reign of Rama III (1824-1851).[8] His son, Chuang Bunnag, sought to adopt for government and his family's use such tools of modern economic enterprise as the square-rigged—and later the steam—sailing vessel and Western-style bookkeeping and established close relations with the growing Chinese mercantile community and with Western merchants and missionaries. Together with Mongkut, his brother Prince Cudamani, Prince Wongsathiratsanit, and a few friends, colleagues, and retainers, he learned English; and some studied other foreign languages and Western science and read European books and magazines and the Hong Kong and Singapore newspapers. All of them were men of assured status and promising prospects in their own society, and they must have come to this experimentation with new ideas and techniques more out of strength than from weakness. All were well educated in the arts and sciences of their own civilization, yet all were both sufficiently uncertain of the adequacy of their own intellectual inheritance and sufficiently confident of their own ability to master the possibilities of change, first to inquire and then to learn and to utilize these foreign ideas and instruments.

The immediate results of this early dabbling and experimentation were of limited consequence. The early exponents of religious change, Western learning, and foreign languages were the leading promoters of Mongkut's accession to the throne in 1851; but their positions in Thai society were such as naturally to lead them to take such a role, and they in fact played down their reformist sympathies in the last years of the reign of Rama III so as not to jeopardize their political fortunes.[9] Their accession to power as a group in 1851 made possible the accommodation to Western demands embodied in the treaties of 1855-56; but it did not fully tip the balance of political power in favor of the reformers, nor was their success accompanied by any aggressive espousal of the principles of fundamental reform.

---

[8] David K. Wyatt, "Family Politics in Nineteenth-Century Thailand," *Journal of Southeast Asian History* 9:2 (Sept. 1968), 208-228.

[9] Cf. Nicholas Tarling, "Siam and Sir James Brooke," *Journal of the Siam Society* 48:2 (1960), 50, 58-59, 63.

Mongkut's generation, although indeed a very small portion of it, made good use of the tools of communication and techniques of organization introduced from the West both to perceive the rapidly rising challenge to the continued survival and identity of their nation and to act to strengthen its ability to resist such threats. These men, however, were sufficiently products of an earlier age, and of its successful surmounting of the clearly defined crisis of the 1850s, to feel that accommodation and pragmatic formalistic change were sufficient to ensure the continued survival of the kingdom without fundamental reform.

Perhaps symptomatic of the approach and expectations of Mongkut and the Bunnags are the plans they made for the education of their own children. With perhaps one exception none was sent to study abroad or to attend the early missionary schools in Bangkok. Many studied with American or English tutors hired primarily to impart a facility in English like Anna Leonowens in the 1860s—but none was given any more systematic or comprehensive instruction than Mongkut and Chuang Bunnag had obtained from the missionaries before 1851. The education of the sons and grandsons of these proponents of accommodation, at least prior to 1868, remained within the broad, loose framework typical of the traditional educational patterns of princes and nobles; and the occasional tutor in English fit within these patterns like a tutor in elephantry or boxing. Although a handful of young Thai were sent abroad during Mongkut's reign for training in naval academies or secondary schools, these for the most part were not men of noble families but rather their clients and retainers, and their subsequent employment generally was as interpreters or clerks in the households and offices of their patrons.[10] They and their patrons continued to

---

[10] Prince Damrong Rajanubhab, "Athibai rüang ratchathut Thai pai Yurop [Explanation Concerning the Sending of Thai Embassies to Europe]," in *Prachum phongsawadan* [Collected Chronicles], National Library edition, part 29 (Bangkok: Kaona, 1963), vol. 7, pp. 338-45; Ratchawòrin, *pseud.*, "Nakrian Thai nai tang prathet khon ræk [The First Thai Students Abroad]," *Chao Krung* [Bangkokian] 12:4 (1963), 35-39.

work within a highly structured and tightly integrated political and social framework in which Western-style educational qualifications had as yet no place, in which the old bureaucratic structure encompassed the entire society and ranked individuals and groups in an elaborate hierarchical system of status and responsibility, and in which social advancement lay through the Royal Pages Corps, admission to which still was restricted as before.

Although Thai society had begun to undergo some "modern" changes by the beginning of the reign of King Chulalongkorn in 1868, these were extremely limited in scope. Some small portions of the royal family and nobility, like Mongkut and the Bunnags, had found new sources of power and strength in money and land, while the labor-based wealth of the remainder of the upper classes was being eroded by rapid economic development and their power sapped by unequal bureaucratic competition with the Bunnags, who by 1870 had a virtual monopoly on political power in the major ministries and departments of government.[11] The successful nobles, like the Bunnags, owed their position to policies of diplomatic and economic accommodation, which by 1870 had reduced the threat of the West to what they seem to have viewed as manageable proportions. The attitudes of the remainder of the capital and provincial elite toward modernizing change must have been shaped by their general lack of direct contact with the West, which may have led them to minimize the necessity for change, and by their experience of the Bunnags and the innovations introduced or patronized by them. If, as seems likely, they resented the imposition of a system of farming tax collections out to Chinese, the growing disparity between their own financial situations and that of the Bunnags, or the manner in which the Bunnags competed so successfully for high office, well may they have yearned for a simpler past and resisted any further encroachments upon their social and economic prerogatives.

---

[11] Akin, *Organization*, pp. 147-154.

In a very real sense, King Chulalongkorn was a generation ahead of his contemporaries. Born in 1853 to a king who had spent most of his adult life in the monkhood, he was only fifteen years old on his accession to the throne in 1868, while his ministers and the elder members of the royal family had been born in the reigns of Rama II and Rama III and had come to maturity well before 1851. Chulalongkorn was thus of the chronological generation of Mongkut's and Chuang Bunnag's grandsons, and his experience lay entirely in a world in which European trading ships and diplomats, foreign languages and newspapers, and international affairs were commonplace. His early reforming zeal suggests that he took seriously the injunctions and exhortations of Anna Leonowens and J. H. Chandler, his English tutors, although his father's deep moral convictions and values indelibly marked his thought. He clearly was determined to embark upon a program of fundamental reform that went far beyond that which his father had initiated. This course sent him into collision with both the progressives and the conservatives of his father's generation, and especially with the regent, Somdet Caophraya Si Suriyawong (Chuang Bunnag), who superintended the young king's acts until he came of age in 1873 and continued to be the single most important political figure in the kingdom until his death in 1883.[12]

Almost immediately upon ascending the throne, King Chulalongkorn took a number of measures to provide for the education of younger members of the royal family and nobility. First, in 1870 a school was founded within the palace walls for the Thai instruction of young princes and nobles in the Bodyguard Regiment of the Royal Pages Corps. Second, on his way abroad for a visit to India in 1872, the king enrolled fourteen of his cousins in the Raffles Institution in Singapore, there to be educated in English until such instruction could be provided for them in Bangkok. Finally, late in the same year the king engaged an Englishman to instruct his brothers and members of the Royal Pages' Bodyguard Regiment in English, French, and mathematics.

---

[12] Wyatt, *Politics of Reform*, ch. 2.

The manner in which these projects were received says at least as much about the state of Thai society and politics in the early 1870s as it does about early Thai attitudes toward modernization. The Palace Thai School for the Royal Pages' Bodyguard Regiment initially was well attended, drawing its 150 students from many royal and noble families which had sent their sons to join the Royal Pages Corps in the hope that they might be singled out for preferment by the new king. They had responded to the Palace Thai School not as an educational institution but rather as a device for gaining the favor of the king in a manner not dissimilar to the way in which they tried to bring their daughters to his attention. For his part, the young king seems to have judged these young men harshly, finding them semiliterate and ill-schooled in "the customs and practices of government," and founded the school in the hope of improving the quality of the royal service.[13]

A Palace English School was provided in 1872 for the same boys with essentially the same intentions. In both cases, the king was appealing for personal and political support, as well as attempting to mold his following in his own image; and he offered this special education only to those committed personally to him in the Bodyguard Regiment. The response of the boys and their families to this act must have been guided by their assessment of the king's political position and prospects. That this was indeed so is suggested by the fact that, following a major confrontation between the king and the more conservative of his nobles in 1875,[14] the enrollments of both schools dropped dramatically as the king's position weakened; the Palace English School was left with three students, all younger brothers of the king, and it finally closed its doors a few months later. The Palace Thai School continued on into the 1880s with reduced enrollments, serving primarily to provide added Thai instruction for the young men of the Royal Pages Corps and Royal Scribes Department. Although

---

[13] *Prachum kotmai pracam sok* [Collected Laws, Arranged Chronologically], ed. Sathian Laiyalak et al. (Bangkok: various publishers, 1935), vol. 8, pp. 81 -82)
[14] Wyatt, *Politics of Reform*, ch. 2.

it did inaugurate a change in the methods of Thai education, introducing printed textbooks for the first time and instructing its pupils in groups instead of individually, the content of the instruction offered was wholly traditional—and, indeed, it could have been little else, for the school's teachers all were former monks, trained in the traditional fashion. In institutional terms, the palace schools functioned within the traditional framework of the Royal Pages Corps, and they appear to have been responded to as such.

In the three years immediately following King Chulalongkorn's confrontation with the conservative nobles, he and his young advisers made two further attempts to introduce modern concepts of education. First, in 1875 a decree was issued calling upon the royal monasteries (selected monasteries that enjoyed royal patronage for Pali and religious instruction) to offer formal Thai instruction in classrooms, using the government textbooks prepared for the Palace Thai School, the expenses of such instruction to be borne by the Crown through the Department of Religious Affairs. In some ways the decree was revolutionary, for it constituted an attempt to formalize in the monasteries secular Thai education, never before a direct concern of government. In his decree, the king explained: "The Thai language is of great benefit to the study of the Tripitaka which works to the support of Buddhism and, if one is a layman, to the utility of the government service, so that it is an advantage to be literate."[15] He expressed the idea that literacy and a general improvement in educational standards worked to the benefit of the society as a whole. It is possible that the schools the decree envisioned were intended to compete with and counteract the missionary schools then being founded in Bangkok. Whatever its intentions, the decree was an utter failure, for not a single school is known to have been founded in response to it. Why? In the light of the fact that an almost identical action was successful ten years later, with most of the same individuals involved, one can dismiss the possibility of

---

[15] *Ratchakitcanubeksa* [Royal Thai Government Gazette] 1875/76, vol. 2, 111 -112.

monastic resistance or poor administration. What was lacking in 1875 was secure prestige for modern education and an established demand for its products in the offices of government.

Lacking institutionalized modern education for the young men of the ruling families of the capital, and having failed in his efforts to provide such by 1875, the king tried another alternative in 1878. He responded to a suggestion of Samuel McFarland, then an American missionary, and supported the foundation in Thonburl of a modern school to offer, "especially for those of noble blood,"[16] Thai and English instruction in such arts and sciences as might be "useful to the country."[17] The school was put under the superintendence of a governing committee composed of several of the king's brothers, his private secretary, and teachers of the Palace Thai School. Initially the prospects of the project were good: in its first year it enrolled 100 royal and noble pupils, including many who had begun their studies in the Palace Thai School. These young men would have responded to the leadership of the king, as well as to the prominence of both the traditional scholars of the Palace Thai School and the more progressive of the king's brothers and supporters on the school's governing committee. McFarland, however, as an American and a missionary, took no cognizance of the social status of applicants for places in the school. Although scholarships were offered exclusively to applicants from the royal and noble families, there was no shortage of monied day-pupils from the Chinese families of Thonburi, and they soon came to dominate its student body.

Not long after the foundation of McFarland's Suan Anand School, Prince Damrong Rajanubhab—then only nineteen years old—founded a new school for the Royal Pages' Bodyguard Regiment in 1881. The reasons he later gave for founding this school suggest what was happening to the sons of the royal and noble families during this period and may partially explain the

---

[16] *Siam Weekly Advertiser,* 27 Dec. 1879.

[17] David K. Wyatt, "Samuel McFarland and Early Educational Modernization in Thailand, 1877-1895," in *Felicitation Volumes of Southeast-Asian Studies Presented to His Highness Prince Dhaninivat* (Bangkok: Siam Society, 1965), I, 1 -3.

poor response to the educational experiments of the previous decade.[18] With a natural growth of the government service in the early years of Chulalongkorn's reign, following upon rapid economic growth and increased demands for government services in the new specialized activities of a bustling port, and greatly increased military and administrative requirements, the demands of the civil service for manpower were considerable. Prince Damrong found that young men were being rushed through a rudimentary monastery education on the old model and through brief periods of service as royal pages directly into promising positions in the expanding bureaucracy. To many, it must have appeared that the traditional system of recruiting and training young men for bureaucratic careers was working better than ever before. The sons of nobles were finding employment without difficulty. Fathers had considerable opportunity to indulge the ambitions of their sons and sons-in-law. And most officials were seemingly slow to perceive the needs of their own departments for men with changed qualifications who could efficiently run a new postal service, survey new boundaries and telegraph lines, or train new soldiers. Although the king's initiatives in the 1870s show his awareness of the importance of foreign languages, modern mathematics, and high intellectual standards enforced through common instruction and textbooks, he was not in a good political position to ensure that his wishes were heeded in such a critical area as personnel when he was still clashing with his father's generation over national policies on which he felt the very survival of the state depended. It was left to the private initiative of the king and others, such as Prince Damrong, to promote a new educational standard, and to await a day when those who responded to such opportunities could be rewarded.

Acting on his assessment of the need for better-trained officers in the Royal Pages' Bodyguard Regiment, Prince Damrong founded Suankulap School in September 1881, with the full support and approval of the king. Although only ten students

---

[18] Prince Damrong Rajanubhab, *Tamnan Rongrian Suankulap* [History of Suankulap School] (Bangkok: priv. pub., 1963), pp. 26-27.

enrolled in the first months, the response soon became overwhelming, and by its second year the school was training nearly 100 young men for civil responsibilities as well as for appointments in the officer corps of the Bodyguard Regiment and ultimately in a new national army. Prince Damrong quickly introduced new methods of teaching Thai, new courses in elementary mathematics and geography, and specialized courses designed to meet the needs of modern civil servants, including accounting, telegraphy, and the writing of precis, letters, and reports. Notably absent in the school was the literary emphasis of the old Palace Thai School and the strong religious emphasis of conventional monastery instruction. Suankulap was a new sort of school, run on modern lines, strongly influenced by the earliest Western and Western-type schools in Bangkok, and introducing into Thai educational traditions and institutions a strong bureaucratic bias that was extremely slow to fade.[19]

Suankulap School may be taken as a sensitive barometer of change in Thai society during the two decades following its foundation in 1881. Of nineteen students gaining the equivalent of a secondary education there before 1890, seventeen were of royal descent. The prominence of royal students at Suankulap in its first decade may not have been wholly accidental. In a speech in 1884,[20] the king explained that his primary motivation in approving the foundation of the school had been "a concern for the future of the royal family." He stated that

> the problem with all these *mòmcao* and *mò mratchawong* [the grandsons and great-grandsons of kings] is that there has been no avenue through which they could enter government service. It is not that there have been no openings for them, but rather that, being of royal blood, there have been no opportunities for them to be trained [through

---

[19] Wyatt, *Politics of Reform*, ch. 5.

[20] King Chulalongkorn, *Phraratchadamrat nai Phrabat Somdet Phracunlacòmklao caoyuhua (tangtæ Ph.S. 2417 thüng Ph.S. 2453* [Speeches of King Chulalongkorn, 1874-1910] (Bangkok: Sophon, 1915), pp. 36-37.

apprenticeships in government offices], because they are royalty and not [the sons of] officials. ... I intend that this school shall be a means of preserving their positions, that they might not be ignored as they have been in the past.

Viewed in such terms, Suankulap might have been the king's weapon against the power of the old noble families who dominated government departments at that time; but he also made it clear in his speech that more than simple power was involved. He felt that the country's fate depended upon intelligent decisions made and executed by well-educated government officers; and with royalty generally willing to follow his lead, their proffered services were not to be refused out of any blind adherence to outmoded social conventions. The school's prestige was well established with this speech (which came only a few months after the death of the leading figure of the older conservative faction, Caophraya Si Suriyawong [Chuang Bunnag]), by the fact that the king began to send his own sons to Suankulap for their Thai and English instruction, and by the open participation of several of the leading princes of the realm in the school's administration By 1888 its enrollment included more than 400 students, among whom junior members of the royal family predominated. The king followed his special provisions for the education of princes with new schools within the palace walls for his own sons and daughters in 1893 and then with major efforts to have all his sons and many of his nephews educated abroad, to the point where there were at least fifty young Thai studying in England in 1897, of whom at least half were members of the royal family.[21] Junior members of the royal family were among the first to respond to the initiatives of the king and others in founding such schools as Suankulap, and consequently were among the first to be educated abroad. Thereby they gained a head start over other elements in Thai society which assured their subsequent dominance in the bureaucracy, and this advantage goes a considerable way toward

---

[21] Wyatt, *Politics of Reform*, pp. 161-164, 200-201.

explaining their prominence in the reigns of Vajiravudh and Prajadhipok, as late as 1932.

On the whole, the old nobility was much slower to respond to the opportunities for modern education, for reasons indicated above. That they were slipping behind is indicated by a curious document issued in 1890, a "Royal Decree Inviting the Sons of Government Officials to Enter the Service of Various Government Offices,"[22] in which the king explained that the old system of apprenticeship in government departments, under which the sons of government officials had worked as clerks in their fathers' offices and gradually rose as they obtained experience, no longer was functioning even to maintain the position of the old nobility in government service. Young noblemen were wasting their time on idle pleasures, disdaining work as common clerks, and relying on their ancestry and family backgrounds to qualify them for public service. Meanwhile, others of common backgrounds were taking up paid clerical positions "out of financial necessity," and by their knowledge and experience were qualifying for promotion over the heads of young men of good breeding (*trakun*). The king was apprehensive lest,

> if this state of affairs continues, the sons of families which have maintained their status for generations will not be able to enter government service. ...
>
> Therefore, His Majesty issues this decree to advise those government officials who have sons and grandsons who should enter government service at the present time that His Majesty would much rather have the sons of government officials of noble family enter the government service in the departments in which their fathers have served or even higher positions than have those of no distinguished family enter the government service.

He urged the old nobility to have its sons and grandsons trained (presumably in schools) before entering government service,

---

[22] *Ratchakitcanubeksa* 1890/91, pp. 195-97.

and to accept clerical positions so as to gain the experience in modern office practice which he deemed indispensable for promotion. But the king closed by warning the nobility that the old days of the hereditary dominance of the nobility were past:

> His Majesty needs many more government officials at the present time, as there is more work to do than people to do it; and, good family or not, if a man has sufficient knowledge and ability, His Majesty will maintain him in government service without regard for his background; but if he is of good family, so much the better.

The opportunities existed, particularly at Suankulap, for young men of the old noble families to educate themselves for positions which would allow them to maintain their status in Thai society. Only slowly did they respond to these, by swelling the enrollment of Suankulap in the early 1890s, and then by attending the new secondary schools that began to appear at the turn of the century.[23]

Much more prompt and insistent in their response to modern educational opportunities in the 1880s and early 1890s were two other elements in the urban population of Thailand: the Chinese and the lesser nobility. It is clear that these were the groups who sent their sons to the early missionary schools in the capital, and it would appear that they soon were patronizing the private schools, the existence of which is briefly and obscurely referred to in reports of the Education Department in the late 1880s and mid-1890s. McFarland's Suan Anand School was reported to be popular among the Chinese and "common people" of Thonburi by 1884;[24] and many of the most prominent of the monastery schools founded under the auspices of Prince Damrong and the Education Department beginning in 1884 were in strongly Chinese neighborhoods of Bangkok and Thonburi, notably Wat Sam Cin Tai (now Wat Traimit). At one private school supported

---

[23] Wyatt, *Politics of Reform*, chs. 6, 10.
[24] *Siam Weekly Advertiser*, 22 Dec. 1883, 20 Dec. 1884.

by the Education Department, the Ban Cin Yæm or New School founded in 1888, Chinese instruction was offered.[25] In the following year, Suankulap instituted a twenty-baht tuition fee intended "to prevent common people (*khon leo*) from attending the school;"[26] and the royal decree of 1890 mentioned above implied that large numbers of non-noble young men were entering the government service as clerks. Chinese students became more noticeable on the student rosters of Suankulap, McFarland's Sunanthalai (formerly Suan Anand), and the New School (later Ban Phraya Nana School) in the early 1890s;[27] and Chinese and non-noble students from Ban Phraya Nana and Assumption College (run by French Catholic missionaries) did extremely well in the competitive examinations for king's scholarships when these were introduced in 1898.[28] These indications from a   fragmentary record suggest strongly that the Chinese mercantile community of the capital and minor bureaucratic families were relatively more responsive to modern educational opportunities before 1900 than was the old nobility. The reasons for this are nowhere made explicit but may be inferred from the context in which these developments occurred.

This was a period during which the Thai bureaucracy was expanding rapidly. Its growth before about 1885 was relatively moderate, as most of it occurred within existing institutions. Once the revived royal program of reform gained momentum in the mid-1880s, however, and new departments and proto-ministries were created in preparation for the major reorganization of the administration in 1892, the demands of the state were overwhelming, as the decree of 1890 suggests. Government expenditures climbed at the phenomenal annual rate of nearly 14 per cent in the 1890s, and the staffs of the new ministries increased

---

[25] Wyatt, *Politics of Reform*, p. 119n.

[26] Wyatt, *Politics of Reform*, p. 121.

[27] Cf. Phya Anuman Rajadhon, *Fün khwamlang* [Later Recovery] (Bangkok: Süksit Sayam, 1967), pp. 244-263.

[28] *Bangkok Times*, 10 March 1898; and cf. G. William Skinner, *Chinese Society in Thailand: An Analytical History* (Ithaca: Cornell University Press, 1957), p. 168.

proportionately. School enrollments, however, owing primarily to political difficulties over the budgetary priorities for the various ministries, remained virtually static, at 2,000 to 2,500, between 1885 and 1897; and the shortage of manpower by 1898 was viewed by the king as desperately acute.[29] Similarly, the demands of Chinese and Western mercantile houses, banks, and shipping agencies for educated young men with foreign languages were considerable. This was an ideal situation for ambitious young men.

In addition, not all social groups were equally open to respond to the possibility of mobility. Until the abolition of corvée labor in the years 1899-1905, commoners would have found it difficult to continue their studies at the secondary level, for these commonly came at an age when young men began to be subject to the corvée. (Indeed, in an attempt to increase school enrollments in 1901, it was proposed that the requirements of compulsory labor be waived for students in secondary schools.[30]) Royalty, the sons of nobles, and Chinese, however, were exempt from the corvée and free to pursue their studies as long as they wished. In addition, a great deal of control over recruitment and training for the public service lay in the hands of the king and his brothers, who probably felt less inhibited in hiring commoners and Chinese than the older conservative nobles might have been. With the availability of modern education from the mid-1880s, in public, private, and missionary schools in Bangkok and the provinces, the educational opportunities were present for those perceptive enough to recognize their value.

The motivational factor, however, is essentially unknowable: Why were members of the royal family, the lesser nobility, and the Chinese relatively more responsive to modern educational opportunities in this period before 1900? *Mòmcao* and *mòmratchawong* could have responded to the king's call for

---

[29] *Caophraya* Phrasadet Surentharathibodi, *Phraratchahatlekha la nangsü krap bangkhom thun khòng Caophraya Phrasadet* [Official Correspondence between the King and Caophraya Phrasadet] (Bangkok: privately published, 1961), pp. 292-300.

[30] Wyatt, *Politics of Reform,* pp. 252-253.

education and public service on a personal level and with the rapidity which springs from a long-resented exclusion, if one is to accept the king's assessment of their recent status. One might be able to infer something of the same motivation on the part of the lesser nobility if one supposes that they suffered from bureaucratic competition with the Bunnags in the 1860s and 1870s and/or took the king's patronage of modern education as an invitation to outstep and bypass their rivals. The chief government appointments of the late 1880s and the 1890s went mainly to those whose major qualifications were educational; and particularly noticeable is the manner in which Prince Damrong Rajanubhab brought into the service of the Ministry of Interior men who had done well at Suankulap School in the period when he had directed it.[31] Some of the Chinese who came through the new schools in this period might be classed as lesser nobility, although the fathers of many of those whose names appear in the school rosters and prize lists of the day are prefixed with the term *cin* "Chinese," rather than with a bureaucratic rank. The political circumstances of the period seem most adequately to explain the responses of the royal family and the lesser nobility, while more practical considerations and a degree of commitment to the values of Thai society must be assumed for that portion of the Chinese community which so responded.

A great deal changed in the few years spanning the turn of the century. The king began, after his first visit to Europe in 1897, to perceive that the manpower requirements of the state were more than bureaucratic, and he began to demand more of education in building the common knowledge and sentiments which could make of his kingdom a modern national unity. A great many more vocations than the civil service required a fundamental basis in modern education, and all of the citizens of the state required education of vocational and moral utility. With the assistance of Prince Damrong, Prince Wachirayanwarorot, and Phraya Wisut

---

[31] Tej Bunnag, *The Provincial Administration of Siam, 1892-1915: The Ministry of Interior Under Prince Damrong Rajanubhab* (Kuala Lumpur: Oxford University Press, 1977), chs. 4-5.

242 of STUDIES IN THAI HISTORY

Suriyasak (*Mòmratchawong* Pia Malakul, later Caophraya Phrasadet Surentharathibòdi), he began to frame, elaborate, and put into operation a vastly increased educational program, including major expansions both in public elementary education throughout the kingdom and in general and specialized secondary education centered in the capital.

Two educational institutions founded around the turn of the century were of particular importance to the royal family and the nobility: King's College, a preparatory school run as an English public school, founded in 1897; and the Civil Service School, founded in 1900. Although heavily subsidized by the government, King's College required an eighty-baht admission fee (equivalent to four months of a teacher's salary), and its student body was drawn almost exclusively from the elite of the capital. Of a student body of seventy-one in 1898-99, twenty-seven were of royal blood (mainly *mòmcao*) and twenty-six were the sons of government officials of the rank of *phraya* and above (equivalent to a department head). It primarily prepared its students for studies abroad with a thoroughly English curriculum and English teachers; and from its foundation it was extremely successful, almost completely dominating the awards of king's scholarships from 1899. Operating on a different level, but for much the same sort of clientele, was the Civil Service School, which had a student enrollment of 182 within a year of its foundation. Data on the social composition of the school are not available, but scattered biographies of its graduates suggest that its enrollment came primarily from what has been termed the lesser nobility. Prince Damrong, however, writing some years later, states that he hoped at the time the school was founded that young men of common backgrounds might through it gain entrance to the civil service.[32] The school's curriculum, though partly academic, was primarily practical, and its students went directly to positions in the provincial administration of the Ministry of Interior.[33] After a time,

---

32 Prince Damrong Rajanubhab, "Rüang Rongrian Mahatlek Luang [Concerning the Royal Pages School]," in *Nithan borankhadi (bang rüang)* [Tales of the Past (Selections)] (Bangkok: privately printed, 1956), pp. 88-91.
33 Tej, *Provincial Administration*, ch. 5.

it came also to serve as a means of integrating the sons of the petty nobility of the provinces into the national administrative elite. These two schools, then, functioned primarily to re-equip the traditional elite and to enable them to maintain their social status in a country which in many ways had changed dramatically over the course of a few decades.

Power and social status were much more broadly dispersed and finely shaded by the end of Chulalongkorn's reign than they had been forty years earlier. The bureaucracy had become a national service instead of a series of local ones topped by the limited circle of the court; and its finely graded hierarchies were reaching down through governors and judges, clerks and school-teachers, to remote country districts and villages. A new national army and provincial police force had been created, and specialist services proliferated. These were staffed, for the most part, with the graduates of a greatly expanded system of secondary and technical education that by 1910 included thirteen secondary schools with more than 1,250 pupils and at least eleven technical schools with more than 1,500 pupils studying such subjects as medicine, law, education, military and naval sciences, and agriculture. These drew their enrollments from all elements of society but predominantly from the urban centers and mainly from Bangkok. Through these schools came hundreds of civil servants each year, as professional services began to develop and become aware of themselves as new elements in Thai society. In the long run they would come to compete for power with the graduates of the elitist academies and with those whose status and power depended to some degree upon the advantages of birth.

As Skinner points out,[34] Chinese society in Thailand by 1910 was beginning to have a coherence and self-consciousness which involved an increasing emphasis on Chinese education. The growth of modern schools around 1910, sponsored by Chinese community and speech-group associations, reinforced what the Thai came to view as Chinese economic exclusivity; and it had the effect of slowing the rate of assimilation of Chinese into Thai

---

[34] Skinner, *Chinese Society in Thailand*, ch. 5.

society. To the extent that assimilation became less urgent for the life and prosperity of the Chinese in Thailand; and to the extent that commercial and economic development, as well as the interests of political and social cohesion, provided incentives to the development of Chinese education distinct from that beginning to be offered by the Thai government—to that degree was Chinese participation in Thai government education reduced. No information is available on the proportions of Chinese students in government schools in Bangkok around 1910, but there is evidence that the government was beginning to be concerned over a slowed rate of Chinese assimilation and hoped to use the schools to correct this trend.[35]

The major government concern in education by 1910, however, was rapidly to achieve universal elementary schooling, and specifically to incorporate into a national educational system the provinces in which more than 90 per cent of the nation's population lived. The revival in the mid-1880s of the policy of extending public secular education in the monasteries had elicited a small but important response in the capital and a few provincial towns; but the numbers involved were minuscule. Through the 1890s the number of monastery schools increased very slowly owing to a shortage of public funds and the lack of a clear commitment to mass education. The first major expansion in provincial education came at the end of the nineteenth century with the king's determination to base Thai nationality and modernity on an educated public. A program separate from the Ministry of Public Instruction was established in 1898 under the leadership of Prince Wachirayan Warorot, the king's brother and patriarch of the Thammayut reform sect, to survey the educational and religious state and needs of the provinces and to found new schools and modernize the Buddhist hierarchy. The reports of the monks who served as provincial education directors provide revealing glimpses of provincial attitudes toward educational change.[36] They are dominated by statements such as the following:

---

[35] Wyatt, *Politics of Reform,* pp. 337-339.

[36] David K. Wyatt, "The Beginnings of Modern Education in Thailand, 1868-1910," Ph.D. diss., Cornell University, pp. 329-331, 344.

"Laymen are satisfied with [traditional] education as it is. They feel no need for higher [i.e., improved] education, and desire only simple literacy" (Ratchaburi).

"There is little interest in education; more in gambling" (Samut Songkhram).

"Only one monk and layman in four is dissatisfied with traditional education" (Uthaithani).

"Two-fifths are satisfied with traditional education" (Tak).

"Although most laymen are satisfied with education as it is, the monks are not satisfied" (Suphanburi).

"The progress of education will be difficult, as it has not yet been proven to the public that education can make a difference to their livelihood" (Nonthaburi and Pathumthani).

"Apart from government officials and some Chinese, there is little faith in modern education. People think that there is no use to be served by educating their children" (Chanthaburi).

"There is more demand for Pali than for Thai instruction. ... The only support for schools comes from officials and local governing committees" (Nakhòn Si Thammarat).

With their supporting evidence, these statements suggest that the provincial demand for modern elementary education as late as 1900 was extremely small. Areas with strong Thammayut monasteries and areas where much modern economic development had taken place seem to have been more responsive to the founding of new schools than less well-developed areas; and government officials, Chinese, and monks generally were more receptive to change than the ordinary town-dweller in the provinces. The demand was beginning to be felt in numerous scattered areas, including some very remote provincial areas in the Northeast (for reasons essentially unexplained); but the numbers enrolled in the new monastery schools as late as 1907 remained relatively small: approximately 20,000 students in 340 schools.

New and clearer concerns motivated a more forceful effort to promote provincial education in the last years of Chulalongkorn's reign. New ideas about the purposes of mass education were articulated eloquently by Prince Wachirayan early in 1906. While he felt government efforts were essentially successful in preparing rapidly large numbers of young men for the public service, Prince Wachirayan was concerned at the government's neglect of vocational education, the result of which he saw to be the economic and technical dominance of the Chinese in Thailand. Education, he argued, was "an instrument of social mobility" (*khrüang plian phün phe*) which the government was using too narrowly. He urged the king to expand the educational system to provide all boys with a good general and moral education, as well as to prepare young Thai men for specialized nongovernmental careers in commerce, technical vocations, the crafts, and the professions.[37] The same objectives were urged on the government in 1910 by Phraya Wisut in arguing for the establishment of a major new vocational school in Bangkok.[38] The vocational aspect of these proposals was slow to be embodied in schools, perhaps from lack of demand; but the general desire to build an educated citizenry through universal (and eventually compulsory) education began to be pursued with vigor in 1909. The new schools in every province and town of the kingdom attempted to provide instruction to groups of children in a common national syllabus, using common textbooks and the national language, and overriding provincial dialects and minority languages.[39] The government was by no means immediately

---

[37] Wyatt, *Politics of Reform,* pp. 325-328.
[38] Wyatt, "Beginnings," p. 591.
[39] Wyatt, *Politics of Reform,* pp. 328-329.

successful in attaining its object; but the institutional framework was created through which further innovations and qualitative improvements could be introduced.

The public response to this major and rapid expansion must have been mixed. The entire kingdom certainly was not induced overnight to accept the proclaimed virtues and value of modern education; yet more than 100,000 boys in Thai villages and towns were attending the formal monastery schools on the modern pattern in 1912. To some extent the idea of the moral, economic, and patriotic value of education may have taken hold quickly; but it would appear that much more crucial to the rapid acceptance of modern education once it was pursued aggressively by the government was the behavior of the leaders of Thai society at all levels. The patterns of authority in traditional Thai society remained relatively intact, and to a considerable extent even the individuals and families remained the same. The moral and political authority of the king, tried and proven over an extremely long reign, coupled with his effective control over the functioning of the civil administration and his strong influence over the Buddhist monkhood and buttressed by the traditional authority and prestige of the monarchy, imbued the royal policies and orders and commitments with a sanctity and "rightness" which made them extremely difficult to resist, particularly when the king had the power to enforce his will if necessary. The leaders of Thai society at all levels, ranged in hierarchies newly tightened and laced with improved communications, responded at least pragmatically to what was expected of them, and they often did so with a confidence born of shrewd self-interest and simple trust. And so provincial governors headed up public subscriptions to build new schools, and village headmen and monks persuaded parents to send their sons to attend them.

The importance of royal authority and "change from above" rightly has been stressed often in treatments of the beginnings of modernization in nineteenth-century Thailand. The delay in reform until the king had established his power over the claims of the conservative nobility attests to this fact. But the greatest advantage the king had thereafter was his control, through carefully selected ministers—most of whom were his own brothers—over the occupational structure of the kingdom

His reform program created a new governmental demand for manpower which could be met only through modern education; and the king and his brothers, partly for political reasons but primarily out of a rational commitment to the idea of government by men qualified through education for their new public roles, shaped the manner in which that demand came to be satisfied. They succeeded in transforming both institutions and values to suit their ends. The traditional association between education and the Buddhist monasteries was maintained, but the content of the new education was secularized and adapted to changed vocational demands and political and social ends. The traditional appeal of the bureaucracy remained, yet the nature of the bureaucratic structure and its roles were changed. The monkhood and the monarchy remained pillars of the moral authority of the state, yet that authority was employed in radically new ways. It was the skillful and creative blending of such "continuities and discontinuities," of which Lauriston Sharp spoke so eloquently and insightfully in his presidential address to the Association for Asian Studies in 1962,[40] that was so distinctive in the modernization of Thailand and has given Thai society for so long such vibrant strength.

---

[40] Lauriston Sharp, "Cultural Continuities and Discontinuities in Southeast Asia," *Journal of Asian Studies* 22:1 (1962), 3-11.

SAMUEL MCFARLAND AND EARLY EDUCATIONAL MODERNIZATION IN THAILAND, 1877–1895*

In His Highness Prince Dhani Nivat's illustrious career in Thai public life the Ministry of Education has a special place, for it was there that His Highness spent six productive years (1926–1932) as Minister. To commemorate His Highness' birthday, nothing could be more appropriate than some account of those to whom that ministry's work owes its origin. Among these is the American missionary and educator, Samuel G. McFarland, one who made an early and important contribution to that work which His Highness was later to take up.

After a short but brilliant burst of reform which marked the beginning of the reign of King Chulalongkorn, the general pace of modernization slowed after 1875. Of the two modern-type schools founded in 1870 and 1872 for the Thai and English education of the Royal Family and official nobility, only the Thai school conducted by *Phraya* Si Sunthòn Wohan (Nòi Achanyangkun) remained, first in a building within the Palace walls near the Phimanchaisi Gate, and then in the Saranrom Palace.[1] The Palace English school, conducted by an Englishman,

---

* In *Felicitation Volumes Of Southeast-Asian Studies Presented To His Highness Prince Dhaninivat* (Bangkok: Siam Society, 1965), vol. I, pp. 1-16. Reprinted with the permission of The Siam Society.

[1] Abbreviations:

CSS: *Cotmaihet Sayam samai* [Siam Times]. Bangkok, 1882–86.

NA: National Archives Division, Department of Fine Arts, Bangkok. Fifth Reign Archives, Ministry of Education Series.

PKPS: Sathian Laiyalak et al., comps., *Prachum kotmai pracam sok* [Collected Laws, Arranged Chronologically]. 69 vols. Bangkok, 1935– .

250 STUDIES IN THAI HISTORY

Francis George Patterson, lasted for only three years. During that time it made an important contribution to the education of the next generation of Thai leaders, for its pupils included the young Princes Devawongse, Damrong, Phanurangsi, and Wachirayan, among others, all of whom were to leave their marks on modern Thailand; but towards the end of his three-year contract Patterson was able to attract only one student, the young Prince Damrong, and he left Bangkok when his contract lapsed in mid-1875.[2] A somewhat similar fate befell the young King's first attempt to inaugurate the reform of the traditional system of monastery education. On 6 July 1875 he issued a decree extending the Royal Patronage to secular, Thai schools in the Royal Monasteries *(phra-aram luang)* offering the monks free printed Government textbooks (the six-volume *Munlabot Banphakit* series of *Phraya Si Sunthòn*), salaries to lay teachers and increased alms to monk teachers, and rewards to those pupils passing government examination.[3] For a variety of reasons, however, the decree had very little effect, and only one such secular monastery school on the modern pattern (at Wat Niwet Thammaprawat, at Bang Pa-in) had been established by 1883.[4] Thus, by 1877 a beginning

---

RKB: *Ratchakitcanubeksa* (Royal Thai Government Gazette). Bangkok, 1858-59, 1874–79, 1888– .

SWA: *Siam Weekly Advertiser.* Bangkok, 1869–86.

On the Palace Thai School of Phraya Si Sunthòn Wohan, see Prince Damrong Rajanubhab, *Khwamsongcam* [Memoirs] (Bangkok, 1962) pp. 160–61; Thailand, Krasuang Kalahom, *Tamnan thahan mahatlek* [History of the Royal Pages Bodyguard Regiment] (Bangkok, 1953), pp. 1–8; "Prakat rüang rongrian [Decree on Schools]," PKPS, VIII, 81- 82: and *Siam Repository*, V: 1 (Jan. 1873), 114; VI: 1 (Jan. 1874), 18; and VI: 2 (April 1874), 284–85.

[2] On the Palace English School, see Prince Damrong, *Memoirs*, pp. 172, 179-90; and *Siam Repository*, IV: 4 (Oct. 1872), 399; V: I (Jan. 1873), 114; VI: I (Jan. 1874), 18, 56; and VI: 2 April 1874), 284–85.

[3] "Prot klao ... ca hai mi acan sòn nangsü Thai læ sòn lek thukthuk phra-aram [His Majesty Pleases to Have Teachers Teach Thai and Arithmetic in Every Royal Monastery],û RKB, II (C.S. 1237/A.D. 1875-76), 111–12.

[4] Thailand, Krom Praisani, *Sarabanchi suan thi 1 khü tamnæng ratchakan samrap caophanakngan krom praisani Krungthep Mahanakhòn tang tæ camnuan pi mamæ benca sok cunlasakkarat 1245 lem thi 1* [Directory, Section l: Government Officials. For Postal Officials in Bangkok, From the Year of the

had been made in educational reform; but this beginning was more remarkable for the ideas it expressed than the results it obtained. The ardent desire of the young King to examine the laws and customs of both Thailand and the West, discarding that which was damaging or unsuitable and maintaining or introducing that which would work for the progress of the nation[5] was frustrated, partly by a lack of strong public interest and partly by the obstruction of "Old Siam."[6] Modern education was not the least such casualty.

It was into this situation that Dr. Samuel G. McFarland intruded in 1877. Dr. McFarland and his wife had arrived in Thailand in 1860, and began their missionary work at Phetburi in 1861 at the invitation of *Caophraya* Phanuwong Mahakosathibòdi (Thuam Bunnag), then governor of the province and later Foreign Minister in the reign of King Chulalongkorn, who asked the missionaries to instruct his sons and the children of local official families in English and "other subjects."[7] During the next sixteen years this educational work expanded greatly and came to include vocational and academic education for girls as well. By 1877 the educational work of the McFarlands of Phetburi was well known, having gained even the patronage of the King when a new brick building was constructed for the girls' school in that year.

Goat, Fifth of the Decade, 1245 of the Lesser Era, Vol. I] (Bangkok, 1883), p. 198.

[5] "Phraratchabanyat phikat kasian ayu luk that luk thai [Royal Ordinance Regulating the Emancipation of Slaves]," PKPS, VIII, 197-207.

[6] "Phya Krasap," *Siam Repository*, V: 4 (Oct. 1873), 451. See also Mr.Sickels to Mr. Payson, 18 March 1880, printed in United States, Dept. of Interior, Bureau of Education, *Progress of Western Education in China and Siam* (Washington, 1880), p. 12. David Sickels, then American Consul in Bangkok, wrote "There is ... a strong party of the old regime who do not approve of education in any form, particularly in foreign languages and studies, who believe implicitly in the wisdom of their ancestors, and obstinately oppose themselves to any attempt at removing the ancient landmarks wherever posted."

[7] Bertha Blount McFarland, *McFarland of Siam*, (New York, 1958), pp. 20–21.

In October 1877, Dr. McFarland wrote a public letter suggesting that Americans might endow "a college at Bangkok for the education of Siamese youth, similar to Robert College in Constantinople."[8] Coming to Bangkok the following month, McFarland was sought out by the King's English-language Secretary, *Phraya* (later *Caophraya*) Phatsakòrawong (Phòn or Chumphòn Bunnag), and was told that the King himself desired to establish such a school and would like to have McFarland take charge of it. After some months of hesitation, McFarland agreed to abandon his missionary labors to establish and conduct the school, and submitted to the King a proposal for such a school.[9]

McFarland's plan was presented to the King in the following July with the comments and suggestions of *Phraya* Phatsakò rawong. The Government agreed to grant McFarland an annual salary of 80 *chang* (6400 *baht*) over a five-year term, and to provide an annual sum of 120 *chang* (9600 *baht*) for the expenses of the school. The old Nantha-Utthayan Palace (generally known as Suan Anand) was refurbished and put at the school's disposal. It was to be run as a combination boarding and day school, instructing the sons of royalty and nobility in both Thai and English. According to King Chulalongkorn's diary, on the advice of *Phraya* Phatsakòrawong "only sufficient training in reading and writing for clerks" was to be offered, and "the teaching of Christianity will be absolutely prohibited." The school was, however, to provide such instruction in mathematics and the arts and sciences as might be "useful to the country."[10]

---

[8] SWA, 16 May 1878. McFarland, p. 48, asserts that the idea of establishing the school was the Kingûs, prompted by an article on American education in Harperûs Monthly Magazine which "fell into the Kingûs hands" early in 1878. The close conjunction between the dates of McFarlandûs public letter (25 Oct. 1877–although it was not published until 16 May 1878) and *Phraya* Phatsakòrawongûs seeking an interview with him (November, 1877) seems more than mere coincidence.

[9] L. (sic.) G. McFarland to Mr. Torry, n.d., printed in *Progress of Western Education*, p. 13.

[10] King Chulalongkorn, *Cotmaihet phraratchakit raiwan* [Royal Diary], VII (Bangkok, 1934), entry for 2 9/ 8, 1240 (8 July 1878), 164–66.

Rather than being made an organ of Government, the school was put under the administration of a governing committee appointed by the King, presided over by Prince Phichit Prichakan and including among its members *Phraya* Phatsakòrawong; *Phraya* Si Sunthòn Wohan and *Khun* Owat Wòrakit (Kæn Owatsan), teachers at the Palace Thai school; and several of the King's younger half-brothers, including Prince Devawongse and Prince Sommot Amòraphan. It was with this committee that Dr. McFarland signed his contract in October, 1878, with the understanding that he would be given a free hand in all academic matters.[11]

The school opened on 2 January 1879, and in its first year taught one hundred royal and noble pupils, of whom half were awarded full Royal Scholarships for tuition and board by the school committee. Many of the boys already had begun their studies in the Thai school within the Grand Palace.[12] They were taught by four Thai and three American teachers, the latter including Dr. McFarland, his son George Bradley McFarland, and John Eakin.[13] Their first year was concluded with public examinations, the first such examinations ever held in Thailand, on 19 December 1879, presided over by Prince Phichit and *Phraya* Si Sunthòn. The results of the examinations greatly pleased contemporary observers, and the school subsequently was advertised as offering a better education than could be obtained abroad, largely on the strength of the fact that its American teachers were proficient in the Thai language.[14]

The school was organized to give a five-year English-Thai course at the secondary school level. Half the day was devoted to English instruction and half to Thai. Great emphasis was placed

---

[11] Ibid.: and McFarland, pp. 48–49. Documents concerning the hiring of Dr. McFarland and the founding and early history of this school, formerly kept in the National Museum, were among those destroyed in the disastrous fire of 1960.

[12] King Chulalongkorn, *Diary*, VII, 166.

[13] CSS, 4 Nov. R.S. 104 (1885), pp. 83–84.

[14] SWA, 27 Dec. 1879, 25 Dec. 1880, and 24 Dec. 1881; and CSS, 4 Nov. R.S. 104 (1885).

on training the boys for complete fluency in both languages, but the syllabus gradually was expanded beyond language training to include lectures on astronomy, geography, and history by 1881,[15] and physics. telegraphy, and military drill by 1883.[16] Parallel to the formal academic activities of the school, McFarland sponsored the formation of a literary society which at annual public meetings exhibited the developing skills of the students in compositions, speeches, and debates, presented entirely in English.[17] It would be reasonable to expect that by means of this ambitious program and the substantial abilities of the school's teachers, both Thai and American, the Suan Anand school attained a high standard of quality, the more significant because the indigenous base of Thai traditional education on which it had to build had not yet begun noticeably to adapt itself to the changing requirements and standards of a new age.

Suan Anand had been founded expressly to provide quality Anglo-vernacular education to the sons of royalty and nobility,[18] and the initial response of these elements of the population to the founding of the school seemed encouraging, as there were more applicants for admission in the first year than could be accommodated, and of those admitted there were twelve "princes of the realm."[19] By the end of McFarland's first five-year contract in 1883, however, it was apparent that this plan had gone wrong. The proportion of Government-sponsored royal and noble pupils had dropped steadily, year by year, until "only seven of the original fifty young noblemen" graduated with the first class in 1883.[20] The school had not lacked for students, but these for the most part were young day-students from the growing and prosperous Chinese mercantile community and from poorer families living in the neighborhood of the school.[21] Disquiet

---

[15] SWA, 8 Jan. 1881.
[16] Paul A. Eakin, *The Eakin Family in Thailand* (Bangkok, 1955), pp. 14–15, 18.
[17] CSS, 4 6/ 1, 1245 (5 Dec. 1883); 4 /5 1, 1245 (19 Dec. 1883); and 4 1/ 2, 1246 (17 Dec. 1884).
[18] SWA. 27 Dec. 1879; and McFarland, pp. 48–49.
[19] McFarland, p. 49; and *SWA*, 9 Jan. 1879.
[20] SWA. 22 Dec. 1883.
[21] Ibid.; and SWA, 20 Dec. 1884.

about the changing social character of the school was voiced implicitly by Samuel J. Smith, editor of the *Siam Weekly Advertiser*, and it was the cause for some serious concern on the part of McFarland himself.[22]

There are a number of explanations for this social change, which was materially to affect the fortunes of the school. First, social discrimination must have played some part in it, a fact easily adduced from measures taken later in the decade to preserve the upper-class character of Suankulap School.[23] Another important factor was the inconvenient location of the school on the Thonburi side of the river, far from the homes of many of the Royal Family and nobility."[24] Another factor may have been the curriculum of the school, which, judged against *Phraya* Phatsakòrawong's initial caution about restricting instruction to subjects suitable for clerks may have been viewed as too radical and too *farang* by more conservative elements of the society. It seems most significant, however, that the turning point in the school's enrollments came during the course of the 1881 school year at the same time as Prince Damrong's Suankulap School in the Royal Pages' Bodyguard Regiment (Krom Thahan Mahatlek Raksa Phra-ong) added English instruction to its syllabus, taught by Baboo Ramsamy Pultar.[25] Suankulap undoubtedly attracted many young princes and nobles away from McFarland's Suan Anand School in these years, particularly because it could offer its students a privileged entree into the Government service. Thus was born the unequal rivalry between the two schools.

---

[22] McFarland, p. 109.

[23] NA 5 S 5, 25/5, "Announcement, R.S. 108" (1889/90), announcing a twenty baht annual tuition fee "to prevent common people *(khon leo)* from attending the school."

[24] McFarland, pp. 56–57.

[25] Prince Damrong Rajanubhab, *Tamnan Suankulap* [History of Suankulap] (Bangkok, var. ed.) gives the early history of this school. See also McFarland, p. 57; and *SWA*, 24 Dec. 1881. Baboo Ramsamy Pultar was variously styled "a native of Calcutta" (McFarland, p. 57) and "Ex-Regent of Muar and Kessang and Heir-at-Law to the Sultanate of Johore and its Dependencies" (*Bangkok Times*, 26 Sept. 1898).

At the close of the 1883 school year Suan Anand was closed, and no date was set for its reopening. Soon thereafter, John Eakin was approached by Prince Damrong and asked to take over the headmastership of the English division of Suankulap School. On asking "what class of students would be admitted, ... the Prince [Damrong] replied that only the sons of princes and the highest nobles would be admitted. John [Eakin] felt that any scheme of education that did not include the sons of the common folk was a mistake. So John persisted in resigning ...."[26] In this incident may be seen an expression of the democratic admissions policy of Suan Anand School which sealed its character.

Suan Anand School was reopened sometime in 1884 and resumed its educational work. That year witnessed a great reawakening of interest in education in Bangkok which Dr. McFarland served and from which he benefited. In late August or early September of that year King Chulalongkorn appointed a committee of seven men, including Prince Damrong, *Phraya* Si Sunthòn Wohan, *Phraya* Phatsakòrawong, *Phraya* Samut Buranurak (Sin), *Phra* Sarasat Photchakan, *Khun* Owat Wòrakit, and Dr. S.G. McFarland. They were asked to devise a program of mass public education for the country, prescribe a syllabus and prepare textbooks, and fix qualitative standards for examinations.[27] Out of their deliberations, in which they could draw from a wealth of varied experience from all their members, came the first government monastery schools by the end of the same year."[28]

---

[26] Eakin, p. 19.

[27] SWA, 6 Sept. 1884; and CSS, 4 -6 10, 1246 (10 Sept. 1884). See also the Kingûs Birthday Speech, CSS, 4 5/ 11, 1246 (24 Sept.1884).

[28] The first of the Government monastery schools is held to have been founded at Wat Mahannapharam late in 1884: see Prince Damrong Rajanubhab and W.G. Johnson, *Prawat sangkhep hæng kancat kansüksa pratyuban hæng Prathet Sayam phak thi 1 (Ph.S. 2414–2434)* [History of the Introduction of Madern Education in Siam, Part I (1871–1891)] (2nd ed.; Bangkok, 1937), pp. 14–15; and Momluang Manich Jumsai, *Prawat kansüksa khòng Thai* [History of Thai Education] (Bangkok, 1959), p. 20. Another such school, sponsored by Phraya Phatsakòrawong, opened at Wat Prayurawong in Thonburi in November, 1884: See CSS, 8 April 1885; *SWA*, 1 April 1885; and Phrakhru Phisanwinaiwat (Hem), *Prawat Wat Prayurawong* [History of Wat Prayurawong] (Bangkok, 1928), pp. 8, 49–52.

By mid-1885, Prince Damrong was acting as "Commissioner of Education" over an Education Bureau in his Department of the Royal Pages' Bodyguard Regiment, superintending the activities of "12 or 16" monastery schools, and submitting regular quarterly and annual reports directly to the King.[29] In the educational development of the eight years from 1884 to 1892, McFarland and his Suan Anand school fared well. Its enrollment grew from an annual figure of fifty pupils between 1885/86 and 1888/89 to 206 in 1891/92,[30] despite increasing competition from Suankulap for upper class students and from the New School (founded by Baboo Ramsamy in 1888) for other students. One of the conditions apparently agreed to by McFarland in 1884 was that his school be brought under the centralized control of Prince Damrong, and his school was included in the rosters of Government schools submitted by the Department of Education as early as 1886.[31] Under this new arrangement, the school benefited from the services the Department could provide, which must have been of particular importance for its Thai curriculum, and it submitted to regular inspection by the Department.[32] It also acquired in Prince Damrong an effective advocate and patron.

---

[29] SWA, 29 Aug. 1885. Prince Damrong's seventh Quarterly Report, reprinted in Rong Sayamanon, *Prawat Krasuang Süksathikan 2435–2507*[History of the Ministry of Education, 1892–1964] (Bangkok,1964), pp. 54–58, covers the second through fourth months of R.S. 105 (1886/87). Counting back, one arrives at the second quarter of the year 1885/86, i.e. June-October, 1885, as the date of the first report, which is not in the Archives. Alternatively, if Prince Damrongûs numbering of his reports included his first annual report, the first quarterly report would have covered the third quarter of the year 1885/86, i.e. October-December, 1885. The Department of Education as a distinct, civil office of government, however, dates only from 1887.

[30] From annual reports of the Department of Education for the years R.S. 105 (1886/87) and 107–110 (1888/89–1891/92) in NA 5 S 8, 16/8 and 18/8; NA 5 S 2, 22/2; and statistical reports in NA 5 S 8, 6/8 and 17/8 II, 7.

[31] Suan Anand School is included in the earliest of the Department's reports (R.S. 105) which I was able to find in the Archives.

[32] See school inspection reports annexed to the report of the Department of Education for C.S. 1248 (1886/87). Suan Anand did, however, continue to hold its own examinations, separate from the national ones.

In 1888 Prince Damrong took to the King McFarland's complaint about the inconvenient location of Suan Anand, arguing that its location kept its enrollments low and brought undue hardship upon its pupils.[33] He succeeded in obtaining for the school the use of the Sunanthalai School buildings, constructed as a memorial to Queen Sunanthakumarirat and intended for use as a girls' school, but which had laid vacant for some years for lack of a teacher.[34] Into these fine, spacious and accessible buildings on the Bangkok bank of the river McFarland's school moved on 4 March 1889.[35] The enrollment of the school immediately tripled. McFarland modified the curriculum to heed the growing demand for civil servants by introducing a "special department in instruction for candidates for the Civil Service of the Government ... The course of instruction will be through the medium of the English language."[36]

By 1890 the school, renamed Sunanthalai, seemed headed for an important role in the developing educational system of Thailand. Prince Damrong began to plan to have the new Sunanthalai, with its American teachers, enter into beneficial academic competition with Suankulap English school and its British teachers, in the manner of the competition between such English public schools as Eton and Harrow.[37] The new English curriculum and examination standards devised by (Sir) Robert Morant and promulgated by the government in 1891[38] were designed at least in part to lay down the ground rules for this competition, although they called for substantial modifications of the Sunanthalai curriculum, inasmuch as they prohibited the teaching of English to students who had not yet passed Standard I of the Thai curriculum (equivalent to the modern *prathom*) and made no provision for the well-developed and varied curriculum which had been taught at Sunanthalai for more than a decade.

---

[33] NA 5 S 2, 22/2, Report, Dept. of Education, R.S. 107 (1888/89).
[34] McFarland, p. 73.
[35] *Bangkok Times*, 16 March 1889.
[36] *Bangkok Times*, 30 March 1889.
[37] NA 5 S 8, 17/8 II, 17, Phatsakòrawong to King, 18 May 111 (1892).
[38] "Phraratchabanyat kansòp wicha [Royal Ordinance on Examinations]," RKB, VIII (R.S. 110/A.D. 1891–92), 26–29. This decree took effect in 1892.

All these plans, however, came to naught with the ministerial changes of 1892. Prince Damrong, who had been preparing to assume the full responsibilities of Minister of Public Instruction in the new Cabinet form of government, found himself suddenly transferred to the Ministry of Interior,[39] and was able to devote no attention to educational affairs during the next six years. As *Phraya* Phatsakòrawong had to be moved from the Ministry of Agriculture and Commerce to make way for *Caophraya* Surasakmontri (Cœm Sæng-Xuto), he was given the new post of Minister of Public Instruction.[40]

Phatsakòrawong was presented almost immediately with a major crisis. His predecessor, with Morant, had entered the Ministry into very expensive commitments for expenditures for teacher education, a new school for upper-class girls, and provincial education. When Phatsakòrawong went to the Cabinet to obtain budgetary sanction for these programs, however, neither his political influence nor his persuasive powers were equal to the task, and the Ministry's budget was drastically cut. Phatsakòrawong was unable to alter the commitments made to hire teachers from abroad, as they were regulated by contract. His only alternative was to cut back on the funds for the government monastery schools and to make drastic changes in English education.[41] Because the teachers for the girls' school were en route to Bangkok while no funds were available either

---

[39] Prince Damrong Rajanubhab, *Thesaphiban* (Bangkok, 1960), pp. 3–8.

[40] Caophraya Surasakmontri, *Prawatkan khòng caophraya Surasakmontri* [The Life of Caophraya Surasakmontri] (Bangkok, 1962), IV, 265. As one will note from the frequent mentions of his name above in connection with educational matters, Caophraya Phatsakòorawong was not at all as unfitted for his new office as his critics thought; e.g. McFarland, p. 96. For his biography, written by Prince Damrong, see the volume published on his cremation, *Khamklòn khòng caophraya Phatsakòrawong* [The Klon Verse of *Caopraya* Phatsakòrawong] (Bangkok, 1922).

[41] The documents on this episode are extensive. Phatsakòrawong himself gives a good summary in his letter to the King's Secretary, Prince Sommot, 21 June 117 (1898), NA 5 S 5, 13/5, 15. The most important letters of the period are: NA 5 S 8, 17/8 II, 17, Phatsakòrawong to King, 18 May 111 (1892); 17/8 II, 19, Phatsakòrawong to Sommot, 6 June 111 (1892); 19/8, 9, King to Phatsakòrawong, 12 June 111 (1892); and 17/8 1, 83, Phatsakòrawong to

for a school building for them or for operating expenses, his only alternative was to hand over to them the Sunanthalai buildings, which possessed a handsome endowment[42] and were, at any rate, intended for the education of women. Phatsakòrawong also had no choice but to dismiss Dr. McFarland from the headmastership of Sunanthalai in June, 1892. He offered McFarland a choice between accepting a position as a compiler in the Textbook Bureau of the Ministry at 4800 baht per year (he formerly had received 7680 baht) or conducting a private school under an annual Government subsidy of 2400 baht.[43] McFarland could only choose the certainty of the former.

Had Sunanthalai School been attended by the sons of the princes and the highest government officials the Cabinet might have had second thoughts about their actions. But they did not. Deprived of the support of his former patron, Prince Damrong, who had his own budgetary battles to fight, McFarland could only acquiesce loyally in their decision. During the latter half of 1892, all English instruction was temporarily centered at Sunanthalai under the headmastership of Glen Culbertson, McFarland's former assistant who, unlike McFarland, was under Government contract. Then, when the girls' school moved to Sunanthalai in December, 1892, the British teachers returned to Suankulap, while Culbertson moved back across the river to the Thammasapha Building at Wat Prayurawong in Thonburi.[44]

King, 20 June 111 (1892). See also King to Phraya Wisut Suriyasak, 11 June 117 (1898), printed in *Phraratchahatlekha læ nangsü krap bangkhom thun khòng caophraya Phrasadetsurentharathibodi ... R.S. 113–118* [The Correspondence Between His Majesty and Caophraya Phrasadet Surentharathibodi ...., 1894–1899] (Bangkok, 1961), pp. 262–63.

[42] NA 5 S 5, 20/5, 21, Phatsakòrawong to Sommot, 6 March 115 (1897); and 20/5, 25, "Expenses and Income of Sunanthalai, R.S. 107–114" (1888/ 89–1895/96).

[43] McFarland, p. 110; NA 5 S 2, 28/2, 4, Phatsakòrawong to Sommot, 31 March 113 (1895); 5 S 8, 17/811, 17, Phatsakòrawong to King, 18 May 111 (1892). Mrs. McFarland attributes her father-in-law's dismissal to Morant's hostility towards "that American preacher" (p. 109) and to Morant's own feelings of "self-importance" (p. 111).

[44] NA 5 S 8, 17/8 I, 95 and 100, Phatsakòrawong to Sommot, 17 Dec. 111 (1892), two letters.

Culbertson resigned in June, 1893, and the school was then put under the direction of an American-educated Thai headmaster, Kòn Amatyakul. A year later it was moved again to an old private residence (Ban Phraya Nanaphitphasi [To]), where it continued on for a number of years.[45]

S. G. McFarland did not long survive the loss of his school, on which he had labored for more than fourteen years. Much disheartened at the treatment accorded him, unjustly, he felt, and weakened by ill-health and advanced age. he resigned his position in the Textbook Bureau in March, 1895, after sixteen years in the government service.[46] He opened a private night school, teaching commercial subjects for a year, and then, in May, 1896, returned to the United States, where he died a year later.[47]

It is not easy to assess the contributions made to the educational modernization of Thailand by Dr. McFarland and his Suan Anand/Sunanthalai School. Both he and his biographer were too modest and the records are too mute. Yet his influence during the crucial decade of the 'eighties, when educational development first began to gather momentum, must have been strong. Because some of Suankulap's teachers had taught earlier at

---

[45] *Bangkok Times*, 5 July 1893, 14 July 1894, and 8 Sept. 1894. Kòn Amatyakul (1865–1922), later *Phraya* Winitwitthayakan, Head of the Examinations Bureau in the Department of Education, was the son of *Phra* Pricha Konlakan (Sam-ang Amatyakul). who in 1879 married Fanny Knox, daughter of the British Consul and heroine of R.J. Minney's *Fanny and the Regent of Siam* (London, 1962). *Phra* Pricha, learning in 1876 that Dr. Samuel House, his former tutor, was returning to America, sent his son Kòn with Dr. House to be educated. After completing a four-year course in mining engineering at Lafayette College in Indiana, Kòn returned to Thailand in 1889, and taught at various schools, including Sunanthalai, before becoming headmaster of the Ban Phraya Nana School in 1893 and he served there until 1903. See George Haws Feltus, *Samuel Reynolds House of Siam* (New York, 1924), pp. 222–23; and Nai Kòn's biography, "Prawat sangkhep ammat-ek Phraya Winitwitthayakan (Kòn Ammatayakun)" in *Prachum phongsawadan*, pt. 36 (Bangkok, 1927), pp. (2)-(5).

[46] NA 5 S 8, 17/8 I, 55, McFarland to King, 16 June 1892; 5 S 2, 28/ 2, 8, McFarland to Phatsakòrawong, 1 Feb. 1895; and 28/2, 4, Phatsakò rawong to Sommot, 31 March 113 (1895).

[47] McFarland, p.112. Mrs. McFarland mistakenly dates his resignation as 1 April 1894.

Suan Anand (e.g. *Phraya* Owat Wòrakit); because of Prince Damrong's friendship with McFarland; and because Suankulap was founded at least partly as a reaction to or in response to Suan Anand and worked towards solution of the same problems and fulfillment of the same needs in somewhat similar fashion, part of the credit for Suankulap School must go to McFarland, although, of course, the major share is Prince Damrong's. Similarly, the whole development of post-primary education in Thailand owes not a little to the examples set by McFarland's work from 1879, in the schools whose work he directed, in his work on Government education committees, in the examinations he instituted, and in the textbooks he compiled.

One can see in the career of Samuel McFarland an antidote for the excessive preoccupation with foreign advisers evident in many Western historical writings on this period. McFarland, to one acquainted with the turbulent years of the reign of King Chulalongkorn, exemplified the effective "foreign adviser." He was effective because he was always content to view his role as service, as an instrument of the Thai government in pursuing ends and policies which it alone could define. McFarland was given a task to perform and he accomplished it. While he had only limited success in attracting members of the royalty and nobility to his schools he rendered a vital service by providing government departments and commercial firms with bright, well-educated young men who could serve their country at the high tide of her rush into the modern world.[48]

---

[48] I wish to express my deepest gratitude to Dhanit Yupho, Director-General of the Department of Fine Arts, and Thawat Sumawong, Director of the National Archives, who so graciously gave me access to documents in the National Archives; to Tri Amatyakul, Director of the Division of Literature and History, and Kachorn Sukhabanij, who were so generous with advice and encouragement; and to Carat Kamphlasiri and Praphat Trinarong, section heads in the Archives, whose friendship and assistance made my work there so pleasant. To all of them is due the credit for making my research there possible. Neither they nor the Foreign Area Fellowship Program, which supported my research in Thailand in 1962–63, are responsible for the views and opinions expressed herein, which are alone the responsibility of the author.

ALMOST FORGOTTEN:
BAN PHRAYA NANA SCHOOL*

In his memoirs, the late Phya Anuman Rajadhon mentioned briefly the first modern-type school—Ban Phraya Nana—that he attended as a youth of nine or ten years in 1897 or 1898.[1] Considering the *caokhun's* formidable intellectual powers, his liberal ideas, and his wide-ranging interests, that school is of considerable interest to those interested in the forces that shaped a remarkable generation of Thailand's leaders around the turn of the century. Looking back upon it from a perspective of seventy years, Ban Phraya Nana might not be considered particularly important in itself, for its existence was brief and its influence limited. Within the context of its own times, however, when it was one of only three schools providing English instruction in Thailand, its significance grows; and even if one comes to regard it as an institution that failed, one can neither forget its immediate influence on the generation of schoolboys which attended it, nor discount the school's value as an educational experiment.

Ban Phraya Nana School was the lineal descendent of the first permanent public English and vernacular school in Thailand, that founded by Samuel G. McFarland in 1879 and known first as Suan Anand and then as Sunanthalai School.[2] Through the

---

* *In Memoriam Phya Anuman Rajadhon,* ed. Tej Bunnag and Michael Smithies (Bangkok: The Siam Society, 1970), pp. 1-8. Reprinted with the permission of The Siam Society.

[1] *Fün khwamlang,* vol. I (Bangkok, 1967), pp. 244, 255, 258-63.

[2] See D.K. Wyatt, "Samuel McFarland and Early Educational Modernization in Thailand, 1877-1895," *Felicitation Volumes of Southeast-Asian Studies Presented to His Highness Prince Dhaninivat (Bangkok, 1965),* vol. I, pp. 1-16.

1880s it was noted as one of the chief centers of English instruction in Thailand, and its enrollment rose rapidly from 50 pupils in 1885 to 206 in 1892,[3] an increase attributable primarily to the dramatic bureaucratic expansion which preceded the reorganization of government in 1892. Late in 1890, two additional American teachers joined the staff of Sunanthalai School to augment the efforts of six already teaching there.[4] Government policy toward English instruction, however, was at that time being reconsidered, and in 1889/90 the Education Department began at Suankulap School to prohibit the study of English by those who had not yet completed the primary school curriculum.[5] This was a direct threat to Sunanthalai, where English instruction usually was given to boys almost immediately upon their matriculation.

In May and June of 1892, when at the urgings of the new Cabinet the Ministry of Public Instruction under *Caophraya* Phatsakòrawong (Phòn Bunnag) began to reduce the budget allocation for English instruction, Sunanthalai was an obvious target for economy measures, as it was the single most expensive charge on the ministry's budget.[6] The Cabinet recommended that all English instruction be concentrated at Suankulap School, but *Caophraya* Phatsakòrawong instead recommended a modification of the existing system, government support being concentrated instead on two schools, Suankulap and Sunanthalai. This arrangement, which preserved some public English instruction for boys not of the upper classes (who went to Suankulap), was made possible by eliminating government support of a third Anglo-vernacular school (New School, founded by Baboo Ramsamy[7]) and by cutting the salary of McFarland and moving him into the ministry offices as a textbook compiler.[8]

---

[3] D.K. Wyatt, "The Beginnings of Modern Education in Thailand, 1868-1910," doct. diss., Cornell University, 1966, p. 152.

[4] National Archives (NA), 5 S, 17/81, 9, Damrong to King, 17 Dec. 1890.

[5] NA 5 S, 18/8, 5, Education Department, Report, 1890/91.

[6] NA 5 S, 17/8,11,17, Phatsakòrawong to King, 18 May 1892.

[7] See D.K. Wyatt, *The Politics of Reform in Thailand (New* Haven and Bangkok, 1969), pp. 124, 167-69.

[8] Wyatt, "Samuel McFarland," pp. 8-9.

But Sunanthalai did not survive the 1892/93 school year without further economies. In December 1892 it was decided to use the Sunanthalai buildings for a new girls' school. The Ministry temporarily transferred Sunanthalai's British teachers to Suankulap School, and the remaining American teachers to a building, the Thammasapha, at Wat Prayurawong in Thonburi which normally was used for the instruction of Buddhist monks.[9] It was just at this moment that Prince Narathippraphanphong, who then was acting as Minister of Finance, suggested to *Caophraya* Phatsakòrawong that the former home of *Phraya* Nanaphitphasi (To Bunnag), which had just reverted to the Crown, might be suitable for use as a school. In passing this recommendation on to the King, Phatsakòrawong noted that the school was on the river, and might not be safe for use as a primary school. He suggested that the buildings might be used as a boarding school where boys from the provinces might study Thai before going on to higher English instruction at Suankulap, or that it might serve as a training school for the civil service.[10] From the range of ideas which he presented, the King decided to concentrate on the immediate problem and authorize its use for Sunanthalai School.[11] The ministry was slow to prepare the new buildings, and so the school remained on at the Thammasapha building under Glen Culbertson as its headmaster until it was able to move into "Ban Phraya Nana" in 1894.[12]

Immediately prior to its move to the Thammasapha in 1893 Sunanthalai had a considerable student body and a strong academic record. It had 8 teachers for its 206 pupils (121 of which were studying English) in 1892; and in the Government English examinations conducted in March of the following year,

---

[9] NA 5 S, 17/8 1, 95, Phatsakòrawong to Sommot, 17 Dec. 1892, no. 649/6279.

[10] NA 5 S, 17/8 1, 100, Phatsakòrawong to Sommot, 17 Dec. 1892, no. 650/6287.

[11] NA 5 S, 17/8 1, 101, King to Phatsakòrawong, 21 Dec. 1892, no. 739/111.

[12] *Bangkok Times*, 14 July 1894.

[13] NA 5 S, 17/8 11, 17, Phatsakòrawong to King, 18 May 1892, and *Bangkok Times*, 25 March 1893.

12 of the 14 students sitting the examinations passed them, proportionally a better record than any of its rivals.[13] The comparative quality of English instruction at the school for some time survived the loss of all its *farang* teachers by 1893 (Culbertson resigned in that year[14]), but its place in the educational system rapidly declined. Culbertson was replaced as headmaster in 1893 by Kòn Amatyakul (later *Phraya* Winitwitthayakan), who was largely responsible for the school's high standards.

Kòn was born in 1864, the son of *Phra* Prichakonlakan (Sam-ang Amatyakul) by his third wife, whose name was Liam.[15] His father was a good friend of Dr. Samuel Reynolds House, an American medical missionary in Bangkok, and when Dr. House returned to the United States in 1876, Kòn was sent with him to be educated. Following secondary schooling, he took a four-year non-degree course in mining engineering at Lafayette College in Indiana, and returned to Thailand early in 1889 only to find his family out of favor at court, and deprived of the extensive mining interests they had held a decade earlier.[16] He found employment as an assistant teacher at Sunanthalai School with Dr. McFarland in April, 1889, and taught there in that capacity until he became the headmaster of the Thammasapha School in 1893.[17] His earliest interests had been in the natural sciences, and he was virtually a native speaker of English; and these strengths cannot have failed to be imparted in his school.

Only one detailed account of Ban Phraya Nana's operations appears to have survived, in the report of an inspection of the school carried out by Prince Chanthaburi Narunat (then Prince Kittiyakòn) in August, 1895, as part of a general survey of

[14] *Bangkok Times,* 5 July 1893.

[15] Tri Amatyakul, comp., *Prawat banphaburut læ sakunwong ammattayakun* (Bangkok, 1964), p. 37.

[16] George Haws Feltus, *Samuel Reynolds House of Siam: Pioneer medical missionary 1847-18-6* (New York, 1924), pp. 222-23; Prince Damrong Rajanubhab, "Prawat phraya aphirak ratcha-utthayan," in *Cotmaihet sadet praphat tangprathet nai ratchakan thi 5 (Bangkok,* 1917), pp. 10-11.

[17] "Prawat sangkhep ammat-ek phraya winitwitthayakan (Kòn Amatyakul)," in, *Prachum phongsawadan,* pt. 36 (Bangkok, 1927), pp. (2)-(5).

government schools in Bangkok which the prince undertook in preparation for assuming duties as Director-General of the Education Department.[18] Prince Chanthaburi reported that "about 50" pupils were in attendance, taught by three Thai teachers and divided into classes, one to each room. There were two classes studying Thai, a smaller class of beginning students studying the elementary reading book *Bæp rian reo* and a larger class studying grammar, the royal chronicles, Thai composition, and general reading. He explained that the pupils did not study Thai for a proficiency sufficient to pass the government primary examinations, but only to be able to read and write prior to beginning the study of English. There were 20 pupils in the English division, studying at various levels. Prince Chanthaburi generally was impressed:

> When I visited, the teacher was not present, but I saw the pupils' work—grammar, reading, [writing to] dictation, arithmetic, algebra, object lessons, drafting, and geography. I tested them on grammar, and they were not good. Their algebra was good. They have very good discipline, even when the teacher was not present.[19]

Ban Phraya Nana was among the best of the schools he visited, surpassed only by Suankulap and Sunanthalai Girls' School in the quality of the education the prince found.

The only other detailed information available for Ban Phraya Nana comes in connection with the annual Government English examinations, conducted usually in March or April. Year after year a small number of the school's students managed to pass the examinations—12 in 1893, 12 in 1894, 18 in 1896, and 27 in 1898.[20] Some of its students performed particularly well in the annual competitive examinations for King's Scholarships for study abroad. The first such examinations were held in March,

---

[18] Wyatt, *Politics of Reform*, p. 148.
[19] NA 5 S, 13/4, 1, Kittiyakòn to King, 31 Aug. 1895.
[20] NA 5 S, 14/5, *passim*.

1898, and at the top of the list of 22 candidates was a "Nai Boa," a tutor in the Royal Palace who had received his English instruction at Ban Phraya Nana.[21] The school's candidates in subsequent years, however, did not fare so well: only one candidate entered from Ban Phraya Nana in 1899, and he finished near the bottom of the list, while the four boys contending in 1900 finished in 10th, 11th, 12th, and 13th places.[22]

That something happened to Ban Phraya Nana School around 1898, at about the time Phya Anuman left it to attend Assumption College, is readily indicated in the examination and enrollment statistics of the Education Department. In 1892, the school had enrolled 121 out of a total of 252 students of English in Bangkok's government schools; but by 1898 it enrolled only 66 out of 403.[23] In 1892 there had been only three public English schools (Suankulap, Sunanthalai, and New School), but in 1898 there were six; and these six included four schools more heavily supported by the Ministry than Ban Phraya Nana—Suankulap, the Normal School, King's College (a new English-style boarding school), and Sunanthalai Girls' School.[24] For the most part, these schools were performing better than Ban Phraya Nana in the annual English examinations; and students from Assumption College, Suankulap, and King's College dominated the King's Scholarship examinations.[25] Alternative educational opportunities were becoming more widely available in Bangkok, better financed by the government, with more trained teachers and Europeans to teach English, and better equipped with textbooks. With a thorough overhaul of secondary education in 1902, it was to be expected that Ban Phraya Nana School should be among the first schools to be dropped.

---

[21] *Bangkok Times,* 10 March 1898.

[22] NA 5 S, 52/5, 18, W.G. Johnson to Kittiyakòn, 24 March 1900.

[23] NA 5 S,95/5, 21 b, Report on Numbers of Schools and Students, 1898/99.

[24] *ibid.*

[25] *Bangkok Times,* 11 April 1899,12 March 1901, 13 March 1902, 10 March 1903; and NA 5 S,52/5,17, Kittiyakòn to Phatsakòrawong, 28 March 1900.

Phraya Wutthikanbòdi (M.R.W. Khli Suthat na Ayudhya, later *Caophraya* Witchitwongwutthikrai), the new Minister of Public Instruction in 1902, gave four reasons for closing Ban Phraya Nana:

(1) The location of the school is not appropriate, as almost all the pupils have to cross over from this [Bangkok] side of the river;[26] (2) The smaller, less bright pupils begin studying English right away, which keeps them in school for a long time and makes [their education] very expensive, as the school has to pay an English teacher disproportionately to the time he teaches; (3) Pupils who study this way learn slowly and get no real education; and (4) *Luang* Winitwitthayakan (Kòn) is a person who has a very good knowledge of English as well as other branches of knowledge, and should teach at a higher level commensurate with the value of his education.[27]

To these arguments the king agreed, noting that the discussion of the proper level at which English should be taught had dragged on long enough, and should be resolved in favor of postponing English instruction to the secondary school—the decision taken earlier in 1888/89.[28] Accordingly, Ban Phraya Nana School was closed early in 1903, and its remaining teachers were transferred to Wat Samphanthawong School in Sampheng, the Chinese quarter of the city, where it became a "special primary school," admitting only students who had finished their primary education. There, boys embarked upon the full-time study of English as preparation for entering the service of the Post and Telegraph Department, the railways, and private business, where a sound knowledge of English was required.[29] *Phraya* Winit went

---

[26] Ban Phraya Nana School was located on the Thonburi side of the Caophraya River, opposite Wat Müang Khæ, or roughly opposite the river end of Surawong Road.

[27] NA 5 S, 85/5, 34, Wutthikanbòdi to King, 25 Oct. 1902.

[28] NA 5 S, 85/5, 37, King to Wutthikanbòdi, 26 Oct. 1902.

[29] NA 5 S, 85/5, 34, Wutthikanbòdi to King, 25 Oct. 1902

on to teach at the Medical School, and then served as headmaster of several secondary schools before entering the Examinations Bureau of the Education Department in 1914, where he served until his retirement in 1921.[30]

Its influence on a number of city boys who went on to careers in business and government aside, Ban Phraya Nana School in the ten years from 1893 to 1903 might be viewed as a somewhat protracted experiment in which the most effective age-level or educational level for foreign language instruction was at issue. One might argue from Phya Anuman's silence concerning English instruction at Ban Phraya Nana that it was hardly memorable there; but much more telling an argument is the specific fact of his transfer to Assumption College around 1898 —a time when boys from Assumption were placing second, third, and fourth in the examinations for King's Scholarships, and when enrollments in English instruction elsewhere were rising rapidly. It would be dangerous, however, to apply the same facts to an argument attempting to prove the government's 1902 case for postponing English instruction to the post-primary level, however, for a considerable number of boys like Phya Anuman were studying English at Assumption College and then the Bangkok Christian Boys' High School in the 1890s and 1900s while their contemporaries were finding English instruction in Government schools delayed until the secondary level. It is highly probable that the Government's decision to restrict English instruction to the post-primary level reflected primarily the difficulty in spreading scarce resources of trained teachers among a number of primary schools as much as it reflected the actual results of the instruction offered. The issue still, of course, is very much alive both in Thailand and elsewhere; and it still tends to be resolved by governments whose first concern must always be the allocation of scarce resources.

---

[30] "Prawat sangkhep," p. (3).

INTERPRETING THE HISTORY
OF THE FIFTH REIGN*

The forty-two year reign of King Chulalongkorn is a period of the most profound significance for modern Thailand. The Fifth Reign saw a dramatic transformation in almost every aspect of Thai national life; and the permanent changes made in Thai governmental institutions, no less than in the structure and composition of the society and economy, still in many ways bear the imprint both of that great king's and his ministers' reforming ideas and of the pressures of the times in which he lived. There is little disputing the real import of the changes thus introduced but the manner of their conception and execution does present serious problems of interpretation which are more difficult for the fact that so little serious detailed historical research on the Fifth Reign has been completed.

In addition to the conduct and resolution of Thailand's external affairs during the high tide of European imperialism, one theme which figures prominent]y in all accounts of the period is the world of domestic modernization which culminated in the 1890s with the reorganization of the central administration and the subsequent reform of the system of provincial administration. In discussing and interpreting these developments, most Western historians have focused their attention on the work of European advisers and on the inhibiting influence of Thai domestic politics. A close examination of the process of educational reform during the Fifth Reign suggests that this emphasis is misplaced, and that the process of reform and modernization in the Fifth Reign

---

* *Sangkhomsat parithat* (The Social Science Review, Quarterly) 6:2 (Sept. 1968), 20-23.

European political imperialism and externally-imposed reform.

Two developments stand out in the history of the reign which are not accounted for in the conventional interpretations. First, a great deal of attention has been paid to the series of important reforms instituted in the years 1873-74, immediately following Chulalongkorn's second coronation as King in his own right. A beginning was made in abolishing the system of slavery, the practice of prostration in the royal presence was done away with, some legal reforms and major financial reforms were undertaken, and the Privy Council and Council of State, embryonic new political institutions, were inaugurated. In 1875, however the processes of reform ground to an almost complete halt, and they did not resume momentum until the later 1880s: the consultative councils ceased to meet, no new major reform decrees were promulgated, and many of the new institutions created just a few years earlier ceased to function. In the mid-'eighties, as an older generation of Ministers of State began to die and pass from public office, the work of reform picked up almost where it had left off a decade earlier, to culminate after a period of frenzied preparation in the reorganization of 1892, and thereafter steadily to accelerate through to the end of the reign. Most accounts of the reign have failed to notice this rhythm of reform, although surely its understanding is crucially important. Why did reform completely cease for a period of ten years?

The British and American diplomatic records and some Thai documents recently published[1] make it quite clear that the uneven pace of reform was determined by a political rhythm. The reforms of the early 'seventies provoked a conservative reaction which was so strong as to halt further reforms until the most prominent of the old conservative statesmen had passed from the scene. For the most part, this resistance was an honest one, maintained out of a sincere belief that fundamental change in Thailand's political, legal, and administrative institutions was not required to forestall further European encroachments on Thai sovereignty. It had theeffect, however, of delaying urgently-required defensive and

---

[1] Natthawut Sutthisongkhram, *Somdet Chaophraya Sisuriyawong* (2 v.; Bangkok, 1961-62).

self-strengthening reform; and the conservative leadership of some nobles seems to have been sufficient to retard the willingness of the bureaucratic elite to send their sons to be prepared by modern education for the modernizing tasks which lay ahead.[2] These two effects reinforced each other; permanent reform started late, and labored under a severe handicap from the lack of trained men available for the specialized tasks of the new, modern bureaucratic institutions. Implicitly and explicitly the reforms of the 'nineties often have been criticized for the inefficient manner in which some of the new ministries worked, for the old-style behavior of some of the men who were in charge of them, and for the semi-nepotism of the King in appointing so many of his own royal brothers to positions of great responsibility.[3] Some of this criticism is justified, but most of it is also uninformed. Reform was inefficient because it was late and desperately hurried; many old men persisted in high office because new men were not ready; and the royal princes were prominent in the new administration because, better than most young men of their generation, they were prepared for their new responsibilities by education and experience. As a group, they were remarkable by any standard. The work of King Chulalongkorn's ministers, however, frequently has been overshadowed in Western accounts by the attention paid to the work of numerous foreign advisers who served the Thai Government, especially after 1892. Many of them were influential, their ideas often were important, and they were involved in a great many important tasks. Although few of them may have been imposed on the Thai Government for political reasons, most of them were hired for specific reasons, for particular skills they possessed which the Thai Government, owing to a severe shortage of trained manpower, wished to utilize. The policy of hiring such advisers was Thai, and the decisions both on the work it was

---

[2] "Prakat hai but kharatchakan khao rap ratchakan tam òpfit tangtang," *Ratchakitchanubeksa* 7, pp. 195-97. See also this authorûs article "Family Politics in Nineteenth Century Thailand," *Journal of Southeast Asian History*, 9:2 (Sept 1968).

[3] See D. G. E. Hall, *A History of South-East Asia* (2nd ed.; London,1964), Ch. 36; and John F. Cady, *Southeast Asia: Its Historical Development* (New York, 1964), Ch. 21.

intended they should accomplish and on the measures they recommended were political and administrative decisions of the King and his ministers. Ultimate responsibility for the reforms belonged squarely to them, and not to the advisers.

The work of J.G.D. Campbell in the Ministry of Public Instruction is a good example of this fact; and is particularly appropriate as an illustration, as Campbell's book, *Siam in the Twentieth Century, Being the Experiences and Impressions of a British Official* (London, 1902), has been used extensively by Western historians of the period. The decision to hire Campbell in 1899 grew out of a lengthy correspondence between the King and *Caophraya* Phrasadet Surentharathibòdi, the Thai Minister in London, in the course of which discussions of Siam's lack of trained manpower and the shape of future educational policies featured prominently.[4] Some of Campbell's suggestion were used to reinforce similar ideas already current in the Ministry; and the Minister, *Caophraya* Phatsakòrawong (Phòn Bunnag), used Campbell's recommendations to force the Ministry of Finance to allocate much-needed funds for some projects, particularly in the field of English secondary education. The King and others among his advisers, however, were more acutely anxious about mass primary and specialized vocational education, and not as sympathetic to the gentlemanly, elitist projects of Campbell as he wished; and Campbell left Siam on the expiration of his contract in 1901.[5] Eventually he was replaced by W.G. Johnson, who long had worked in the school of the Ministry, was fluent in Thai, understood Thai educational problems and opportunities, and was sympathetic to educational policies which were closer to those of the King and more appropriate to the real needs of Siam early in the twentieth century.

---

[4] *Phraratchahatlekha la nangsü krap bangkhom thun khong Caophraya Phrasadet* ... (Bangkok, 1961). See also *Phraratchahatlekha Phrabat Somdet Phra Cunlachòmklao Caoyuhua la lai phrahat Somdet Phrapitutcacao Sukhuman Marasi, Phra Akkharatchathewi* (Bangkok, 1950).

[5] See this authorûs doctoral disserta*tion*, "The Beginnings of Modern Education in the Reign of King Chu]alongkorn, 1868-1910," Cornell University,1966, pp. 378-84, and 390-406, based on the Fifth Reign records in the National Archives, Bangkok.

Campbell's and Johnson's expertise was of considerable aid in the development of modern Thai education, but the decisions on educational policy and on the implementation of specific program remained firmly where it belonged, with the King and his Ministers. Responsibility and credit for the reforms, and for the school which by 1910 enrolled 83,966 pupils, belongs primarily to them. Western-language accounts of the reforms generally have been based on the writings of the advisers and of those foreigners in Bangkok on whom the advisers daily vented their frustrations. The advisers rarely credited the King and his Ministers with the policy which had resulted in their own appointments. and they seldom understood the enormous obstacles to the full implementation of their recommendations. Working in a single ministry, they neglected to consider the fact that other ministries also were clamoring for funds for projects which they deemed vital to the nation's security and development and they failed to do justice to the heartbreaking task of the King in balancing the competing priorities of modernization.

Both the political rhythm of the reign and the work and role of the foreign advisers serve to illustrate a critical accomplishment of King Chulalongkorn for which he commonly has not been given credit. The King had to work in times that were extremely difficult. Being firmly committed personally to reform and vitally convinced of its importance to the survival of the nation, he had to battle and overcome the resistance to change and modernization. This was a slow, painful, and delicate task, to which few men would have been equal. He accomplished it with great skill, consummate patience, supreme determination, and a single-minded dedication to the ultimate good of the nation. Better than any of his contemporary critics, he had a full appreciation of the difficulties he faced and the dangers he had to overcome. From his nation and people he won the participation in, commitment to, and support for his cause which ultimately were to bring him and it success. The true measure of the greatness of King Chulalongkorn is more readily seen when viewed against the background of the difficulties he overcame and the responsibilities he assumed. He truly was a rare and great man and King.

KING CHULALONGKORN THE GREAT:
FOUNDER OF MODERN THAILAND*

King Chulalongkorn acceded to the throne of Siam on the death of his father, King Mongkut, or Rama IV, in 1868, and the centenary of his accession was celebrated eight years ago. But another centenary is much more important: that which marks the date upon which King Chulalongkorn, having come of age, was crowned king in his own right, was released from the supervision of a regent, and began actively to initiate fundamental change in the structure of the kingdom. This occurred on November 16, 1873. The distinction between his accession in 1868 and his full coronation in 1873 points up the basic transformation of the monarchy that Chulalongkorn undertook.

The Regency Period

The young prince Chulalongkorn was a boy just turned 15 when he was elevated to the throne late in 1868. It was a dangerous time for his country, for the Thai monarchy, and for the young king himself. Although his illustrious father—well-known from Margaret Landon's book, a Rodgers and Hammerste in musical comedy, two films, and a happily-aborted television series—had worked to diminish the threat of Western imperial expansion in the preceding two decades by opening his kingdom to the West, to Western trade, and to Christian missionaries, none could be fully confident of the kingdom's survival, and in fact the heaviest pressures of the European colonial powers were to fall in Chulalongkorn's reign.

---

* First published in *Thailand Since King Chulalongkorn*, ed. Lauriston Sharp (New York: The Asia Society, 1976), pp. 5-16. (*Asia*, Supplement no. 2, Spring 1976)

In meeting the Western challenge, old Siam was perilously weak, in ways that few at the time fully understood. As much as anything else, this was an institutional weakness. Much more than is generally recognized, old Siam was less an absolute monarchy than it was a nominal monarchy ruled *de facto* by a small oligarchy of noble families who controlled the departments and ministries of state, sons succeeding their fathers for generation after generation. In fact, the accession of King Chulalongkorn in 1868 marked the pinnacle of this oligarchy's success: By placing a young boy on the throne who was seriously ill and expected to die and by naming at the same time an heir apparent who was far removed from the normal line of succession and totally beholden to the preeminent noble family, the ruling oligarchy expected that they would be able to continue to rule as they had before, without any fundamental changes in the existing structure of the kingdom.

The political dominance of the nobility and their resistance to fundamental institutional change were serious handicaps to the survival of the kingdom and the king. Both were very weak. The kingdom was only loosely centralized: Amateur military forces, finances, provincial administration, and even the legal system were under the control of semi-independent individuals and families. Personal relationships, subordinate and super ordinate, characterized the political system. The king's decree was law only when it did not infringe upon the customary prerogatives of entrenched interests. The crown could not prevent outlying provinces from undertaking actions which might, and often did, run the risk of involving them in conflict with foreign powers. Neither could the crown undertake the basic reforms involved in centralization that alone could strengthen the kingdom's defenses and minimize the dangers of conflict with the West.

King Chulalongkorn's personal vulnerability was considerable. This is what he had to say about his situation in 1868 (recalling it a quarter-century later in advising his sons):

> When I ascended the throne I was only fifteen years and ten days old. My mother had died. Of my

maternal relatives, they were either unreliable or they were in unimportant positions. My paternal relatives in the Royal Family had fallen under the power of the Regent, and had to protect their own interests and their own lives, and most did not support me in any way. As for government officials, although there were some who were very close to me, most of these were but minor officials. Those who had important positions did not have the ability to support me in any way. My brothers and sisters were all minors, younger than I, and not one of them was able to do anything. As for myself I was but a boy. I had no great knowledge or ability in governmental affairs by which I might carry out my duties except for what my father had been able to give me. I was sick almost to the point of death. I grieved constantly because of my father's death. At that time I was like a headless person, my body propped up as a puppet king ... and there were enemies whose intentions were openly bared around me, both within and without, in the capital and abroad, and my bodily illness was afflicting and tormenting me beyond endurance.[1]

I think that the young King Chulalongkorn felt this way particularly because his conception of the nature of the monarchy and the functions of the monarch went beyond that of his father. Chulalongkorn was struck, and disturbed, by the discrepancy between the theory and practice of monarchy—all the more so, perhaps, because of his youth. He had expected power, and during the regency (of 1868-1873) was granted only authority, with the old nobility doing everything in his name. His determination to exercise real power on coming of age in 1873 began with his education by his father and his governess, Anna Leonowens, and took shape with his experience during the regency.

---

[1] King Chulalongkorn, *Phrabòrommarachowat nai ratchakan thi 5* [Royal Advices of the Fifth Reign](Bangkok, 1960), pp. 20-21.

พระบรมราโชวาทในรัชกาลที่ 5

During that period, he felt the strong negative effect of his elders' conservatism and reluctance to yield power and received a strong positive example from his first-hand view of European colonial administration during his visits to Malaysia, Indonesia, Burma, and India in 1871-72. His subsequent actions were to prove that he was both morally and intellectually committed to changes based on, or inspired by, the examples of European colonial administration he saw then.

The five-year regency must have seemed endless for the boy-king. He spent his time well, allowed by the regent at least to experiment in his own household, the Grand Palace. There he introduced minor innovations, such as dressing his courtiers in Western clothing and shoes, and sponsoring Western-style education for his younger brothers and friends. He moved also to strengthen his political (and military) support, seeking out like-minded young men (and some opportunists) who sympathized with his ideas of refashioning the kingdom. As his 1873 coronation approached, the young king entered the Buddhist monkhood for a brief spell, as Thai young men approaching maturity were expected to do. There was considerable questioning in the capital as to what the young king would do upon his accession to power. No doubt the old guard—the "Old Heads" *(hua boran)* as the King and his friends called them—thought he would make a fool of himself by introducing laughable innovations and alienating popular support, whereupon power would fall all the more firmly into their hands. Each side, King and nobility, underestimated the power and intentions of the other; and each side perhaps also had an exaggerated idea of what it might be able to accomplish. The "Old Heads," given their way, would have had no change at all—certainly no institutional change. For his part, young King Chulalongkorn seemed to have thought that he might be able to turn his kingdom into a miniature European colony, without the Europeans, making it a modernizing, "civilized" (in Western terms), Asian state. The stage was set for a serious conflict, and the drama began unfolding immediately upon Chulalongkorn's second coronation on November 16, 1873.

First Reforms

Although the grounds of the conflict were fundamental questions about the nature and powers of the monarchy and whether the state should be defined in traditional Siamese terms or in terms of the modern Western "nation-state," the contest came immediately to turn upon concrete practical issues that reflected the more fundamental questions. What King Chulalongkorn demanded was *power:* power of the purse and power over the semi-independent ministries and departments of state—which is something of a misnomer, for they were actually the ministries and departments of individuals and families. Some have argued that Chulalongkorn was primarily interested in gaining power for its own sake, in the Machiavellian or (to use a term derived from the handbook of statecraft indigenous to the area) Arthasastran sense. Nothing could be further from the truth. King Chulalongkorn had a strong moral conviction as to what power was for. He strongly felt that it was right, in both Thai Buddhist and Western terms, that the king exercised his power as a sacred trust—that he ruled, not for himself and his family, but for his subjects, and that they and he were locked together by strong mutual bonds of obligation. He was firmly convinced that fundamental change was both right and necessary: "right" in terms of common Buddhist and Western standards of justice, honesty, and human dignity; and "necessary" because the kingdom's failure to exemplify these standards would imperil the kingdom's survival. Certainly the young monarch did move to strengthen his own power; but he did so in the service of ends which far transcended his personal interest.

Chulalongkorn's very first reform decree, promulgated at his coronation in 1873, was not particularly important or far-reaching, nor especially effective (given present practice!), but it perfectly symbolized the new ideas of human dignity and citizenship with which he wished to imbue his kingdom. At that moment, he abolished the centuries-old practice of prostration in the royal presence and commanded his subjects to stand on their feet before him. Most people were shocked at what they considered an affront to the monarchy, and to this day most Thai still are uncomfortable in obeying this particular royal decree. Its symbolic significance is obvious: The king is not a god-king, not a *devaraja;* rather, he and his subjects are both human beings and should treat each other as such.

The reform decrees that followed, through the rest of 1873 and all of 1874, began more substantial institutional change and attacked directly the existing state of public affairs. Along four separate approaches, they undermined the strength of the semi-independent, oligarchic nobility. First, by announcing the progressive abolition of hereditary slavery and by severely re stricting the conditions under which the nobility could hold debt bond-servants, the King undertook to free the ordinary Thai farmer from traditional constraints on his political and economic life—an action which struck against the chief source of the nobility's wealth, which was their control over manpower. Second, he established special law courts to clear the enormous backlog of litigation in Bangkok and its concomitant delays, which oppressed all the litigants involved and profited the noblemen and petty officers who controlled the myriad jurisdictions of the kingdom's legal system. Third, he worked to build up the financial resources available to the central government, at the expense of numerous private pockets, by attempting to centralize collection and disbursement records, by standardizing rates of taxation, by ordering that tax collections farmed out to private individuals be let by public auction, and by establishing a central audit office (in which the King himself, with the assistance of his teenage brothers, pored over ledgers and receipts). Fourth, and finally, he moved to consolidate his own political support against the old men left in office by his father by establishing two advisory councils to consider public legislation and policy, the Council of State and the Privy Council. His intention in this respect was to bring older, more conservative officials into a larger body where they could be outvoted or influenced by his young friends and loyal supporters.

All four of these series of reforms of 1873-74 attacked established interests; each of the four engendered considerable passive and, in some cases, active resistance from the "Old Heads;" and each of the four attempted in some way to define and establish the king's sovereignty. The entire program of reform was called into question by what proved to be the most extreme attempt to challenge royal sovereignty: the so-called "Front Palace Crisis" of December 1874 to February 1875.

Threat and Crisis and Delay

I have already mentioned that when Chulalongkorn was elevated to the throne in 1868 by the oligarchy in council, they at the same time moved to insure his good behavior (and perhaps to wager against his health) by appointing as his heir-apparent an elder cousin, Prince Wichaichan (also known as Prince George Washington). Prince Wichaichan was the eldest surviving son of the man who had been elevated in 1851 to rule conjointly with King Mongkut as "Second King," an arrangement which had rapidly collapsed. Wichaichan was given, in 1868, what amounted to a semi-independent government of his own, with his own troops, corvée manpower, bureaucracy, tax revenues, and law courts, as well as virtually certain succession to the throne in the event of Chulalongkorn's untimely demise. The existence of Prince Wichaichan in this office, in the "Front Palace," only a few hundred yards from the Grand Palace (on the present site of the National Museum and Thammasat University), was an ever-present and visible threat to royal sovereignty—particularly as the King and his reformist supporters began to worry about a possible political challenge to the far-reaching reforms he had been undertaking. The King and his young friends argued on sound legal and historical precedent that the king, and he alone, had the power to appoint his *uparaja,* or heir-apparent. Either with or without Chulalongkorn's encouragement, a verbal attack was mounted against Wichaichan in the Privy Council in November of 1874 which soon thereafter escalated into active military preparations undertaken by both sides. The subsequent course of events still is not perfectly clear, but we do know that the country came to the verge of civil war, Wichaichan suddenly took asylum in the British Consulate, and French and British intervention that might have brought about the partition of the kingdom was narrowly averted by the timely arrival of the British governor of Singapore, who fortunately dampened the confrontation but refused to intervene in the dispute and left the two parties to negotiate a compromise settlement under which Wichaichan remained heir-apparent, but with a drastically reduced military force.

The "Front Palace Crisis" is of major significance for several reasons. First, this conflict (politely ignored in almost all Thai histories of the country) demonstrates the high degree of danger present early in Chulalongkorn's reign, danger both domestic and foreign. It offers us at least a glimpse of the strong political opposition to Chulalongkorn and his reforms, which one might logically have expected but of which there is otherwise very little mention. It is of primary importance, however, for an understanding of the particular course and timing of Chulalongkorn's subsequent reforms.

Although the evidence for this still is not entirely satisfactory, it seems clear that Chulalongkorn survived the crisis of 1875 only by deciding, or perhaps agreeing, to postpone further reform until time had removed from power his strongest opponents and enemies. What evidence we have is largely inferential: For nearly a decade after 1875, Chulalongkorn undertook no further reforms save within his own personal establishment, and most of his previous reforms were allowed to wither on the vine. It seems that, denied the possibility of institutional reform, Chulalongkorn then decided to work with individuals, preparing, training, and testing them for power by work in the Royal Audit Office, his personal secretariat, the Royal Pages' Bodyguard Corps, and a few new schools supported from his personal purse. Given the apparent political triumph of the King's conservative opponents, it was natural that the young men of the nobility continued to avoid Western education, preferring to join the departments where their families held sway. It was also natural that Chulalongkorn, despairing of the nobles' political orientation and their lack of progressive inclinations and suspicious of their loyalties, should have counted for support and future leadership on his younger brothers and junior members of the royal family, and on members of minor noble families and parvenu Chinese families—all alike excluded from real power by the conservative establishment. The most   important power at the King's command remained the power of appointment: Although he could not remove men from their family's strongholds in government, he could put new men in their positions when they retired or died, for only his signature legitimized a noble. As the old guard passed rapidly from the scene between about 1883 and 1889, he filled their posts with those who had rallied around him in the bleak years after 1875—men whose loyalty he counted upon and whose modern orientations he assumed.

By any standards, this was an extraordinary generation of talent, the quality of which might to some be suspect because of the fact that the most prominent of them were brothers and other relations of the King. But there is very little correlation between age or relative status within the royal family and the ultimate rank and office a prince achieved, and this group of able ministers included such princes as Damrong and Devawongse, whom all Western observers agreed were among the most capable men they had ever encountered anywhere.

The real leadership in reform and modernization came from the King, who chose his men carefully, educated them, tested them in lower positions, and then promoted or demoted them, prodded them to prodigious efforts, advised them, criticized them, encouraged them, and gave them free rein or held them in check, while at the same time he was taking particular care to ensure that the subsequent generation of Thailand's leaders would be even better educated and prepared for public office than they were.

Founding of the Modern State

Again by any standards, the accomplishments of King Chulalongkorn and his brothers and ministers in the two decades or so from about 1890 to his death in 1910 were phenomenal. In that short space of time, despite severe foreign crises that almost spelled the end of the kingdom (particularly the Franco-Siamese crisis of 1893, which resulted in the cession to France of Laos) the entire structure of modern Thailand was brought into being—almost literally from scratch—and a traditional Southeast Asian kingdom; ringed by dependent tributary states, was transformed into a modern nation. Provincial administration was brought under centralized direction and control and serviced by specialized functional ministries staffed by competent specialists. Modern law codes were drafted and put into force by administrators, judges, and lawyers. Fiscal administration was centralized, and modern accounting, budgeting, and auditing procedures introduced. Railways and telegraphic communications were constructed. A broad range of educational institutions was founded to serve all the varied needs of the state, and modern military and naval forces were created. Except for subsequent changes in technology and the role of the crown itself, there is little in the Thailand of the 1970s that was not present at least in formal structure and some reality by 1910.

On this enormous accomplishment alone, King Chulalongkorn's reputation as the founder of modern Thailand would be assured, given the fact that virtually every piece of the legislation and the action that created this state carries with it some ingredient, some component, of the King's own ideas, or thought, or hard work, or painful decision, or determined will that it must be done. What seems to me to lift his work to the level of genius is symbolized in two decisions, made at about the same time, which express his own faith in his people and his hope for the future of his country. These were the decisions, taken right at the turn of the century, to commit the kingdom to universal, and ultimately compulsory, primary education, and to universal, and also ultimately compulsory, military conscription. Both these decisions went against the advice of Chulalongkorn's European advisers at the time. It was argued that both were prohibitively expensive and that both were potentially dangerous in political terms in the extent to which they enhanced the possibility of opposition to the regime, at least in the long run. Chulalongkorn knowingly, willingly, and insistently ran those risks. In those two decisions he expressed a quintessentially modern idea of popular sovereignty: an idea of a nation of citizens with both the right and the obligation to put their talents to work for the benefit of the whole community as fully as possible and to defend that community if necessary with their blood. Modern Thailand is at least as much a product of these two commitments, educational and military, for good and for ill, as it is of the more structural products of his institutional reforms. We might consider the hypothesis that these two commitments had different germinating times, and that the fruit of military development came with the coup d'état of 1932, and that of educational development with the upheavals of 1973, but that remains to be seen.

The conventional interpretation of King Chulalongkorn's reign that is expressed in Thai school and university teaching and widely accepted in the West is that the great modern reforms of King Chulalongkorn's reign came about almost by magic, as though the institutions of old Siam, by the logic of their autonomous development and perhaps some dialectical influence of Western models, transformed themselves under a benevolent great king. This interpretation does not admit of the possibility that such obviously good accomplishments could have been resisted or opposed by anyone, and implies that the nation, with a single will, lifted itself up by its bootstraps (or sandal-thongs) into the modern world. The conflict and opposition which the reforms encountered and the difficulties inherent in their achievement are simply ignored in a totally ahistorical fashion. The accidental by-product of this interpretation is an impaired appreciation of the greatness of King Chulalongkorn: By ignoring the difficulties of his tasks, one underrates the scale of his accomplishment. This interpretation is the product of the transitional period of nation-building in Thailand—the fruit of the necessity of inculcating in the Thai educational system precisely those qualities still in some measure deficient in the nation. Because the nation has been constructed to bridge social divisions, ethnic divisions, regional divisions, and political and economic divisions, the past has been interpreted to emphasize the unity of the state. Fortunately, this particular interpretation is beginning to fade as unity becomes a reality.

Unfortunately, in the recent reinterpretation of Thai history, especially from a leftist perspective, Chulalongkorn still has not been treated completely fairly. Recent criticism has centered on his failure to introduce a constitutional monarchy when challenged by some of his young friends to do so in 1885. It is argued that he selfishly hung on to power for himself and the royal family when he should have attempted to build the nation on a broader base of public involvement. In my view, this interpretation of King Chulalongkorn's reign also is ahistorical. It does not consider the actual choices open to Chulalongkorn in his own time. He was perfectly aware of these, and on the specific issue of constitutional change his judgment, uttered in response to the 1885 petition, has been fully justified in the constitutional history of Thailand between 1932 and 1973.

One of the truly outstanding men of the world in his day, ranking among such world figures as Garibaldi, Bismarck, Gladstone, Disraeli, the Meiji Emperor, Li Hung-chang, and Abraham Lincoln, Chulalongkorn was by no means a man without faults, but his merits and accomplishments are almost staggering in their dimensions. He was a man of immense personal power, leadership, and vision. He worked enormously hard at his tasks—his daily diary entries always close with some such statement as "then retired upstairs to go over papers with so-and-so until 2 a.m.," and he personally read and acted upon many hundreds of pieces of official correspondence every day. He was a man of high intelligence, especially in his pained consideration of the problem of distinguishing between "borrowing from the West" and "making modern" his state.

While thoroughly familiar with the latest of Western thought and technology, he was at the same time the leading scholar of his own culture. He intelligently discussed railway specifications, wrote Thai literary and historical commentaries, and even composed a comic Thai version of Gilbert and Sullivan's "The Mikado." What Chulalongkorn accomplished he had to do almost without the support of indigenous institutional structures; commonly in opposition to them, he had to create a nation almost from the ground up. I can think of no one else in the world, in his day, who, at his age, did single-handedly so much in so creative and visionary a fashion. I am convinced that he fully deserves the epithet "the Great" with which only a few other Thai monarchs have been honored.